Slavic Excursions
essays on Russian and Polish literature

Also by Donald Davie from Carcanet

POETRY
Collected Poems 1970-1983
Selected Poems
To Scorch or Freeze

CRITICISM
Under Briggflatts: a history of
poetry in Great Britain 1960-1985

AUTOBIOGRAPHY
These the Companions

SLAVIC EXCURSIONS

DONALD DAVIE

Essays on Russian and Polish Literature

CARCANET

First published in Great Britain in 1990 by
Carcanet Press Limited
208–212 Corn Exchange Buildings
Manchester M4 3BQ

British Library Cataloguing in Publication Data

Davie, Donald *1922-*
    Slavic excursions : essays on Russian and Polish
    literature.
    1. Russian literature – Critical studies   2. Polish
    literature – Critical studies
    I. Title
    891.709

    ISBN 0-85635-864-9

The publisher acknowledges financial assistance
from the Arts Council of Great Britain

Typeset in 10pt Bembo by Bryan Williamson, Darwen
Printed and bound in England by SRP Ltd, Exeter

Contents

Foreword

To these pieces on Russian and Polish literature I have given the name 'excursions', meaning by that to acknowledge that in them I stray through fields where, by one not unreasonable set of professional rules, I have no rights and no competence. Of the Russian language I know little more than what I picked up, as a World War Two sailor in the Royal Navy, during eighteen months ashore in or near Murmansk and Archangel; and of Polish I know not a word except *solidarność*. What impudence, then, to suppose that my reflections on Russian or Polish texts have any validity or any value! And to be sure I am well aware that every one of my transactions must betray my lack of inwardness with the native tongues in which those texts are at home.

However, these excursions did not when I undertook them, nor do they now when I review them, present themselves to me as off-beat vacations from the serious professional business of describing and accounting for literature in English. Excursions, they may be – but diversions, no! I should dislike it extremely, if this collection should seem to perpetuate a long-established tradition of merchants and diplomats in their retirement whiling away the time by turning their hands to versions of, or essays about, Pushkin or Mickiewicz or Leskov or whoever. The products of such well-intentioned hands still burden the shelves of libraries, and too often convey the stultifying impression that Russian or Polish gentlemen of any period were essentially – ah, essentially! – not different from British or American gentlemen at the same date. Properly professional Schools of Slavic Studies are steadily, though not altogether rapidly, banishing such amateur publications to the dustier extremes of the library stacks.

And a good thing too, I'm sure. Yet I'm forced to remember that when, having returned from Russia in love with its melancholy spaces, I looked for some guidance into the culture that I'd grasped the skirts of, it was these graceful amateurs that alone could help me. Maurice Baring, Edwardian man of letters, and in a later generation C.M. Bowra – these I turned to, since they held the field, except for pedestrian Czech *emigrés* (the first professional Slavists) turning a dry-as-dust penny. My debt to Baring and to Bowra is doubtless very great, and complicated. It gave me unwarranted confidence. What I knew or was beginning to know – I speak of the 1940s – was, thanks to F.R. Leavis and Yvor Winters and Ezra Pound, the necessary structure, and the necessary compact texture, of an admirable poem, whether in English or any other tongue. And so I came to the presumptuous but right conclusion that, whereas Baring and Bowra had forgotten more Russian than I would ever learn, about *poems*, their structure and their texture, they knew rather little. It was thus that, after extolling quite compellingly the international significance of Tyutchev or Blok, the versions they produced to enforce this verdict were of an insipid fluency. I didn't know enough Russian, but I knew enough poetry, more than they did; and that was my warrant for entering the lists against them.

In another dimension altogether was the ultimately tragic figure of D.S. Mirsky. Prince Mirsky was insolently confident and well-informed about the cultural climate of England, as he knew it while he lived in London in the 1920s. And that assurance gave incisiveness and point to his *History of Russian Literature* and *Contemporary Russian Literature* (the latter dedicated to Maurice Baring) – two books to which, as an ex-serviceman in Cambridge, I devoted time that I could ill spare from acquainting myself with the literary classics in English. This was nostalgia of course – for my war-time self and for my *barishna* or girl-friend, Glaphira Alexeyevna in Archangel. All the same, there was more to it than that. Mirsky did not disappoint the trust that I put in him. For his facility with British analogues was only one of his accomplishments. And though I seldom nowadays consult him – in the book that is on my shelves, the one-volume abridgment *A History of Russian Literature*, edited by Francis J. Whitfield in 1949 – I am ready to trust my memories so far as to think that Mirsky was a great literary historian. For him to be that, he had to display (and did) capacities that we think un-Russian if – like most of us in those years, and perhaps even now – we take as quintessentially Russian the moody, tempestuous and capacious novels of Tolstoy or Dostoevsky. (To be sure, both of these have their elegancies, and Turgenev has more than either.) Mirsky could marshal his voluminous material only because he was driven by a passion for order and subordination, economy and incisive clarity. His was, in these ways, a *classical* intelligence. And whereas I had murkily discerned this bent of mind in the famously untranslatable Pushkin (whom I had dutifully tried and failed to translate already, under the Northern Lights), it was only when Mirsky set Pushkin among his peers and associates that I envisaged a specifically Russian sort of elegance which, because it mostly expressed itself in verse, had been for non-Russian readers overborne and hidden from view by the later novelists. Of Pushkin's circle the only poet that I could make a fist of translating was the somewhat marginal, though engaging, Prince Vyazemsky. But trying to grapple, always at second hand, with what Mirsky claimed for these aristocratic poets was very fruitful for me; for instance Pushkin's untranslatability, making me wonder what in any poet made him less or more translatable than the next, certainly contributed to my first book about English poetry, *Purity of Diction in English Verse* (1952).

I began to dabble in Polish literature only later, and as an extension of my always baffled but not frustrated fascination with Pushkin. Wacław Lednicki's *Russia, Poland and the West*, which by chance I got for review from a London periodical, introduced me to the matter of Pushkin's relationship with his great Polish contemporary Adam Mickiewicz – a relationship fraught and tormented by politics yet apparently secured by the mutual esteem between poet and poet. Lednicki, who was Professor of Slavic Languages at Berkeley, was grateful for my review, and in 1957-58, my first year in the States when I was down the coast in Santa Barbara, we got to know each other. I liked Lednicki very much, and have tried to convey my affection on a page or so of my book of memoirs called *These The Companions*. What endeared him to me was that, although he was a sharp and captious critic of fellow-Slavists, he accepted it as natural and praiseworthy that I, not knowing a word of Polish, had been tinkering with a Polish masterpiece. This was Mickiewicz's *Pan Tadeusz*, to which – by the luckiest of chances, that I can't now account for – I had gained access in the admirable prose translation by a Californian Slavist of an earlier generation, George Rapall Noyes. To Noyes, whom of course I never knew, I am even more indebted than to Lednicki. All I did, where I found the opportunity, was to lift Noyes's sturdy prose into verse – into such English verse as at that time I could command and feel comfortable with. At a later stage, which included crossing from Liverpool to New York in the old Cunarder *Britannic*, I laid these pieces end to end, making slight metrical adjustments, so as to compose a continuous though certainly elliptical narrative, which I called *The Forests of Lithuania*. What this represented was, out of the numerous facets of Mickiewicz's wonderfully rich poem, that aspect which corresponded to a novel by Walter Scott – all refracted however, though I didn't realize it at the time, through a sensibility that had taken the imprint of Ezra Pound's exhortation 'never a word too many'. Pushkin too had responded to the novels of Sir Walter Scott; and the difference between the Russian's and the Pole's response to that common stimulus was something that I teased out to my own satisfaction, there in California and later, after my return to England. The book built around that, called *The Heyday of Sir Walter Scott*, gets classified as 'Comparative Literature'. And I am happy with that, except that my experience tells me there is no worthwhile literary study that is *not* 'comparative'. I recount the story in this much detail because I believe it shows that there are relations between an English-language and a foreign-language author that cannot be comprised in any of the categories that we commonly recognize: not translation, adaptation, imitation, plagiarism, nor 'influence'. Certainly the pressure of Mickiewicz's imagination compelled me to contrive, in my English verse, effects such as I've found no chance to duplicate since.

In 1958, returning from our Californian year, my schoolboy son and I took ship from New York in the French Line vessel, *Flandre*, and landed in Plymouth – my wife's native town, whither she and our young daughter had preceded us by air. I remember vividly the bright but keen autumn morning when, as I waited for the London train, I bought from the bookstall on Plymouth North Road railway station the newly published English version of Pasternak's *Doctor Zhivago*. (No chance nowadays of finding such a book on North Road station, nor indeed of finding any bookstall whatever, in that sense.) I had read about Pasternak ten years before, in Mirsky; and had even tried at that earlier time to engage with the earliest translations of him, by Stefan Schimanski and Vladimir Nabokov. From that earlier encounter I had recoiled, not just frustrated but aggrieved. If that was what modernism with a Russian accent sounded like, I could do without it; it came over to me as pretentious and mannered. So it must have been distrustfully that I settled in to read *Doctor Zhivago*. And I cannot pretend that the reading bowled me over, as with a blinding light. My accommodation was much more gradual. I was fortunate that the poems in the seventeenth and last chapter of *Doctor Zhivago* were the chastened products of a poet regretting the modernist or *avant-gardiste* ebullience of his blazing youth, by which he had made his reputation with Russian-speakers like Mirsky. Moreover it was fairly plain that Max Hayward, who had translated the prose chapters, had virtually 'signed off' when he got to these poems; and I began to see with excited interest how, if the originals permitted it, Hayward's versions of the poems could be improved, and in ways that might illuminate the otherwise enigmatic connection between Chapter Seventeen and the chapters before it. So I was intrigued by *Doctor Zhivago*, rather than bowled over by it.

Shortly thereafter (1960), there appeared *Kogda Razgulyaetsa*, called *Poems 1955-1959* by Michael Harari, whose translations read well as poems in English and who was, I was heartened to hear, not much less amateurish in Russian than I was. These poems too were products of Pasternak's last, 'chastened' period. And it would be another ten years before, with the help of Angela Livingstone at the University of Essex, I could reluctantly and distrustfully track back from these poems to the more exuberant and audacious collections of Pasternak's youth, such as *My Sister Life*.

Before that ensued several years, in the early 1960s, when I apprenticed myself quite deliberately to the poet of *Kogda Razgulyaetsa* and *Doctor Zhivago*. I had mastered for my first two collections a style which, I came to feel, had mastered *me*. The ageing Pasternak, while observing for the most part stanzaic and metrical patternings that I could not comfortably abandon, showed me how to accommodate within those constraints ranges of experience that I had up to then ruled out as too risky. The foreign poet showed me a way of shucking off my first achieved style (which, after a while, 'wrote itself') in favour of another style that was more open-ended. In this crucial respect my debt to Pasternak was, and is, very great indeed. And I do not believe there was an English-language poet who could have served me so well in that emergency.

Why could Pasternak thus help me, where Mickiewicz could not? Partly, no doubt, because Pasternak was undoubtedly 'a modern', whereas Mickiewicz wasn't. But that was only part of the story. At that time I still thought of the poet, the poet I wanted to be, as a *lyric* poet: an impassioned 'I' who, situating himself in a physical or psychological or mythological landscape, has emotions about it, which he then expresses. But whereas this is a true description of what Pasternak does in the poems we value him for, it is clear that the Mickiewicz who wrote *Pan Tadeusz*, no less than the Pushkin who wrote *Eugene Onegin*, conceived of the poet quite differently – not as a magisterial ego, but as a sounding-board on which there registered voices quite different from, and even antipathetic to, the poet's.

This apprehension, that the lyric poet is only one sort of poet, was of course available to me in my native tradition, pre-eminently in the case of Shakespeare. But, shamefully perhaps, I have to put it on record that the perception was forced home on me by once again a Slavic poet: the Polish/Lithuanian, Czesław Miłosz. I acknowledged that debt – which I suppose could figure as my release from the delightful fetters of the lyric Pasternak – in my small book, *Czesław Miłosz and the Insufficiency of Lyric* (1986). Miłosz has tolerated my temerity, as Lednicki did.

D.S. Mirsky, feeling no doubt the increasing strain of exile from his native land and his native tongue, moved nearer and nearer to reconciling himself to the politics of the Soviet Union; and some time about 1930 he returned permanently to Russia. It is said that he was guaranteed the protection of Maxim Gorky. If so, it did not protect him for long. For a few years his name cropped up in Soviet periodicals. But quite soon he dropped from sight, and his fate could not be determined by Francis Whitfield in 1949. So far as I know, *glasnost* has not lifted this veil. I recount this so as to make good what may seem to be a deficiency in my account thus far. Have I not perversely omitted to recognize how all the authors I have named, from the remote as well as the recent past, suffered from political oppression, sometimes of the cruellest kind? No, I have not forgotten this. Nor am I trying to 'de-politicize' poetry, or literature generally. Literature from Eastern Europe in our day has been unavoidably – in the persons of Akhmatova and Tsvetayeva, Solzhenitsyn and Mandelstam, Miłosz and Zbigniew Herbert (to go no further) – literature of *witness*. And that witness is what Anglo-American readers, in their so much more comfortable circumstances, need to attend to. But to attend to them *only* as witnesses – to atrocious circumstances we can only guess at – is to sell them short, in a way that they themselves resent. They want and deserve to be recognized as *artists*, engaged in a corporate endeavour which, in its essentials, has not changed since the Ancient World. That there were such individuals, enlisted in that enterprise even under the worst inhumanities of Stalinist Russia and Poland, is precisely what they crucially bear witness to.

DONALD DAVIE
Exeter, 1989

1   Russian Poetry in English Translation

When you asked me to talk this year about Russian poetry, I was very pleased; because Russian poetry has been an absorbing interest of mine ever since, as a very young man and a sailor in the Royal Navy, I spent eighteen months in Arctic Russia in 1942-43. But as soon as I began to think of what I could present to you this evening, I realized that there could be no question of my trying to do justice to the whole history of Russian poetry through the centuries; and accordingly (I hope you won't be disappointed) I am going to limit myself to Russian poetry of the present century, and indeed to Russian poetry since the Bolshevik Revolution of 1917.

Such a survey must begin – so nearly every one would agree – with two poets who were at or very near the height of their creative powers in 1917 or 1920. These were Alexander Blok and Vladimir Mayakovsky.

I'm not going to read any poems by either of these great poets, for the good reason that I know of no English translations which do justice to either of them. And I·can't delay any longer before pointing out to you how we all talk out of two sides of our mouths on this matter of verse-translations. On the one hand we tell ourselves that poetry is intrinsically untranslatable; on the other hand our bookshops and libraries are full of books that claim to be verse-translations, books which we happily buy or borrow on the assumption that translating poetry, so far from being impossible, is really quite easy. This is a very complicated matter, and I'll rush through what could be a long argument to tell you how I stand. Very dogmatically, then, I declare that, no, poetry *isn't* untranslatable, but translating it is very, very difficult indeed – from which it follows that most of the books that offer themselves as translations of poetry, though their publishers offer them in all good faith, are in fact so unfaithful that they are worthless. This has got to be the case, because what we ask of a translator of poetry is that he have all the skills of a poet in his own language *plus* skills in identifying himself with a foreign language and a foreign culture. How can we wonder then that the good poetry-translator is just about the rarest creature to be found in literature? And please note that when I say most translations of poetry are 'unfaithful', I don't mean that they haven't carried over the literal *sense* of the original (though some of them, it's true, can't do even that) but, far more often, that they've got the sense right and have even reproduced the external form of the original but have somehow lost precisely the *poetry* – which is what after all we are looking for. I'm assuming that a faithful translation of a great or good Russian poem must be at least a good poem in English. This is a lot to ask, and yet we dare not ask for less. So it's neither shameful nor surprising that among the men and women who have tried their hands at putting Blok and Mayakovsky into English, I can't find one that measures up. And on the other hand when in a few minutes I read you translations that I think *do* measure up (translations of other Russian poets), please have a proper gratitude and respect towards these English translators who have succeeded where so many have failed.

Alexander Blok was a famous and admired poet long before the Revolution. And he wasn't himself an active revolutionary. But he saw the Revolution coming, he saw that it was inevitable, and so when it happened he accepted it – though on his own rather special terms. In 1918 he wrote an essay, 'The Intelligentsia and the Revolution', which Henry Gifford has described as 'an impassioned appeal to the Russian intellectuals that they should strain every nerve to hear what the Revolution was about. He conceives the process as akin to a blizzard, a maelstrom that destroys or saves the individual at random. But of its grandeur Blok has no doubt at all. This terrible destructive roar is the music of history.' At the same time Blok was writing a poem, *The Twelve*, which has been called 'the first masterpiece of Soviet literature'. It is a masterpiece certainly, but hardly of 'Soviet literature' as distinct from Russian literature. The revolutionaries themselves were disconcerted by it – as well they might be, for in the poem twelve ragged and brutal Red Guards patrol the wintry streets of Leningrad, and at their head walks...Jesus Christ! And the relation between Christ and these twelve who follow him cannot be taken care of by supposing that His presence vindicates the brutalities of these, His seeming 'disciples'. Blok accepts the Revolution, yes – but on his own terms, which were not the clear-cut and simplified terms of the revolutionaries' propaganda.

The poet who tried to take the Revolution on those terms was Mayakovsky, who deliberately challenged comparison with Blok by replying to *The Twelve* in a long poem called *150,000,000*. 'But', says Professor Gifford, 'the 150 million inhabitants of the Soviet state to whom is accredited the authorship of his poem coalesce into the one symbolic figure of Ivan who engages in combat with President Wilson. And the voice of the narrator who dominates the poem is a single voice, that is to say Mayakovsky's.' Mayakovsky in this and subsequent poems went further than any comparably gifted poet has ever done in the direction that is sometimes pressed upon us English poets also – of suppressing his own personal concerns so as to speak for the otherwise inarticulate masses of his countrymen. And it would be too easy to say that, when he shot himself in 1929, it was because he had recognized the impossibility of this task that he had set himself. One of his contemporaries, Pasternak, who did not share Mayakovsky's notion of what the poet should do, wrote of Mayakovsky's death much more compassionately than that, in a poem and also in prose reminiscences.

As for Blok, Pasternak was continually aware of him also, as a living presence long after he was dead. Once again he recorded this both in a sequence of poems and also in the prose of his novel *Doctor Zhivago*. However, rather than read any of Pasternak's poems to Blok, I want to read a poem by one of Pasternak's contemporaries, Marina Tsvetayeva, translated by Elaine Feinstein:

> Your name is a bird in my hand
> a piece of ice on the tongue
> one single movement of the lips.
> Your name is: five signs,
> a ball caught in flight,
> a silver bell in the mouth
>
> a stone, cast in a quiet pool
> makes the splash of your name, and
> the sound is in the clatter of
> night hooves, loud as a thunderclap
> or it speaks straight into my forehead,
> shrill as the click of a cocked gun.
>
> Your name how impossible, it
> is a kiss in the eyes on
> motionless eyelashes, chill and sweet.
> Your name is a kiss of snow,
> a gulp of icy spring water, blue
> as a dove. About your name is: sleep.

That poem, you may think, isn't really about the poet Blok at all, but only about the plopping or clopping or clapping sound that his name happens to have when we speak it. And so we might think that Tsvetayeva's poem is slight and trivial, unworthy of its subject. But this is the first lesson that we need to learn when we approach Russian poetry from the perspective of our own poetry in English:

the Russian poets care a great deal more than most of our poets do, for the *sound* of what they write, the sounds of that Russian speech out of which they make the compositions of sound that are their poems. I don't mean simply that they try to make the sounds of their poems pleasing or seductive or expressive of what the poem is saying (for that is what all self-respecting poets try to do, whatever language they are writing in); and I don't mean, either, that Russian poets are less ready than English-language poets to abandon the melodies carried in verse-forms perfected in the past (though that is certainly true). I mean that Russian poets attend to, listen to, the sounds that their language makes, in the faith that the sounds themselves carry meanings – or rather, that the sounds do not just *carry* meanings, but create meanings, or reveal them. A similarity in sound between two words – something that our poets dismiss as accidental, though of course worth exploiting – this the Russian poet dwells upon and attends to, as significant, meaningful. And so Marina Tsvetayeva's meditation on the sheer sound of a poet's name is a good deal less trivial and more meaningful than we are likely to suppose.

Accordingly, we know that some Russian poets of our time have begun composing poems by in the first place walking about making sounds – grunts and moans and squeals, hissings and cracklings – which only at a much later stage in the composition are transformed into words strung together to make a sort of prose sense. (Incidentally this seems exactly analogous to the use of shapes in paint by a Cubist painter like Juan Gris.) One Russian poet of whom we know this is the famous and tragic Jew Osip Mandelstam, killed by Stalin in 1938, whose widow still lives in Moscow. Mrs Mandelstam, who speaks and writes English well, has written her memoirs in two brave and bitter books, *Hope Without Hope* and *Hope Abandoned*; and in the first of these she speaks of her husband composing in the way I have described. The only English-language poets, so far as I know, who in the act of composing paid anything like so much attention to sound and soundingness were William Wordsworth and the great Anglo-Irishman W.B. Yeats. This mouthing and noising of sheer sounds is something that Mandelstam speaks of himself in a little eight-line poem that he wrote in the 1930s:

> I love the way the weave, when two or three or
> Four sometimes great gulps can't draw it tight,
> Comes up, comes clear; when I achieve a more
> Shuddering breath, and get it sounding right.
> So much good that does me, yet I fetch
> Much weight upon me, as the moment nears

When the arched breastbone, onerously a-stretch
Through my slurred mumblings, reaches to your ears.

Because that translation is by me, I'll give you an alternative version
of the same poem by another English poet, John Riley:

I love the way the fabric unfolds
when after two three or
even four convulsions there
comes the sigh that sets it straight –
when that instant's near what
relief, what pain – and the sudden
shock of arching breath
sounds in my mutterings.[1]

You would hardly think it was the same poem, would you? But at
any rate, in John Riley's version as in mine we hear Mandelstam
talking of the making up of a poem as in the first place a sort of
deep-breathing exercise, a straining of the lungs and the vocal cords,
a shape made out of sounds before it is a shape made out of meanings.
And this is a view of poetry that he shared with Tsvetayeva, who
wrote the poem about Blok's name, and also with Pasternak.

Mandelstam, Tsvetayeva, Pasternak – add to these the name of
another woman, Anna Akhmatova, who outlived the rest and died
only a few years ago. She wrote a poem called 'There are Four of
Us'; and the four poets that she means are these four: Mandelstam
and herself from Leningrad, Pasternak and Tsvetayeva from Moscow; one man and one woman from each of European Russia's twin
great cities – the two cities which, now as in the past, represent two
alternative or complementary directions for the Russian imagination, the one looking westward and outwards (Leningrad), the other
looking eastward and inwards (Moscow). And this doesn't exhaust
the really quite spooky symmetry about these four names; for in
each of the two pairs there is one poet who either ultimately or
immediately defied the communist regime (Tsvetayeva and Mandelstam), and another poet who went to all lengths to work with
the regime until the authorities made it impossible (Pasternak in
Moscow, Akhmatova in Leningrad). Of course it was arrogant and
provocative of Akhmatova to name only these four, perhaps not
exclusively but pre-eminently, as the four poets who had kept the
faith in her lifetime with the calling and the duty of Russian poetry;
some students of Russian poetry in this country, and doubtless some
poets inside Russia, have protested against this grouping. But it

---

[1] John Riley, *Mandelstam's Octets: a version*. Pensnett: Grosseteste Press, 1976.

seems certain that not just Akhmatova but each of the other three poets did in fact see the other three as their true peers – this despite great differences among them politically, and despite the fact that they were hardly ever all four in one another's company.

And in case you are tempted to write this off as just poets ganging together in a clique so as to promote each other's work (which happens often enough in this country), you need to take account of the quite different situation that poets experience in a dictatorship like the Soviet Union. Professor Gifford, whose admirable essay I have quoted from already, evokes that situation very vividly:

> Lydia Chukovskaya tells in her reminiscences of Akhmatova how on a July day in 1953 they tried vainly to reconstitute a poem from 1940, 'The Cellar of Memory'. Akhmatova was then subsisting upon translation, like Pasternak; but whereas he could undertake the work with a will, however irksome it may have been at moments, Akhmatova felt that in this activity a poet simply eats his own brain... Seven years before Zhdanov had blasted her and the satirist Zoshchenko. Since then officially she had ceased to produce original work. A poem on her situation says:
>
> > You hung me like a slaughtered animal
> > On a bloody hook,
> > So that tittering and incredulous
> > Foreigners might wander round
> > And write in esteemed journals
> > That my incomparable gift had burned out,
> > That I had been a poet among poets,
> > But it had now struck thirteen.
>
> Anything she did compose for herself had to be hidden away, in manuscripts entrusted to courageous and reliable friends, or (more safely) learned by heart.

And Henry Gifford goes on to tell how Akhmatova's own poem could not be retrieved in full from the poet's own memory and the memory of her friend, until two years later, in 1955. Under a government like that of Stalin and his monstrous Minister of Culture Zhdanov, which can and does destroy poems in their physical embodiment as black marks on sheets of white paper, we can hardly expect poets to behave towards each other with the sort of deprecating modesty and ready tolerance that we expect as mere good manners in a more fortunate society like our own. The very *being* of Russian poetry was at stake; and in those circumstances how could Akhmatova be polite towards graceful and (sometimes) well-meaning versifiers, whose work was approved by the authorities simply because it was innocuous?

In 1953, when Akhmatova and her friend were trying to put together from memory the poem of hers that it had been too dangerous to commit to paper, two of her chosen quartet of poets were already dead. Mandelstam we know about already; he was last reported seen in 1938, scavenging for food in a garbage heap near Vladivostok at the far side of Siberia. The next to go was the other woman, Tsvetayeva. She was the only one of the four to oppose the Revolution implacably from the first; she emigrated, like other sympathizers with the defeated Tsarist regime, and lived many years in exile, in France and Czechoslovakia and elsewhere. But shortly before the Second World War she decided to go home to Russia, and in 1943, alone and destitute, she hanged herself in an obscure Russian village called Yelabuga. That place-name, 'Yelabuga', echoes through the poem that I'm going to read now, and in the course of the poem comes to seem the name of some monstrous poisonous spider. The poem is by the living woman-poet Bella Akhmadulina, and the translator is once again Elaine Feinstein. There is another allusion in the poem, where Akhmadulina speaks of 'your beloved African, that great genius of / kindness, whose own end was unkind'. As even poorly educated Russians would realize, the reference is to the greatest of all Russian poets Alexander Pushkin, who in the 1820s virtually created the language for poetry that Russian poets have used ever since. Pushkin had a negro strain in his heredity, as portraits of him show quite clearly – hence the expression, 'beloved African'. 'I Swear', by Bella Akhmadulina:

> by that summer snapshot taken
> on someone else's porch, skewed to one
> side, that looks so like a gibbet, and
> points a way out of the house not into it;
> where you are wearing some violent sateen dress that
> cramps the muscles of your throat like armour;
> and are simply sitting there, with the endurance of a
> tired horse after the labour of
> singing out to the end all your grief and hunger.
> I swear: by the photo, and your delicate pointed
> elbows, which are as child-like as the smile of surprise
> that death uses to lure children to itself and leaves
> as a mark upon their faces for evidence.
> I swear: by the painful burden of remembering
> how I gulped your airless grief from the
> breathless rush of your lines, and had to

keep clearing my throat until it bled.
Yes, by your own presence, which I have stolen,
burgled, taken for myself, as if forgetting that
you belong to God, who cannot get enough of you;
and by that starved emaciation which
killed you at the end with its rat tooth.
  I swear: by the blessed Motherland herself, even if
she grossly abandoned you like an orphan;
and your beloved African, that great genius of
kindness, whose own end was unkind, now
as a statue watching over small children.
By those children! And the Tversky Boulevard!
And your own sad rest in Paradise, where
there is neither trade nor torment for you!
I swear: to kill that Yelabuga, your
Yelabuga, so that our grandchildren
can sleep soundly. Old women may still frighten
them at nights, not knowing the power of her
'Sleep little child, quietly, quietly, for
blind Yelabuga is coming to catch you.'
And with all her tangle of legs truly she will
hasten towards me crawling with horrible speed.
But I shall bring my boot down on her
tentacles without saying any more, and
put my weight on my heel, and my toe-cap into
the back of her neck, and keep it there.
Then the green juice of her young will burn
the soles of my feet with their poison, but I'll
hurl the egg that ripens in her tail
into the earth, that bottomless earth!
And not say a word of the porch in the photograph.
I will not speak of Marina's homeless death.
I swear it. Even while in
the dark, and in the stench of silt,
with the toads in the well about her, she
has one yellow eye fixed in my direction:
The Yelabuga
swears her own oath – to kill me![1]

To speak for myself, the finest dimension of that poem comes into
sight when Akhmadulina says 'Yes, by your own presence, which

[1] Elaine Feinstein (trans.), *Three Russian Poets*: Aliger, Moritz, Akhmadulina.
Manchester: Carcanet New Press, 1979.

I have stolen, / burgled, taken for myself' – reproaching herself, I take it, for taking a fate so appalling as Tsvetayeva's to serve as but the pretext or occasion for a poem of her own; or else, and also, for seeing in Tsvetayeva's death only an example of the fate that awaits all poets including herself – this being, as I read the poem, the reason why at the end, when she imagines the Yelabuga coming for her, she says she will *not* 'speak of Marina's homeless death'. I need hardly point out what courage it takes for a poet still living in the Soviet Union to write such a poem, and publish it.

To return to Akhmatova... After the death of Stalin, conditions for writers and other artists in the Soviet Union improved; and there has never been a return to the vindictive bullying that was the rule under Zhdanov in the first years after 1945, though of course no writer in Russia is 'free' in the sense that our writers take for granted. Akhmatova profited a little by this change in the climate of opinion, and in her very last years she was permitted to visit the Free World – to receive for instance an honorary degree from Oxford University. She was even able to get into print some parts of the long poem that she had begun in 1940 in beleaguered Leningrad, and continued to work on intermittently almost up to her death in 1966. This work is called *Poem Without a Hero*, and it is a poem to and about the city that Akhmatova made her own, the city called St Petersburg when she knew it as a young woman in 1913, and Leningrad in 1941 when it was under siege from the Germans just as London was. Akhmatova was very vividly aware of that connection, of Leningrad with London. She wrote at the time when both cities were being bombarded a poem, 'To the Londoners', in which she said:

> Time is now writing with impassive hand
> Shakespeare's black play, his twenty-fourth
> ... Only not this one, not this one, not this one –
> This one we do not have the strength to read.

And at the head of Part 2 of *Poem Without a Hero*, she wrote 'My future is in my past' – which, as we know from her notebooks, is her adaptation of the famous motto of Mary Queen of Scots, 'In my end is my beginning', something that she knew from the use of it by T.S. Eliot in his poem 'East Coker', written and published in war-time London. Similarly, in the passage I'm going to read now, from Part 3 of the poem, there occurs the place-name 'Tobruk', scene of some of the fiercest battles between British and German forces in North Africa. In this passage Akhmatova is addressing her dear city from thousands of miles away, Tashkent in Central Asia, to which she had been evacuated so as to escape the worst months of the siege of Leningrad in 1942, sufferings that she imagines guiltily because she suffers them only in imagination. The translation of this extremely difficult poem is by D.M. Thomas, a distinguished Cornish poet:

To my city

Inside the House on the Fontanka
    Where with a bunch of keys, a lantern,
        The evening lassitude
Begins, with an out-of-place laugh I
    Hallooed to a distant echo, shattered
        The unbroken sleep of things;
Where, witness of all in the world,
    At dawn or twilight, an old
        Maple looks into the room
And, foreseeing my absence,
    Stretches out his dried and blackened
        Arm as if to help.
Earth hummed beneath my feet and
    The red planet was streaking
        Through my still unbroken roof.
It listened for its own password – that
    Sound that is all around us...
        And in Tobruk...it is everywhere.
You, not the first nor the last dark
    Auditor of bright madness,
        What vengeance do you prepare for me?
You will only sip, not drain to
    Its depths this bitter taste of
        Our separation. Understand
There is no need to set your
    Hand upon my head. Put an end to
        Time, let it forever remain
Here like a bookmark in a book at
    The silence of the cuckoo
        In the arson of our woods...

And at this point Akhmatova breaks off into another metre to address some one unnamed, who fairly clearly however is a representative of the thousands on thousands in the Siberian prison-camps, of whom her own son was one and the dead Mandelstam another:

    And behind barbed wire
    In the dense taiga's heart
    – I don't know in what year
    Transformed to a pile of camp-dust, an

Anecdote from the terrible fact –
My double goes to interrogation,
With two thugs sent by the Noseless Slut,
And I hear from where I stand
– Isn't that a miracle! –
The sound of my own voice:
  I have paid for you in cash,
  For ten years I've looked
  Neither right nor left,
  Your ill fame at my back...

And then she resumes her address to the city of Leningrad:

You, the grave I sprang from,
  Dearest, infernal granite,
    Have paled, have died, lie still.
It's only imagined, our separation,
  Nothing can split us, efface my
    Shadow that's on your walls,
My reflection in your waters,
  Steps in the Hermitage halls, where
    My friend and I once strolled;
And in ancient Volkovo Field,
  Where there's no end to weeping
    The still fraternal graves.[1]

It's time for me to say something about a suspicion that I'm fairly sure has been growing in the minds of some of you: the suspicion that I'm giving this talk out of a political bias; that I'm deliberately putting before you those Russian poets who are in opposition, out of sympathy with the regime there, and ignoring other poets who support the regime. If I assure you that I've chosen to talk about only those poets whom the best British and American scholarly opinion singles out as the best, I may be told that all such scholars have been brainwashed by the capitalist press of the USA and the UK, which has an interest in painting the Soviet Union in the blackest colours. Certainly our press *has* such an interest; sometimes it shows, and leads to unfairness, and I urge you to be on your guard about that (though our own Leftwing press is just as bad on the other side). But the real question is: *are* the poets that I've put before you the voices of the internal opposition, vowed from the first and at

---

[1] Anna Akhmatova, *You Will Hear Thunder* (trans. D.M. Thomas). London: Secker & Warburg, 1985; reprinted as *Selected Poems* by Penguin Books, 1988.

all costs to oppose and slander the Russian Socialist State? The answer is: they are not. For instance, the poem I've read from last, Akhmatova's *Poem Without a Hero*, is very bitter and unsparing about the decadence and depravity of pre-revolutionary Petersburg as the poet remembers it – something that makes her castigate Alexander Blok as a representative figure of that world, in terms much less flattering than those in which he was spoken of by Tsvetayeva and Pasternak. Her poem doesn't in the least praise Tsarist Petersburg against Socialist Leningrad – its effect is to tell us that all such black-and-white, cops-and-robbers accounts of politics or of history are childish and yet murderous simplifications – the realities of how we manage to live together without killing each other are just too complicated to be got hold of by politicians or conveyed in political slogans. And of course the Russian politicians hated her for saying that, just as our politicians – British and American alike – hate us poets when we say the same thing.

The proof, I think, may appear from looking now at the last of the quartet that Akhmatova singled out in 'There Are Four of Us' – that's to say, Boris Pasternak. Pasternak, as we have heard already, was in disgrace under Zhdanov just as Akhmatova was, though he wasn't like her singled out for Zhdanov's personal abuse and also, whereas she hated the translating which was all that was permitted them, Pasternak took much pleasure in it. (And indeed his translations of some of Shakespeare's plays are reckoned to be the best Russian versions ever made.) Pasternak had been as it were contemptuously tolerated ever since the Revolution, and it now seems incontrovertible that, strange as it must seem, the monstrous dictator Stalin himself had a sort of grudging respect for him. Ugly rumours circulate that Pasternak didn't use this connection as strongly as he might have done, to save Mandelstam. This and other curious episodes in Pasternak's career can best be explained on the assumption that, unlike Akhmatova and Mandelstam, he was politically naïve. He seems to have been naïve enough, for example, to think that the much-advertised 'thaw' under Khrushchev, after Stalin's death, would restore to writers something like the freedoms they had had before the Revolution. Accordingly he submitted to a State publishing house the manuscript of his *Doctor Zhivago*, which he had been working on for twenty years; and appears to have been genuinely surprised when it was found unacceptable. This book of Pasternak's is usually decribed as *a novel*, and I myself called it that a few minutes ago; but this can lead, and has led, to fruitless comparisons with great Russian novels of the past, like Tolstoy's *War and Peace*. It would be more accurately described as 'a poem mostly in prose'; and if that sounds like special pleading, we'd do well to remember that Pushkin's greatest poem, *Eugene Onegin*, was called by its author 'a novel-in-verse'. If *Doctor Zhivago* is indeed a novel in any sense, it certainly isn't a *realistic* novel; for we can see that Pasternak went out of his way to make his plot turn upon obviously improbable coincidences. More to the point is something that is much clearer in the Russian-language original than in the English translation: in the original, the poems that the hero Yuri Zhivago has written are printed as the last chapter (Chapter 17) of the whole work, whereas in the English-language version these poems, very perfunctorily translated, are offered us as a sort of unforeseen optional appendix. Eighteen years ago I wrote a whole book on this matter, and proved to my own satisfaction (if not to everyone else's!) that Pasternak meant Zhivago's poems to be the pay-off and vindication of his whole life, and that accordingly any attempt to make sense of the plot of the previous sixteen chapters without taking note of the poems must be doomed to failure.[1] In order to write this book, I found I had to make my own translations of all the poems that Pasternak puts in the mouth of his hero, Zhivago; and I'd like to read you one of them. It is called 'Miracle', and it deals with what is perhaps the queerest of all Jesus's miracles as recorded in the Gospels – his cursing of the barren fig-tree:

He fared from Bethany to Jerusalem,
Foreshadowings of affliction weighing on him.

Burrs of brushwood scorched on the steep bluff's oven,
Over the hovel nearby no blown smoke stirred:
Hot breath of the air, and the reedbeds there unmoving,
And on the Dead Sea repose immovably anchored.

With sourness at heart that vied with the salt sea-water
He fared, while behind a few clouds raggedly followed,
Along the dust-choked road to some man's shelter,
Fared to the town, where some He instructed gathered.

And so far sank He, self-absorbed and brooding,
A wormwood smell came up as the field saddened.
All stilled. Alone He midway along was standing,
And the terrain stretched, sheeted in unfeeling.
All swam and merged: the balmy air and the barrens,
The lizards, the gushing springs, the waters running.

---

[1] These translations and notes are reprinted as Chapter 6 of the present volume.

A fig-tree rising no great distance off,
Utterly bare of fruit, nothing but leaves and wood,
He said to it: 'Do you do me any good?
Is your stockstillness anything to be glad of?'

'I hunger and thirst, and you – you barrenly flower.
Encountering you is comfortless as granite.
What a trial you are, and how devoid of talent!
Stay as you are to the world's last hour.'

Throughout the tree ran the quake of condemnation,
As the levin-flash along a lightning-rod
Flashed on the fig-tree sudden incineration.

Had leaf and branch and root been granted
One moment's freedom, then the laws of Nature
Had made all haste, and doom been intercepted.
But a miracle is a miracle, a miracle is God.
When we are all at odds it comes upon us
Instantaneous, and when least expected.

You may well wonder what there is in such a poem for the Soviet authorities to take exception to – to the extent that, when Pasternak had got *Doctor Zhivago* printed abroad, and a few months later was awarded the Nobel Prize, the rulers of Russia should insist that he refuse the award on pain of being banished from his native land for ever. What's more, those of you who have read the whole book will realize that, so far from being (as is commonly supposed by those who haven't read it) a sustained criticism of the Communist Revolution and the Communist State, it is a celebration of the private life, and of human relations – particularly the relations of man and woman in love. But this is just the point! It will not satisfy the Soviet censors that you abstain from criticizing the Soviet way of life; you must positively *applaud* that life – and it's an unwritten law of that life that public life takes precedence of private life, and that *social* relations are more important than *human* relations.

What Pasternak as a poet does criticize is the damage that is done by this view of things to *language* – to the Russian language of Pushkin which he inherited. And this is not anything limited to Russia; we too perceive, day by day, how woolly bureaucratic jargon is supplanting, in our own mouths and the mouths of our children, the language of Shakespeare. Indeed, I have given you quite the wrong impression if I have not made it clear that the example of these Russian poets is a constant inspiration and provocation when

I think of what it is I am doing, and must do, as a poet of England. These poets of Russia took it upon themselves to be the conscience of their nation; English poets, in their so much more comfortable circumstances, are called to the same duty.

A talk given to the Barnsley Literary Society, 1983.

2 The Poetry of Prince Vyazemsky (1792-1878)

The business of verse translation always requires an apology. The translator, I suppose, acknowledges to himself that his versions will not be read as poems but as documents of literary history. No doubt all poems, or at least all poets, can be considered as having value for the literary historian, a value more or less independent of their value as poets. Vyazemsky produced some poems which are very fine and moving in themselves. I have attempted to translate some of these poems, such as the 'Stanzas to Davydov', but it is in respect of these that the translator feels inevitably the inadequacy of his undertaking. Vyazemsky, has, however, an interest for the literary historian which is greater than that of many other poets intrinsically finer than himself. Of the circle of poets and writers who associated with Pushkin in the so-called Golden Age of Russian aristocratic literature, between 1810 and 1840, Vyazemsky was almost the only figure to survive into the later years of the nineteenth century. He thus saw the phenomenally rapid development of Russian literature, through the rise and fall of an aristocratic culture, and into a totally different phase of bourgeois realism. Moreover he was, from the first, perhaps the most acute critical intelligence of the Pushkin circle, after Pushkin himself, and throughout the sixty years in which he played a more or less prominent part in Russian letters he was the spokesman of an attitude remarkably consistent and enlightened. It will appear, therefore, that the reader who is unaware what Vyazemsky 'stood for' in Russian letters between the year 1840 and 1880, the years which saw most of the masterpieces of Russian realism, can have no complete idea of the cultural milieu in which Turgenev, Goncharov, Dostoevsky and Tolstoy were living and writing.

Vyazemsky's attitude to the cultural, political and social state of Russia in these years can be described as that of an intelligent anti-democrat. On the other hand it could be claimed equally well that he was a democrat from first to last. His democracy was that of the enlightened liberal of the reign of Alexander I, an attitude which he probably shared with many of the Decembrists. This 'democracy' was something quite different from the radicalism of Western Europe or of such a Russian thinker as Belinsky. Vyazemsky's change, therefore, from the liberal to the conservative camp, after the European revolutionary movements of 1848, does not in the least brand him as a renegade. On the contrary, it was entirely consistent with his earlier views. In this respect, Vyazemsky makes a better showing than Pushkin, who abandoned the liberalism of his early years and applauded the brutal severity with which Imperialist Russia subdued the Polish rebels of 1830. Vyazemsky had interested himself in the plight of the Poles ever since he assisted in the false offer of a Polish constitution by Alexander I, and the way in which he dissociated himself from the anti-Polish measures of 1830 is one of the most admirable incidents in Vyazemsky's life.

Prince Peter Andreevitch Vyazemsky was born in 1792 into an ancient and noble Russian family. In 1802 his mother died, and in 1805 Vyazemsky was sent by his father to St Petersburg and studied for a time under a Jesuit. In 1806 he was recalled by his father to Moscow. His father died in the following year. Between 1807 and 1811 Vyazemsky led the life of a rich young aristocrat, and in these years he learnt the technique of verse from Batyushkov and Zhukovsky. In 1812 he married, and in the same year served with the Russian Army at Borodino against the invading French. In this year his first child was born. The child died in 1814, when Vyazemsky attended the entry of the Russian troops into Paris. On his return Vyazemsky entered state service, and in the same year was one of the organizers of the famous 'Arzamas'.

The 'Arzamas' was a literary society intended to organize the opposition to the other literary society of the time, the 'Beseda'. The latter was conservative, and represented those writers who maintained that Russian poetic diction should be based upon old Slavonic vocabulary, and who upheld the rigid distinction between the lofty and the base style, as quite separate instruments each adapted for certain genres of Russian verse. The 'Arzamas', on the other hand, believed that the language of Russian poetry should benefit from the innovations of Karamzin, who had attempted to bring the language of poetry closer to the colloquial Russian spoken by the Russian gentry. The most considerable poets of this period, such as Batyushkov and Zhukovsky, belonged to the 'Arzamas', and the young Pushkin was also representative of this current of opinion. But after 1825 Pushkin took up a position between the 'archaists' and the 'innovators', drawing for his diction upon Slavonic turns as well as upon the colloquialism of Karamzin and Vyazemsky, and enriching it still further from the language of the peasant. Moreover, recent Soviet research has shown that Pushkin was sympathetic to certain writers among a younger generation of archaists, such as his friend Küchelbaker. Vyazemsky, on the other hand, was always one of the keenest propagandists for the doctrines of the 'Arzamas', and it was not until the controversy had been dead many years, that he evolved the elegiac mode of his later serious work. It is necessary to keep this chapter of literary history in mind when attempting to deal with Vyazemsky's early verse. This verse presents peculiar difficulties to the translator, and there are no examples of it in the present selection. Because each poem represented a blow struck in this wordy battle, the pieces often appear trivial, and lose their value when not seen in the context of controversy. The poetry read at the meetings of the 'Arzamas', for example, consisted almost entirely of parodies of the style of the rival school.

In the same years as Vyazemsky was thus involved in literary dispute, he was frequently in Warsaw on civil service work, and his dislike for the Russia of Alexander I and Arakcheev became steadily firmer, being defined by his experiences in Poland (he had learnt Polish), and his readings in French political science. This development can be clearly traced in his correspondence with A.I. Turgenev, and in some of his poems from 1819 onwards. After 1820 he was closely associated with Pushkin, writing an appreciation of *The Prisoner of the Caucasus* (1822). In 1824 Pushkin published *The Fount of Bakhchisarai* with an introduction by Vyazemsky.

In 1825, the year of the attempted Decembrist coup, in which many of his closest friends were involved, Vyazemsky was seriously ill. In the same year he began to assist Polevoy with the *Moscow Telegraph*. Polevoy's undertaking was the first attempt in Russia to publish an independent journal, and Polevoy was one of the first bourgeois to appear upon the Russian literary scene. Vyazemsky's co-operation with him needs to be set against the aristocratic hostility which he expressed to the other bourgeois of the period, Bulgarin and Grech, venal journalists who were in the pay of the government.

Vyazemsky's dislike of Bulgarin was well founded, for he spent two years from 1828 to 1830, clearing himself of the libel brought by Bulgarin, to the effect that he was the author of subversive writings. Vyazemsky cleared his name before the Emperor and was allowed to remain in state service, though not in the Ministry of Justice, as he had hoped, but in the department of finances. In 1831 appeared his translation of *Adolphe*.

Herzen and others have borne witness to the cramping and suffocating atmosphere of Russia between 1830 and 1840, under the rigid military autocracy of Nicholas I. In Vyazemsky's poems of this period appear for the first time the elegiac note and the poet's vision of himself as the sole survivor of a great age. This note becomes stronger still after the pitiful death of Pushkin in 1837. Vyazemsky was abroad for long periods during these years, travelling in Germany, Italy, France, and, in 1838, Britain.

Until 1847, Vyazemsky continued to work for the Finance Ministry, but a change of ministers in 1845 did not improve his position. The death of his daughter in 1840 was only the first of a series of bereavements, which took from Vyazemsky those who remained of his companions from the milieu of Pushkin. Yazykov died in 1843, Boratynsky in 1844, A.I. Turgenev in 1845. Almost the sole survivor was P.A. Pletnev (1792-1862), with whom Vyazemsky collaborated on the 'Sovremennik', and whom he highly valued. At the same time he drew close to the self-effacing Tyutchev, who is now considered the finest Russian poet of that time. In Vyazemsky's verse of this period, together with the characteristic themes of solitude and of age, appears some religious feeling. But the prose is probably more important, since to these years belongs Vyazemsky's most ambitious and provocative criticism, which attacks, in the name of the earlier aristocratic literature, the natural school of the 1840s, the critical attitudes of Belinsky and his disciples, and the intrusion into criticism of political and sociological considerations. The European revolutionary movements of 1848 led Vyazemsky to disown explicitly the liberalism of his youth. In 1849, the death of his eldest daughter impelled Vyazemsky and his wife to travel to Constantinople, where they stayed with their son, the only child remaining to them. From there Vyazemsky visited the supposed field of Troy, and also Jerusalem, before returning to Russia in the next year. In 1851 he was abroad again, in Paris, recuperating from a serious illness, and for the next few years he travelled, as a sick man, in Italy, Germany, France and Switzerland. In 1854, he published in Brussels a collection of letters on the political state of Europe, *Lettres d'un vétéran de l'armée Russe en 1812*.

In the next year, on the death of Nicholas and the succession of Alexander II, Vyazemsky returned to Russia, to become Minister of Education (a post which involved some dealings with the censorship), and an intimate adviser of the Imperial family. He resigned his Ministerial post in 1858, and was again abroad for over a year. In 1861 the Russian Academy celebrated the fifty-year jubilee of Vyazemsky's introduction to the theatre of Russian letters; in all the liberal organs the festival was made the occasion of severely satirical attacks upon Vyazemsky as man of letters, as publicist, and as politician. For the last fifteen years of his life, Vyazemsky was never in Russia for long. He lived more and more in the past, reading memoirs and writing studies of the same sort on the scenes of his youth. In his last years his time was spent in preparing for the press a collected edition of his works, for which he wrote an autobiographical introduction; but the complete edition had still not appeared when he died in Baden-Baden on 10 November 1878.

There is no need to emphasize that the range of topic and sentiment in Vyazemsky's verse is not wide. Apart from the early verse there appears on the one hand the scorn, sometimes savage, sometimes light-hearted, of his invective and satire; on the other hand, laments for vanished glories, a sense of personal insufficiency, isolation, and sterility, the thought that he has outlived his own best period, tributes to those who seem to retain the unfashionable attitudes which he prized, and a wholesale disillusionment with the Russia in which he wrote. It is inevitable, therefore, that the reading of Vyazemsky's verse in bulk becomes monotonous. At its best the verse is remarkable for the purity of its diction, and its inventive vigour of movement. Modern English criticism has taken to heart the Aristotelean remark that in metaphor the poetic power is most evident. Too often such criticism takes the 'image' as the unit for appreciation, beginning and ending by showing the poet's command of metaphorical language. No attitude could be less serviceable for appreciating the Russian poets in general. In Vyazemsky, as in Pushkin himself, the image is not greatly used. Where it occurs it is drawn from a limited conventional range. It is not organic, nor decorative, nor striking; it illustrates. Images are not swollen into symbols, nor worried into conceits, nor daubed on to the poem for the sake of a sensuous opulence or accuracy. The poet makes his effect by working inside a comparatively limited vocabulary and an artificial rhetoric. In this respect, the English poets who most nearly resemble Vyazemsky or Pushkin are to be found in the eighteenth century, but the themes of the Russian poets are not the themes of Dryden or of Pope, of Johnson or of Cowper. And the Russian poems are suffused with a sort of romantic feeling impossible before the Europe of the French Revolution. When all is said and done, therefore, the English poet whom it is most helpful to keep in mind is still Byron. In one of his poems Vyazemsky treats of Byron and the Byronic vogue in Russia. His attitude to the English poet, as to the Russian fashion, is by no means uncritical. But only in Byron do we find Romantic themes and feelings, together with a respect for the values and methods of the poets of the preceding century. On this account I have tried to keep in mind the characteristically Byronic rhetoric, while translating.

Brighton

Deep peace on Brighton has descended
And, wearied by the brawls of day,
The people sleep, wants, sins, all ended,
And to me, only the sea's extended
Booming, through the mist, makes way.

Of what, thou sea, art thou complaining?
Wherefore these sobs which fill thy breast?
Against nocturnal quiet straining,
Crying, groaning, and exclaiming,
Tossing in dreams but not at rest?

The strains are eloquent and loud,
When the heaven and earth give tongue,
When rolls 'mid fires the thunder-cloud,
And, with the storm, dispute aloud
The woods, in one concerted song.

But all's as nought, oh sea, before
Thy plaint, when thou dost nightly pine,
And sudden strifes dismay once more,
And urge thy sobs of grief, so sore
My soul could mingle tears with thine.

1838

Stanzas to Davydov

Versifying, I invoked you,
Denis, from a distant clime,
Not knowing that – your state how altered! –
The cypress held you, not the vine.

Back the echo came, from my
Indigenous acres. There, they say,
Brother, my own dear cemetery
Sepulchres your clay.

Hunting my friend brought back his day.
Grievous, the day retrieved!
Friend crossed with good companion is
The composite shade I grieve for.

Cold the poet's sparkling cup,
Cold the guerilla's blade unsheathed.
From glass and pipe the fumes rose up,
The living speech no longer breathed.

No longer, firing and delighting,
Flares out, strewn like stars, your keen
Language of light horse – still lighting
Down to sting the philistine.

No more shall stories ever new,
Ever in spate, transport us
From rigours of the Finnish snow
To tempt the flaming Caucasus;

Nor tell of that year, stamped in blood,
When, fired for vengeance on her foes,
While overhead the Kremlin glowed,
The Russian earth in love arose,

When unconditionally all,
Great and humble, offerings brought
To native shrines and, one in soul,
Deadly the folk went forth, and fought.

In tales that stirred the heart, your learning
In the people and their ways
Brought shadows from their graves returning
In brightness that excludes our gaze.

Out of the past that Achilles,
Bagration, came; Seslavin, then;
Kutuzov, our sly Ulysses;
Kulnyev – the brave and simple men.

Of you, great lords in years of glory
And years of force, survives not one!
And see, your peer, who sang your story,
Into the darkling tomb is gone.

Our dignities has Death all blasted.
Our eyes with listless tears are filled
Where the glass is spurned, untasted,
And all escutcheons are annulled.

Within your unmanned halls I waited.
I called – the one-time strain was still.
Belatedly my verse encounters
No smiles from lips gone chill.

This song, my votive tribute soaring,
Records the bright and vanished past.
This my libation, Denis, pouring,
Take to your heart, beloved dust.

1854

To Fyodor Ivanovich Tyutchev

Your song-bird, trailing wounded wings,
Sings with such a plaintive note,
To us so sympathetic rings
The sorrow in the singer's throat,

Our coldness with that anguish burns,
Of the song's pain enamoured grown,
And the heart in us, echoing, yearns
And weeps for woes that seem its own.

Poet, misfortune's ulcerous sore
Anointing with secreted balm,
The tears that from your soul you pour
Ring pearls about an inward harm.

1864

To P.A. Pletnev and F.I. Tyutchev

To you, twin peers out of that pleiad blest,
Where I played once my part among the rest,
Preservers of the taste, the views, the ties
In which our circle started and grew wise,
Unblushing, yet not boldly satisfied,
To you my book of verses I confide.

Whatever pressures moved my mind or heart,
The fleeting gleams which in bright colours start
When Inspiration's hour in dreams appears,
What moved my mind to laughter, what to tears,
The genial fits, delusions and mistakes,
The unmeant faults that human frailty makes,
Things somewhat prized, yet as no partisan,
All that my mind or feelings chanced upon,
The good thing loved, the loathéd escapade,
My whole confession, all of me betrayed,
You are to read in my perfidious book.
Rough numbers rise where you, my judges, look,
The wilful word, the sense or stress to gloze,
Harsh turns, and in the stanzas tags of prose.
Spare no regret nor blame, but still be hard;
From little sound the much corrupt discard.
But seek the man behind the bard to ken,
Redeem the pang from the defaulting pen.
....
....

Zhukovsky was my judge, and Pushkin too;
Now I have lost the old, nor come by new.
You have I left: in you their flame is bright,
You pair my public Areopagite.
Still in you, sacred, glows the native love
That brightened our domestic hearth above.
Still, with you by, may I the past recall,
To whom, from strings long-snapped, the echoes call,
Still bandy talk of a familiar cast
And stories cherished from our common past.
The public I esteem, at ball or play;
But for its favour will not dearly pay.
....

I fled the idols of the multitude,
Its views in vogue, its men of note eschewed.
I never served as tool, footstool, or spring,
Nor, in my turn, their parrot, learned to sing.
It pleased me best to tread the untrodden way,
And what I felt, to sing; what thought, to say.
As best I knew, with flowers of the fall,
I have bedecked the ingle of my entrance hall,
Inviting whom but you, to modest cheer,
You, who are ancients of a better year?
Of others dear, none from their tombs will burst,

For none may close again what time dispersed.
Well-satisfied and pleased shall be my muse,
If spleens have sympathy, or pranks amuse.
Therefore my gift accept, with frankness due,
With no less love than tenders it to you.

1864

Reminiscences from Boileau

> Qui n'aime pas Cotin, n'estime pas son roi
> Et n'a, selon Cotin, ni Dieu, ni foi, ni loi.
> *Boileau*

Beneath the moon is nothing new,
All to one pattern knave and fool.
Sometimes our taunts can take their cue
From butts of Boileau's ridicule.

Our publicists, as all agree,
Cry how just deed or honest page
Only with publicists can be,
He our sole citizen and sage:

He who, forthright, or on the sly,
The publicist cannot endorse,
By that same token does deny
Russia, tsar and God, of course;

Those who, in one particular,
Have dared join issue with his force,
In deathly dooms all labouring are,
Traitors or thieves or something worse.

II

When two self-publicists are met
Self-publicising talk is heard:
'How strong I am in my gazette,
My journal – standard, staff, and sword.'

Bright Bismarck of the Russian press,
Not to say the Bonaparte,
Here I scourge, and there I bless,
And legalise the laws by art.

Man with a mission, man of fate,
Public opinion's guide and head,
Minds hungering from birth await
My hand to feed them daily bread.

Russia, but for me, had been
Prostrate, or in fragments strewn;
Who did the falling state sustain?
What valiant hand if not my own?

Strictly logical in judgment
I am not, nor do care to be;
Small store of notions am I lent,
But do without them skilfully.

The names on my subscription list
Need, not ideas, but a word
That from their reading may persist,
And in their table-talk be heard.

Part by skill and part by luck
My hand has plucked the popular string;
Now I take care that note once struck
To strike again on everything.

....
....
....
....

....
....
....
....

Here, fuddled, 'Change!' erupt the cries,
And line by line, learnt off by heart,
Foaming, hysteria writhing lies,
And – 'Stop-press Moscow' – takes our part.

III

Now 'Patriotism', 'the forward trend',
For me too have a weighty sound,
When honest voices to them lend
Meanings hallowed and profound.

But kindling visions, wit in kind,
Must to the actual scene relate,
That from the first the sturdy mind
Their infirm fevers may abate.

A patriotic heat abjures
An endless sounding of alarm,
Nor, in and out of season, roars
Rumours of intrigue, hints of harm.

The crimson tocsin and the white,
Each fiercely clamorous, inflame
The people's passions, and affright
With evils which they cannot name.

All things observe due time and rate,
Which it is fatal to disown.
The zealot in his frenzied state
Shows Truth herself a cozener grown.

In the year 'twelve, the foe, dismayed,
And thwarted by a timely scheme,
Saw flame those fires by patriots laid,
Immortalizing Rostopchin.

But would the case be just the same,
Or what should we have said of it,
If he had each year fed the flame,
And stoked the Moscow he had lit?

IV

These self-advertisements displease me,
And scribble on my soul, 'Untrue';
I'm dubious when clairvoyants see
The earth infected through and through.

In nature's world and thought's I see,
As if to prove I'm wrong to scoff,
A sudden pestilence of three,
Cholera, Bismarck, and Katkov.

1866

Hlestakov[1]

No, Hlestakov has never died:
The *Moscow News* you need to scan,
Any number – look inside:
And find him there a living man.

In all, his self-importance see,
On self-importance fuddled grown:
Familiar with the powers that be,
Himself the power of every throne.

'Tis he the Ministries have sought
To forward their affairs of state.
To him is each oration brought,
When the address still lacks a date.

We never patriotism knew,
He first invented the idea;
Sound slumber reigned all Russia through,
But he knew how to make us hear.

He 'Yuri Miloslavsky' wrought,
From him the 'Rossiada's' come.
His inspiration Peter taught
Swedes at Poltava to o'er-come.

In the year 'twelve, who kept at bay
And – 'nuff said – beat the Frenchman off?
Excuse me, Kutuzov, did you say?
By no means – 'twas this Hlestakov.

---

[1]   *Hlestakov*: the hero of Gogol's comedy, *Revisor (The Government Inspector)*. The last stanza pushes home the point of the comparison with the play.

Whose terse dispatches at this hour
Hit nails on heads and pierce the foe?
No question: Hlestakov must score
On targets only he can show.

From Batu's days to ours, we all
By him were saved from might and strife.
And Russia still survives at all
Because he has insured her life.

His finger, raised, reproves a fault.
And Shedo-Ferotti and Mazade,
The Pole, The Georgian, the Balt
Fly back before him, shamed and sad.

He schools us all, so all believe.
He takes dislikes – he's fearful then;
Napoleon shuddered to receive
His sheets, and paled before his pen.

All this is rot, but here's the rub –
Bobchinsky's and Dobchinsky's race
Gape before him on his tub,
With credulous and vacant face,

And prick their ears, and take due note,
Accept his bragging gabs for true,
Till Russia's saviour, every throat
Hails him, at home and outside too.

....
....
....
....

See, he devises other tricks,
His ardours rise in him once more;
No longer hoaxing certain districts,
But grown all Russia's 'Revisor'.

1866

So-and-so's dead...

('he departed for Rostov'. – I. Dmitriev)

So–and–so's dead. And what of it? He lived and is dead.
He's dead, and there's no more to say. For such is the common lot.
From the book of the living a number's selected,
And 'departed for Rostov' is entered on the spot.
We are all bound for Rostov together; though earlier some,
Some others by so much belated, we lodge in one inn.
There are bills for fresh horses in the pocket of each one,
And at all our baptizings our funerals begin.
And after? The question. There's a shroud shrouds all.
And all pilgrims on earth have to wonder the same:
'Does Rostov the riddle tell us nothing at all?'

1876

From *Hermathena* (LXXVI), 1955, revised.

3   Pan Tadeusz *in English Verse*

Mickiewicz is a poet too important to European consciousness as a whole, and to the whole European poetic tradition, to be available only to those who can speak and read Polish. Though I dare say there is no Mickiewicz scholar who would dispute this, yet it is hard for them to give due weight to this aspect of the matter. For it is a basic assumption of any responsible literary scholarship, and (what is not altogether or always the same thing) of any responsible literary criticism, that the poetry resides in the particular words used by the poet, and nowhere else. Yet this, though it is the only right and proper basis for the scholarly and critical disciplines, is after all belied by the facts. No one can deny that something of the poetry of Homer, of Horace, of Shakespeare, of Dante has 'come through' to readers unable to understand a word of the original, even to readers so out of touch with the cultures from which these poets sprang that they can be seen to misread quite flagrantly – and yet not so flagrantly as to miss everything the poet has to offer. The name of Mickiewicz deserves to belong with these great names; and yet it is apparent that his name does not belong with them, that he is not enjoyed by readers who know no Polish, as Shakespeare is by those who know no English, or as Dante is by those who cannot read Italian. It is this consideration that nerves me to write on Mickiewicz, even though I know his work only in English translation.

If Mickiewicz is little known in English, that is not the fault of his translators; and I, who enjoy Mickiewicz only by favour of their exertions, should be the last to blame them. *Pan Tadeusz*, at any rate, exists, in the prose translation by George Rapall Noyes (London, 1917), as an enthralling and beautiful narrative. Moreover, this translation is available to British readers, very properly, in the most widely influential series of cheap classic reprints, the Everyman's Library. Yet the fact remains that *Pan Tadeusz* is virtually unknown to the English poetry-reading public. What else, it may be asked, can anyone do in the matter? Where can the blame rest, except on the laziness and imperceptiveness of the British reader?

It rests, I am inclined to think, on the contemporary British poets. In getting classic authors out of the hands of the scholarly specialists and over to the common reader of poetry, much depends on the poets currently writing. If Dante is now read widely in English, that is above all because the English poets from Keats and Shelley to Eliot, Ezra Pound, and Yeats (the last an Irishman, but widely read in England) have so repeatedly used Dante as a model, and alluded to him, by implication or explicitly, in their own verses. Similarly, I dare say, nothing brought Goethe to so many English readers as the allusions to his work in the poetry of Matthew Arnold. No English poet, to my knowledge, has made such use of Mickiewicz. If he is to contribute anything to the English conception of what poetry is and has been, it rests with the English poets to show that they, at any rate, have taken account of him in this way. The next move is with them.

It will be seen that I have not in mind, in the first place, the business of verse-translation, in any strict sense. I detect a tendency nowadays to look askance at translation into verse; and I think this is healthy. It derives from the recognition that the first question to be asked of verse-translation is not, 'Is it faithful to the original?' but, 'Is it poetry in its own right?' (This is obviously just, for a translation which is not even poetry is by that token obviously unfaithful in the most crucial way to its poetic original.) We have thus come to realize that the only worthwhile translation into verse will be the work of a man who is a born poet in his own right; and thus that the true verse-translator is an even rarer bird than the true poet. Moreover, any unprejudiced reader must think that Professor Noyes's English prose is a great deal more poetic than, for instance, the *Master Thaddeus* in English blank verse of Maude Ashurst Biggs (London, 1885). It is more poetic and, to just that extent, more readable; the rhythms of the blank verse, in the other version, where there is no poetic content to justify them, are a ruinously irritating distraction.

Yet a poetic talent that is very slender indeed, or even merely latent, may be awakened by the stimulus of an inspired original. It was an instance of this that first stirred my interest in Mickiewicz, when twelve years ago I encountered by chance F.H. Fortey's versions of the first two of the *Crimean Sonnets*. I quote the second of these:

The Sea in a Calm

(From the Rock of Tarkankut)

The flag scarce stirs; the bosom of the main
    Rises and falls in silence, like a bride
    Who dreams her life of rapture will abide,
Then, sighing, wakes and, smiling, dreams again.

The sails are furled (so calm the watery plain)
  As when war's ended flags are furled and tied;
  The sailing-vessels all so stilly ride
As if they anchored were with iron chain.

O Ocean! In the midst of thy bright homes
  A polyp lives: it sleeps deep down in storm;
    In calm, its arms gigantic upward start!

O Mind! Deep, deep in thy abyss there roams
  The hydra of the Past – a sleeping form
    In strife; in rest – its talons reach the heart!

This is an arresting English poem in its own right – though of the 1830s, not the 1920s when it was written, when locutions like 'bosom of the main' and 'watery plain' had long passed out of the usable poetic vocabulary. Yet Fortey, to judge from the rest of his little collection (*Gems of Polish Poetry. Selections from Mickiewicz*, Warsaw, 1923), was in general a thoroughly uninspired versifier. This, however, only supports my main contention, which is that it is in the highest degree unlikely one will ever see a verse translation of *Pan Tadeusz* to surpass Noyes's prose version. Verse translation at its best must always surpass prose translation; but that 'best' is so hard to come by (being either a work of rare genius in its own right, or else, as in Fortey's achievement, the outcome of a fitful and temporary sympathy), and verse-translation short of the very best is such tedious reading, that in calling upon the English poets to help the English reader to Mickiewicz we should not ask them in the first place to provide verse translations.

   If their contribution is to be thought of as 'translation' at all (and after all it is translation in some sense that we ask of them), we must understand 'translation' in its widest and loosest sense, as covering all the activities variously described as imitation, adaptation, sustained allusion, paraphrase. For it is in these fields that they can do most good. As it happens, or so I think, English or American poetry can boast at the present day one brilliant example of that very rare genius, the true verse-translator. I mean Ezra Pound. Unfortunately Pound never turned his attention to any of the Slavonic literatures. But his achievement reinforces the point I wish to make; for while he has done some work of strict verse translation, he has done much more by way of adaptation, allusion, imitation. And – however it may hurt the scholarly conscience to admit this – he has been not least successful, nor least 'faithful', when he was working from an original in a language he hardly knew, taking it all at one or several removes through the notes of a commentator, as he did when writing *Cathay*, his early sequence from the Chinese.

It is, at any rate, on speculations and arguments of this kind that I fall back, in order to justify my own tinkerings with *Pan Tadeusz*. Having lived with Noyes's prose version for many years, I have found myself tempted several times to draw out more saliently the poetry which I felt to be lurking just below the surface of the English prose. What emerges from these experiments of mine is obviously not translation in the ordinary sense, and perhaps not translation in any sense. It does not much matter what name is given to it. I did this work in the first place for my own satisfaction; and if I now contemplate publishing some of it, it is because I hope by doing so to bring Mickiewicz, for the English literary consciousness, into his rightful place among the masters of European poetry.

And yet of course my motives are not wholly altruistic. It would be absurd if they were. Mickiewicz does not stand in need of anybody's charity; and no one asks the modern English poets to read Mickiewicz as a public duty. Mickiewicz has much to teach them – yes, even in translation – and if they have a duty towards him, that is only part of their general obligation, as poets, to perfect their own technical equipment. For English poets of today must be engaged, just as their Polish contemporaries are (if we may believe Czesław Miłosz), in fighting their way back, from surrealism and *poésie pure* and belated Victorianism, to a classical dryness and to the formula coined by T.S. Eliot and echoed by Miłosz, 'the perfection of a common language': 'The style of Mickiewicz is manly and simple. He knew how to use conventional phrasing and, without straying beyond its limits, how to transform it into something completely new. That is not easy. Many poets maintain their standards only at the price of being unconventional, and drop into dullness as soon as they venture to use traditional methods. Through a slight retouching of words, a genuine poet is able to invest a commonplace sentence with charm. But genuine poets are rare, and there are periods of history when such an operation is impossible, because the use of a 'common style' is then beyond the reach of even the great poets'. (I quote from Miłosz's 'Mickiewicz and Modern Poetry', in *Adam Mickiewicz, Poet of Poland*, edited by Manfred Kridl, New York, 1951.) These observations, and the implication behind them that Mickiewicz can today be an unusually fruitful model, are as timely and as apposite in London as in Warsaw. The example of Mickiewicz can be a great help to the English poet of today who is conscientiously trying to learn his trade.

It was precisely because I was feeling my way towards this 'common style' that I undertook my first imitation from *Pan Tadeusz*, a

version of the Judge's speech on courtesy in Book I. I can point to
the very sentence of Noyes's prose which set me to work: 'And our
elders did study: in noble mansions the discourse furnished the
listener a living history of his land, and the talk among the gentry
formed the household annals of the county.' I believe it was the very
rhythms of this English sentence which determined the metre of my
paraphrase; yet doubtless this passage would not have appealed to
me if in my own verse at that time (several years ago) I had not been
trying to convey the meaning of tradition, in the shape of unwritten
laws of decorum binding together a long-established community.
My version (first published in *The Spectator*, London) is as follows:

> The Lithuanian judge
> Offers by way of reproof
> To the young Pan Tadeusz
> Decorum, the difficult science,
> No matter of graceful posture
> Or ease at the affable counter,
> But bearing of old Poland;
> Courtesy, being extended
> To all, not without distinction
> But in the mode most proper,
> As to master with man, or to children
> With parents, or each to each,
> In public, husband and wife.
> Discourse in noble mansions
> Was then a persistent history,
> And talk among the gentry
> The annals of their provinces;
> Gentlemen watched their step,
> Knowing such pains were taken
> To judge of their deserving.
> But neither name nor stock,
> Associates nor achievements,
> Are now inquired after,
> And each goes where he pleases
> Short of the known informer
> And the scrounger by profession.
> Vespasian never questioned
> Out of what hands his riches
> Came to him, having decided
> Money was 'not to be sniffed at'.
> So men approve a title
> And value their connections

By current estimates,
As if to strike up a friendship
Were also a transaction.
But a sense of personal worth
Is arrived at only by weighing;
The beam is only plumb
With a counterpoise in the pan,
A worthiness in another.

It will be seen that the liberties I have taken here (chiefly the running together of two separate speeches by the Judge, and the omission of his final reference to the decorum governing courtship) are only those demanded if the excerpt is to be self-contained.

Much more recently, I tried to do something with the Chamberlain's rejoinder to this speech by the Judge:

And one recalls the pro-French element.
"All men are equal": thus in conversation
Self-styled 'the marquis,'
Democrat later, but after this
By Bonapartist dispensation
'Le Baron.' The doctrine ancient;
But the application?

Worse than the Nogai tartars
That Frenchified generation,
Mocking the faith of their fathers,
Foes to all precedent.
Ring-worm in the great peruke;
Brochures and dissipation
Procured a servile Lent.

Better as now, at last
From France to earn
Glory, than learn
New fads as in the past.
Napoleon moves fast.
Valour bears glorious fruit.
Liberty grows from the laurel's root.

Plainly, this excerpt cannot stand by itself, with its own title. And yet I have here taken much greater liberties; have left much out, rearranged the order of the Chamberlain's rambling remarks, and tried to draw together several floating references into one forceful image, 'Ring-worm in the great peruke'.

A more serious drawback is the tone of my version. I aimed at a man-of-the-world's urbanity, with a sort of weary indignation, thinking that this might represent the difference in social status and background between the Chamberlain and the Judge. But now I read in Professor Weintraub's *Poetry of Adam Mickiewicz* (The Hague, 1954), p.237: 'A few times the poet-narrator interrupts with grave lyrical digressions, such as the passage opening Book XI, which re-creates the atmosphere of the spring of 1812, full of great expectations; or the moving apostrophe to the trees of Lithuania (IV, 1-41). But generally, he wears a mask, that of a naïve, old-fashioned prattler, who is emotionally and intellectually one with the world he describes.' If this is indeed the mask, the persona, through which the poet speaks, then I fear the tone I give to the Chamberlain's conversation, as reported by the narrator, is quite out of keeping.

In fact, Professor Weintraub's remarks on this score supply something which no one could gather for himself from reading the Noyes version – partly, no doubt, just because that version is in prose, and the 'prattling' tone is carried in the very minutiæ of verse form. (See, for instance, Weintraub's remarks on certain of the rhymes: 'Such rhymes give the text a touch of rustic simplicity. They are of a piece with the general stylization of the poem, a tale told by an old rustic.', p.260.) It is, I think, just because from Noyes one cannot determine the prevailing attitude and tone of the narrator, that in his version the poem presents itself as such a baffling achievement. For one is struck, of course, by the great variety of the materials that have gone into the poem; and one is at a loss to conceive in English of a poetic convention at once so firm and so flexible as to govern these heterogeneous elements and mould them into one. I do not think in fact that such a convention exists. The readiness to find poetry in the homely and the commonplace reminds one of Wordsworthian blank verse; in other poems by Wordsworth, *The Thorn*, for instance, or other pieces from the *Lyrical Ballads*, one finds a tone that could justly be described as 'prattling'; and yet in *Pan Tadeusz* there is prattle of another sort, sly and laced with wit, which makes one think rather of Byron's *Beppo* or *Don Juan*. Faced with the problem of reconciling Byron's conventions with Wordsworth's, no wonder the English poet is baffled! And of course, if we cannot read the Polish, Professor Weintraub really takes us no nearer; he can only tell us what the convention is, he cannot present it in action.

As a result, I have found it impossible to versify passages of any length, and instead have tried to find and draw out more or less self-contained extracts. This is unfortunate because, like the notorious anthology, *Beauties of Shakespeare*, it may suggest to the innocent reader that the poem is a collection of separable beauties connected by passages of relatively dull or unimportant material. Among such fairly obvious set pieces (they are not that in the original, but they seem so when extracted) are the episodes of the mushroom gathering in Book III, and of the count watching Zosia in the kitchen garden in Book II:

> Swimming knee-deep, she trawls among the fronds,
> In wrinkled waves for vegetable fish.
> First the foot finds, and then the hand responds;
> She stoops and gathers for a luncheon dish.
>
> Her right hand raised as if to pluck the air,
> Attentively she dawdles down the rows;
> Her eyes look down, her bright and straying hair
> Stirs in the straw hat's shadow, as she goes.
>
> The count is watching, like a crane that stands
> With neck outstretched, outside the feeding flock,
> One leg cranked up, a stone in its lean hand
> Clawed close, to fall and wake it with the shock.
>
> A voice distracts. He turns. She's there no more.
> The leaves return to quiet like a flood
> Cut by a wing. The basket that she bore
> Rides the green swell, capsizing where she stood.

But here, alas, the most brilliant and challenging passage – the introductory enumeration of the different vegetables, precise, humorous, and poetic all at once – this has defeated me.

I have made one attempt at versifying, with much telescoping and conspicuous omissions, a sustained passage from Book II, in which Mickiewicz moves from one kind of material to another, shifting his mood as he does so. I will close by giving this in full:

> Breakfast the judge
> Against the grain
> Admits alfresco:
> Sportsmen home again
> Move to and fro
> And serve the ladies, bear
> In Dresden ware
> Cups, capped in cream,
> Of coal-black, honey-thick

Coffee, as aromatic
As mocha, amber-clear
On charming trays;
Themselves the gentlemen
Take as they may prefer
Ham, goose, or tongue,
All cured in juniper,
And then stewed beef in gravy.

As for the coursing match,
Unsatisfactory;
The dogs called off
The hare in standing corn,
The whole match off.
                              And the count:
They order these things better
(That is, the chase)
In Muscovy, respect the grain
By ukase and decree
As to time and place
'On a higher plane.'

So Telimena,
Installed in a summer villa
Outside St Petersburg;

When Fate must send,
To live next door,
Dog-loving dull *chinovnik*;
Alarming dogs conspire to rend
The night, and drive her frantic.

Worse is in store.
The lady swoons
To see her spaniel mangled
By cruel beagles, and before
Her eyes abruptly strangled.

But brought to book,
The culprits shook:
The tsar's own hunting master
Was bending his tremendous look
Upon both hound and master.

'You coursed a doe!'
'Milord, a dog.'

'What, sir, you contradict me?
The hunting laws, I'll have you know,
Are here enforced quite strictly.'

Four weeks C.B.,
For *chinovniki*
Who course game out of season;
And for their dogs, a summary
Death, for the same good reason.

(Thus Telimena
To the room at large;
Thus, with composure.)

Who'd not condone
The dubious note
In such a lovely cause?
Triumph of tone!
Her anecdote
Draws laughter and applause.

Meanwhile the swain
Forgets the maid
And courts this ampler fair,
Who sets in train
The ambuscade
Of love, and baits the snare.

Now she delays
The murmured phrase
Which he must stoop to catch;
Her gaze, his eyes,
His lips, her sighs
Mingle, and make the match.

Oh that a fly
Should come between
So close a tête-à-tête!
Pursuit, pass by,
Nor intervene!
Domestic hygiene, wait!

He swats. They start
And jump apart,

Halves of a riven tree.
The lightning stroke
Has cleft an oak
Of love's own forestry.

Here the problem of course was the management of transitions. To take the significance of this passage, the reader needs to have had established for him the character of Telimena. Because the reader of my excerpt might not have this information, and also because he might miss the point of Telimena's ambiguous, more than half approving attitude to the 'civilization' of St Petersburg, I have inserted the stanza about 'Triumph of tone'. But this, I'm afraid, is open to the same objections, on the score of inappropriate tone, as is my version of the Chamberlain's speech. And even so, in my rendering it is difficult to believe that the person who narrates the fly-swatting is the same person as describes the serving of the coffee.

Just as a climber who spends all day on one cliff gets to know through his fingertips the mass and poise of a whole mountain, so to scramble in this way over the face of a poem is to become incomparably familiar with it. And if the end of all our endeavours is the admission that we have no idea how it was done, that only means perhaps that we, who have no recourse to the original, are even more conscious than those who have, of what is inexplicable and miraculous in so prodigious an achievement as *Pan Tadeusz*.

From *Adam Mickiewicz in World Literature*, ed. Wacław Lednicki. Berkeley, Los Angeles: University of California Press, 1956.

4 *The Forests of Lithuania*

Note

This poem, like the *Pan Tadeusz* of Mickiewicz, from which it is adapted, is set in Lithuania in the years 1811 and 1812. At this period Lithuania was under Russian occupation, but the sister Kingdom of Poland had been liberated by Napoleon, and Lithuanian patriots frequently escaped to join the Polish legions fighting with the Napoleonic armies as far afield as the West Indies. In 1812, when the French launched their march on Moscow, Lithuania was also briefly liberated. The poem is to be supposed written, as Mickiewicz's poem was written, by a Lithuanian in exile, twenty years later.

Foreword   Mickiewicz in England

Don John of Chesterton was riding to the wars
For Christendom and the Latin heritage
When Monica Gardner spoke of me. *Le Coq*
Gaulois of Belloc crowed around the clock
'Too late, too late'; for Gorky held the stage
And 'Never a patch of plot', said James, enthralled,
'To draw blood', in a story
By Turgenev.
           Scythians invest
Small perfect Europe, for whose sake
All Souls' High Table hears expressed
Dreams of 'Divide and rule'.

Did Belloc baulk, did Pound protest
When Saintsbury found Sienkeiwicz unlicked?
Who quoted Kochanowski, and to cap
What Latin tag? Who cared
That he was salvaged from Cyrillic script,

The Ronsard of Czarnólas?
                              What orisons
Rose, modishly baroque,
                              for our lady of Czestochowa?
                    Who could see
The Hun turn East? Who egged him on?
Who raged at Chamberlain for a guarantee
To Poland, honoured?
                    Europe's paladin,
                    the champion of the *civitas*,
He killed Cock Robin.

The man on the touchline sees most of the play
But may not know the rules. The Antipodean
Anti-Semite brilliantly alleges
The best of Europe's all around the edges,
The rest a ghetto, 'mittel-European'
His curse on Martin Buber.
                              In the white
Nights of the Neva, quays of Amsterdam
And lions of Venice violate a site
Stolen from quagmire and the Finn; an *urbs*
Not Augustinian yet not without
Pushkin's *urbanitas*.
                    Some work their passage
Home out of Kronstadt, through Crimean sonnets,
Or recognise in Florence with a start
The Piazza Demidoff. And Europe's heart
Is wherever community happens in any age.

I   *The Homestead*

    White walls shone from far
    White against green of poplars'
    Windbreak against Autumn.
    The house no great one, but the barn
    Great, and with stacks beside it,
    Gross country, full with foison.
    Enter to these the youth
    Beneath ancestral portraits,
    Ancestral, and of heroes:
    Kosciusko sworn and sworded

To drive three powers from Poland
Or fall upon that sword;
Rejtan, a Life of Cato
And the Phaedo before him,
These, and a knife turned inward;
Jasinski smiting the Russians
With Korsak, on the ravelin
Of Praga burning behind them.
Enter to these Tadéusz,
And to the grandfather clock
That plays Dombrowski's march,
And to his room when a boy...

But this, so feminine?
Can this be the place? a piano,
Sheet-music upon it, books...
And see, across a chair
The white gown freshly shaken.
Cross to the window. A brook
That ran through nettles once
Borders a garden plot
Of grass and mint. Those beds
Were lately rained upon:
The watering pot that stands
Half-full has felt
Just now her hand, the gate
Swings from her touch, on the sand
– Dry, white as snow – the print
Is light but clear of some
Unshod, unstockinged foot
That lately ran. His eyes
Rove, and as they rise
See her upon the wall
Balanced, in her white
And morning disarray
That will not screen,
Though crossed arms veil the breast,
Swan's throat and shoulders. Hair
In curling-paper rays
A small head, in the sun
Thus crowned, an ikon. Turning
From wall to turf, across
Stile and parterre, and up
A leaning plank, like a bird

Flying, and like a ray
Of moonlight darting through
The windowframe she gains
The very chamber. He
Blushes and bows, retires
And will not look, but hears
Cry as of a child
Half-wakened. When he looks
No one...

His uncle's house, the judge's,
Where he is entertained
In the stately manner: Assessor,
Seneschal, Notary,
Apparitor, in order,
Gaily but in order,
Not without heat discussing
Hounds and guns and tomorrow
A coursing-match; but his thoughts
Running on women, the girl
He has glimpsed already, women
And one place left at the board.

The Lithuanian judge
Offers by way of reproof
To the young Pan Tadéusz
Decorum, the difficult science,
No matter of graceful posture
Or ease at the affable counter,
But bearing of old Poland;
Courtesy, being extended
To all, not without distinction
But in the mode most proper
As to master with man, or to children
With parents, or each to each
In public husband and wife.
'Discourse in noble mansions
Was then a persistent history,
And talk among the gentry
The annals of their provinces;
Gentlemen watched their step,
Knowing such pains were taken
To judge of their deserving.
But neither name nor stock,

Associates nor achievements
Are now enquired after,
And each goes where he pleases
Short of the known informer
And the scrounger by profession.
Vespasian never questioned
Out of what hands his riches
Came to him, having decided
Money was "not to be sniffed at".
So men approve a title
By current estimates,
As if to strike up a friendship
Were also a transaction.
But a sense of personal worth
Is arrived at only by weighing;
The beam is only plumb
With a counterpoise in the pan,
A worthiness in another.'

To whom the Chamberlain speaks
From the place of honour: 'Recall
The pro-French element.
"All men are equal" – thus
In conversation one
Self-styled the marquis,
(Democrat later, later still
By dispensation
Of Bonaparte, *le baron*).
The doctrine doubtless ancient,
But the application...? Worse
Than the Nogai tartars that
Frenchified generation,
Hating the faith of their fathers,
Foes to all precedent.
Ringworm in the great peruke!
Brochures and dissipation
Brought servile Lent. Far better
As now at last to earn
Glory from France, than learn
New fads as in the past.
Napoleon moves fast.
Valour bears glorious fruit,
Liberty from the laurel's root.'

And so to the legions!
So to news of the legions!
And yet not here, not now.
Who swam across the Niemen?
Gorecki, Pac, and Obuchowitz,
Piotrowski and the Mirzejewskis,
Brochocki and the Bernatowicz brothers,
Not here, not now. Perhaps
Later in private Robak
The Bernardine, the almoner
Of a foreign house, his bearing
So soldierly (and a sabre's
Cut on the brow), will take
A knife to scapulary. Now
Talk of the coursing, talk
Of the old dispute with the Count
With a foible for the Gothick
Who wants our ruined castle.
Tomorrow the folk may read
Their own gazette's citations
In the bearing of their betters
With pride, or brokenly. Or else
An old maimed beggar stands
Having his crust; and then
Out with it – Dombrowski
Assembling on the plains
Of Lombardy; Kniazewicz
Among the captured eagles
In Rome; or Jablonowski,
His Danube Legion locked,
Among the sugar canes
And the pepper plants, with the blacks.

II   *The Castle*

Who does not remember his boyhood, gun on shoulder,
  Whistling through unobstructed fields?
Overstepping the bounds, yet offending no leaseholder
  Of Lithuania, where the chase was free?

There ocean-goer, unmarked ship, the hunter
  Ranged at large; an augur,

Read skies and clouds; or to townsmen occult, an enchanter,
    Heard the earth-whisper.

Look in vain for the landrail, as lost down the meadow calling
    As pike in the Niemen, and look
In vain overhead for the lark whose carillon falling
    Around us rings in the Spring.

There an eagle wing rustles, appalling the sparrows,
    A comet dismaying the stars. And a falcon,
Fluttering butterfly pinned, when a hare moves in the meadow
    Stoops like a meteor.

When will the Lord God have us return, inhabit
    Ancestral fields, bear arms
Against the birds, and only to ride down the rabbit
    Muster our horse?

    Breakfast the Judge
    Against the grain
    Admits alfresco:
    Sportsmen home again
    Move to and fro
    And serve the ladies, bear
    In Dresden ware
    Cups, capped in cream,
    Of coal-black, honey-thick
    Coffee, as aromatic
    As mocha, amber-clear
    On charming trays;
    Themselves the gentlemen
    Take as they may prefer
    Ham, goose or tongue,
    All cured in juniper,
    Or else stewed beef in gravy.

    As for the coursing match,
    Unsatisfactory:
    The dogs called off
    The hare in standing corn,
    The whole match off. And the Count:
    'They order these things better
    In Muscovy, respect the grain
    By ukase and decree

As to time and place,
"On a higher plane".' And thus
Telimena, the lady of fashion,
Installed in a summer villa
Outside St Petersburg:

When fate must send
To live next door
Dog-loving dull *chinovnik*,
Alarming dogs conspire to rend
The night, and drive her frantic.
Worse is in store:
The lady swoons
To see her spaniel mangled
By cruel beagles, and before
Her eyes abruptly strangled.
The culprits brought to book,
The tsar's own hunting-master
Bends his tremendous look
On hound and master. 'What,
You coursed a doe?' 'Milord,
It was a dog'. 'Indeed,
So you prevaricate?
The hunting laws of Muscovy
Are meant to be obeyed.'
Four weeks detention cures
Suburban householders
Of hunting out of season;
Their dogs endure a summary
Death, for the same good reason.

Thus Telimena
To the room at large,
Thus, with composure:
Who'd not condone
The dubious note
In such a lovely cause?
Triumph of tone!
Her anecdote
Draws laughter and applause;
And now the swain
Forgets the maid
To court this ampler fair
Who sets in train

The ambuscade
Of love, and baits the snare;
Now she delays
The murmured phrase
Which he must stoop to catch;
Her gaze, his eyes,
His lips, her sighs
Mingle, and make the match.
Oh that a fly
Should come between
So close a tête-à-tête!
Pursuit, pass by
Nor intervene!
Domestic hygiene, wait!
Too late. The Seneschal
Has stalked his chosen fly
Too far. The blow must fall,
And fall it does. A start!
They jump apart,
Halves of a riven tree:
The lightning-stroke
Has cleft an oak
Of Love's own forestry.

Meanwhile by the castle wood
The Count as he rode to the coursing
Had checked at sight of the Keep
That rose from the morning mist
And seemed as tall again.
The roof of tin
Flashed in the sunlight over
Prismatic shards in the casements;
Mist hid in the lower stories
Jags and dilapidations.
Cries of the hunters from far
Windborne, returned by the walls,
For all the world from within
Sounded, as if the fog
With rapid restorations
Had pieced and peopled. The Count
Who aspired to be thought Romantic
Was reckoned an eccentric
Though honourable. Often,
Running the fox or the hare,

He would check and gaze at the sky
As mournfully as a cat
That sights a bird on a pinetree,
Or else as a motionless heron
Devouring fish through the eye.
And the horse he had turned from the road
Trod to the threshold. Alone
He sighed, gazed at the walls
That had once been his, and reached
For paper and pencil – yet started:
Twelve paces away another
Amateur of the picturesque
Counted the stones. Yet he knew him.
The ancient servitor
Of gentle birth, Gerwázy,
Who snatching his cap from a head
Bald and scored with the sabre
(A chopping block) recounted,
Conducting him through the courts,
Their sequestrated glories:

  'Here my old lord
  Sat, having dined,
  And here dispensed
  Rough justice. Jests
  And curious anecdotes
  Exchanged with guests
  Pleased his good humour, while
  In the court below
  Young men with staves
  Gave blow for blow
  Or else broke in
  His Turkish ponies.'
Entering the hall:
  'Less are the stones
  That pave this hall
  Than it saw tuns
  Of wine broached once
  At festival,
  Diet, or meet,
  When guests would haul
  By their belts cast
  Around them, from the vault
  Cask after cask.

As wine went round
Musicians played;
A tucket's sound
Hailed Vivat first
The King, and then
The Archbishop, then the Queen,
And then all gentlemen;
Last the Republic – when,
The fifth glass drained,
The health is "Let us love
Each man his friend", a toast
While day remained
First drunk, but still proposed
As dawn came up
And coach and horse
Stood at the doors.'

Inflamed to re-achieve
His patrimony, stirred,
The impressionable Count
Wandered away. The scene
Round him, unseeing,
Changed slowly. Here the green
Tresses of carrot snared
Slim beans that stared
From a thousand eyes; the sage
And venerable cabbage,
That seemed to meditate
On vegetable fate,
Bared his bald head; the bold
And portly melon rolled
Far from his home, to wait
Upon the flushed estate
Of beetroots; while,
Drawn up in file
(Their leaf the snake, their scent
Repels the flies) the hemp
Screened every bed, and a girl
That was Zosia wandered.

Swimming knee deep, she trawled
The wrinkled waves and fronds
For vegetable fish;
Exploring feet directed

The hand's response,
To pick for a luncheon dish.
Her right hand raised
As if to pluck the air,
She dawdled down the rows.
Her eyes looked down, her bright
And straying hair
In the straw hat's shadow
Stirred as she went. The Count
Stood watch as a crane will stand
With neck outstretched outside
The feeding flock, one leg
Cranked up, clawing a stone
In its lean hand, that, falling,
With the shock will wake it.
A voice, and he turned, then looked
Once more. But she was gone.
Returning to quiet, a flood
Cut by a wing, the leaves
Rocked. The basket she bore
Rode the green swell alone,
Capsizing where she stood.

III *The Gathering of Mushrooms*

Noon. And as from the hawk
Hanging under cloudbank,
Sighted in a hard eye skyward,
Of whom the alerted cock
Crows warning, in the rank
Barley, while the sky
Flashed fierce with summer, hens
And peacocks, geese
And even the pigeon caught
Out of reach of the eaves
Had sought the shade, to bathe
In sand, or on
The cropped turf pant. Among
These heads, rose children's heads,
The short hair white as flax
Bare upon bare shoulders. At their backs
A peacock, preening, spread

His spectral tail, a ground
Whose deep cerulean picked
The pale heads out. And lent
Light from that stellar wreath
Of all its eyes, the heads
(With one that was taller, Zosia's)
Shone where a diafan
Burned in transparency
Of aether that was gold
With maize, with mercury
Coraline, shot silver
By grasses, mallow-green.

Colours and forms in a screen
Of silver and gold grisaille
Plaited upon the air
Swam, a thrown veil. Above,
Nimbus or baldachin,
Hung butterflies, their bright
Cobweb and glass
And quadriparted wings
Stirring and not stirring
Whispered in air. In her hand
A grey whisk screened the heads
Against that golden rain
As with the other hand
To each in turn she proffered
A golden trumpet shape
Like Plenty's very horn.

Dulcinea to a Quixote
Out of the burdocks, who
Four beds away
Stood bowing. Like a lark
Skimming the leaves she'd have flown,
Had not the apparition
And her betrayed intention
Startled her charges. A spirit
Reluctantly hearing the magus,
She sat again and, soothing
The most distressed, she calmed
The small knee-hugging fledglings
Under her lee with 'Come,
That's rude. The gentleman

Will think you rude. For look,
It is no beggarman
But a guest of ours, and kind,
And look how pretty too.'
The pretty gentleman,
The Count, smiled pleasantly
To be so praised. She stopped.
Pretty he was, however;
Tall, and his face an oval,
Ruddy and fair, with mild
Blue eyes, and in his blonde
Hair worn long, the leaves
And grass, in his painful passage
Over the plots torn loose,
Showed green, a tattered wreath.

'O thou', he hailed her, 'by
Whatever name I shall
Address thee, whether
Of nymph or goddess, speak,
Spirit or phantom. Was't
At thine own will thou cam'st
Hither, or hath some fell
Lord or harsh guardian chained
Thee by his spells within
This forest's pale?' And she:
'But
Excuse me
What are you doing in *our* garden?'

*   *   *

His soul like the earth after sundown
Darkened and chilled; his abstraction
Brought him bad dreams; he awakened
In anger that sought its occasion.
Much had he expected, much
Conjectured, as heart high
Head burning, he had wound
After his pastorella. Such
Charms as he'd projected! Now...
Pretty enough and slender
He'd found her. Yes, but how
Inelegant, and her face

So apt to colour
In an excessive, in
A vulgar transport. Clearly
Her mind still slumbering, and her heart
Inactive. . . . And besides,
Oh the rusticity
Of those rejoinders! 'Come,
Why fool myself? Too late
I learn the truth, my nymph
A goosegirl.' The enchantment
Fled with the principal, those bands
Of lucent light and those
Thrown nets of silver and gold
Revealed as straw, he gazed,
Wringing his hands,
On cornflowers bound with grass,
The fly-switch he had thought
An ostrich plume. And gone
Down a child's throat the horn
Once Amalthea's, now
In short a carrot.

Meanwhile the judge had mustered
Mushroom-gatherers, whom,
Once more self-communing,
The Count mistook. For see!
Strange walkers these, in their
Processional parade
To and fro under low boughs,
Around them the birches white
And the turf green under.
These should be ghosts by moonlight.
Strange their attitudes: see
Slowly revolve on its bole
The human tree; all around
Downcast looks; and the dreamer
Direct in trance
Treading his lane
Undeviating. Strange
Decorum this that, prodigal
Of bows, will have them meet
Impassively, without
Acknowledgement, a nation
(So self-absorbed) polite

And yet unsociable.
Field full of folk, in their
Immunity from harm
Crestfallen and serene.
Who would have thought these shades
Our lively friends? Are these
Acres Elysian fields?

Mushrooms at any rate
In plenty: first
The *lísica* pursued
Rightly by swains if song
That marks the worm and fly
Abhor it, wisely prize
Its pallor as the badge
Of maidenhood; yet maids
Preferred *borówik*, slender
And ever under pines,
Called in the song
'The colonel'; all pursued
The smaller *rydz* as yet
Unfamed in song though sweetest
Of fungus kind, in winter
Salted, fresh in the Fall.
Alone the seneschal
Was to the flybane drawn,
Intoxicant toadstool. Some
As poor relations scorned
For ill effect or taste,
Yet deem not useless if
They shade flies, nourish beasts,
Enamel groves. The meadow's
Linen sustained the ware,
Stained yellow, red and silver,
Of *surojádki* lifting
To hold the various grape
Their crystals; like a cup
Inverted, swelled
The *kózlak* and, designed
For vintage of Champagne,
A kind called 'funnels'; white,
Shallow and broad, the cups
Of the *beliáki* proffered
The milk-laced mocha; while

The pepper-dredges
Of round *purcháwki* held
Their ebon dust.
                    Not these
Nor the succulent kinds engage
A lady's interests. Reared
Above the stream,
From Telimena's shoulders
A shawl's carnelian
Unwound, dropped to the turf.
As coral's amplitude
Might draw a winter swimmer
Reluctant, so the scarf's
Colour seemed to draw
Her stooping, who by stages
(Lilith upon a shawl)
Unwound, subsided. One
Palm to her temple, one
Elbow upon the turf,
She bent her head to a page
Of vellum's alabaster
Where her black ringlets wound,
Her ribbons coiled. The grass's
Smaragdine sheen, a shawl's
Carnelian, and a gown's
Fullness whose coral tint
Picked out the black of the shoes
The black of her hair, concurred
With flanking whitenesses
Of hose and linen,
The hand's and the brow's pallor –
So variously on distance
She crawled, a caterpillar
On a maple green.

Towards her Tadéusz first
Obliquely edged, as under
A movable hide
Slung between wheels, the sportsman
Approaches the bustard, or as
Out after plover, his gun
On the saddle or under
His horse's neck, he pretends
To be harrowing, riding the bounds,

His horse between him and the birds,
Thus Tadéusz; but straight to the mark,
A white-skirted smock in a flutter,
A kerchief tucked in a girdle,
A straw hat broad in the wind
Like a leaf of burdock, flapping
Back on his shoulders and forward
And over his eyes, in a hurry
The Judge arrived.
                              He began
A long tale too, and involved:
Of how Tadéusz,
Being the Judge's brother's
Son entrusted
To the Judge's care, should be married
To the Chamberlain's daughter. Protesting
'You want a hick?'
His kinswoman prescribed
Rather a course of polish
In the great world, perhaps
In Warsaw or, still better
With her in the coming winter
To gather in St Petersburg
An order or an office.

Young men, the Judge allowed,
Should see the world and learn
A certain poise. Himself
When young had been in Dubno
About the court and on his own affairs,
And once at least
In Warsaw. Not a little
He'd profited, as doubtless
His nephew should – though not
By job or decoration
From Moscow. What distinction
Of old or indeed today
Attached to such an office? Rank
In local affairs conferred
By suffrage of his fellows,
That was another matter.
                              'As you like',
Returned the lady.
              Yet

This same elusive brother
Retained, it appeared, surveillance
Over his son, and sent
Robak the Bernardine
With a direction, thus:
Tadeusz to be wed
To Telimena's ward
Who, still a child, should now
Be groomed and move
Into society, in short
Why, Zosia.
             And the storm
Broke, as the fair consultant
In what seemed panic spurned,
Hands flailing as if at midges,
His every word: 'For the boy
Let him be bailiff, serve
For all I care
Behind a bar! But Zosia,
That's my concern'. And the Judge,
Distressed and murmuring: 'If
They like each other, then...?'

Out of the question, he was told. And yet
As tempers cooled, there was a sort of truce:
No one will use compulsion. It's agreed
The girl is young. And so the Judge departed.

IV   *The Forest*

'O happy skies of Italy!
Rose gardens of the Caesars!'
'Classic cascades of Tibur,
And Posilippo's crag...'
Thus far that knight of the pencil,
The Count, and Telimena.

Yet round them even as they sigh
Lithuania's forests lie,
Currants wave their hop-crowned tresses,
Quickbeams blush like shepherdesses,
The hazel in a maenad's shape

Crowned with her nuts as with the grape
Twirls a green thyrsus, and below
The striplings of the forest grow –
The may, whom guelder-roses clip;
The blackberry, his ebon lip
Pressed to the raspberry's. Linking hands
(That's leaves) the trees and bushes stand
Like dancers, maid and man, around
The married pair in middle ground,
Two that for straightness, hue and height
Surpass their sylvan neighbours quite;
The silver birch, the well-loved bride,
Her man the hornbeam by her side.
Grave seniors sit some way apart
To watch their progeny disport,
Matronly poplar, hoary beech
Who gazing find no need of speech;
And a moss-bearded oak that bears
The weight of full five hundred years
Rests, as on tombstones overthrown,
On his own forebears turned to stone.

In the Botanical Gardens at Wilno
Trees from eastward and southward
And the trees of Italy grow,
And which of them all is preferred
Before our trees? Is the aloe
Its stem like a lightning rod
Their match? Or will they show
The lemon of the lacquered leaf,
Strung about with its wealth like a widow
Short and ill-favoured but moneyed?
Or is it that emblem of grief
(Of boredom, some would have said)
The long lean much belauded
Cypress, that over the dead
Like a German flunkey is set,
Not daring to stir his head
So strict the etiquette?

Blue, that Italian sky
Clear, as is frozen water;
But in this country
As the wind or the storm passes,

What images, what actions
The sportive wrack composes;
Shower-logged, sluggish in Spring
Clouds like tortoises labour
Over a sky where tresses
Of the long rain sway earthward;
The bowling hailstorm crosses
The heavens by balloon
Blue, but with yellow flashes;
And then, what metamorphoses
Pursue the white quotidian
Clouds that like a gaggle
Of swans or geese the falcon
Wind hard presses;
Harried, they multiply
Prodigies, and crested
With sudden manes as serried
Legs bud beneath them, coursers
Over the steppes of the sky,
Necks arched, they gallop.

                    *   *   *

Does the great oak, Baublis, survive
In whose age-scooped bulk
As in a stout house
Twelve sat at table? The grove
Of Mendog, does it bloom
Still by the churchyard wall?
And in the Ukraine does it rise
Still on the banks of the Ros,
That linden, pride
Of the Holowínskis, spreading
So wide its leaves
Before their houses that a hundred
Young men have danced
Beneath, with a hundred maidens?

Monuments of our fathers!
How many among you yearly
Fall to contractors' axes?
Will such officious vandals
Unhouse all forest-warblers,
Bird or bard, to whom

Your shade was grateful? One,
The linden of Czarnólas,
Jan Kochanowski's descant,
Is singing still, and singing
Though to the bard of the Cossack
Of marvels still. And I,
A wretched shot, escaping
My comrades' gibes, how many
Fancies have I not taken,
A nobler game,
Out of your quiet! Bearded
Mosses around me silver,
The berries crushed and blue-ish
Streaked them, as the tussocks
Of heather reddened, strung
With the huckleberry's coral,
Rosaries. Around
Darkness lay as, low
Green clouds, the branches
Hung over me. Above
That stable vault,
The wind was somewhere wailing
Roaring or howling – odd
And stunning noise, as if
A sea suspended
Over my head swung, tossing.

Below, the remains of cities
Oak overthrown;
Breached wall and shattered column;
And branching stumps,
Beams half-powdered
In a hedge of grass.

Looking within is fearful:
Lords of the woods,
Wild boar and wolf
And bear, dwell here;
Unwary guest,
Bones half-gnawed at the entry.

A double column of water
Behind the green grass
Rises – a pair of antlers,

Stag; and a sunbeam falling
Athwart the trees
Extinguished, a beast passing.

And again, quiet.

Rapping on the fir-tree, woodpecker,
In flight, there...!
Lost. And the rapping
Starting again,
The hidden child
Needing to be sought for.

Squirrel, a nut in its forepaws,
Cuirassier crested
With its own tail,
Fearful although so armoured,
Darting its eyes;
It flies the intruder;

Tree to tree, a dancer,
Like lightning flashes;
Into a fissure
Unnoticed in a tree-stump
Sidles, returning
To tree-form this Dryad.

And again, quiet.

Who has plumbed Lithuania's forest,
Pressed to the thicket's core?
As the sea-floor is known to the fisherman
Meagrely, even inshore,
So the hunter can know of the forest
Only the face of its waters
Never their bed. Of its centre
What fable and rumour have said
Has authority. Once past
The manageable tangles,
The rampart rises – logs,
Roots, stumps, which a quagmire defends –
And water, and nets
Of rank weeds and ant-hills, and knots
Of snakes, and the wasp's and the hornet's

Nests. And then small meres
Grass-choked yet unplumbable, thought
To harbour devils, hold water
Rust-spotted, emitting a thick
And stinking steam. In the fumes
The trees are bald and sicken,
Dwarfed, wormlike; bare
Of bark and leaves, they wear beards
Of filthy fungi, and a knot
Of bunched-up mosses – witches
Around their pot, the pool,
Thawed by a graveplot brew.

These pools no eye can pass,
Still less a foot; morasses
Here raise, miasmal, shrouding
The further reaches, clouds
That rumour says obscure
From view a purer air
And fruitful earth, where all is
As in the ark. Metropolis
Of beasts and plants, the region
Sees brutes forget their rages
And learn civility. The seed
Of every plant that seeded
Throughout the earth is there
Preserved; and the primal pair
Of every creature copulates
In pre-lapsarian state.

Tradition will allow
The ancient buffalo
The bison and the bear
Alone the right to wear
The purple. All around,
Treed that they may command
The land's approaches, wait
Their ministers of state
The lynx and wolverine;
Beside them where they reign
Fed on their broken meats
The two court favourites,
Eagle and falcon, skulk;
Boar, wolf and antlered elk

Each in suburban fief
Owe vassalage. The chief
And patriarchal pairs
Stay home among their peers
But send their progenies
Far out to colonise.

Themselves they know repose
Locked in their ancient ease
Never by cut or shot
To die, but of old age
In nature's course. They have
Likewise a place of graves
Wherein, when near to death,
Wildfowl bring home their feathers
And brutes their fur. The stag
Who barely moves his legs
Limps thither, and the bear
Who cannot chew, the hare
When his blood thickens, grey
Ravens and hawks that grow
Half-blind, and when cross-billed
So far as to withhold
The meat it craves, the old
Eagle. Inferior kinds
Whose bones no woodward finds
Within his walls, repair
When sick or hurt to expire
In that, their fatherland.

A polity well planned
Keeps order in the lair:
Meum not *tuum* there
Embroil, and unaware
Of duelling or war
As once in Paradise
Keeping the peace, too wise
To butt or bite, the tame
And the wild consort. The same
Harmony would extend
Even to humankind;
Should ever human hunter
Although unarmed there enter,
Unhurt he'd pass between

The animals, and be seen
With that astonishment
Which their first fathers bent
On Adam when he first
Upon the sixth and last
Day of Creation ran
Through Eden. But to man
Death, Toil and Terror ban,
How luckily, access;
Nor can he ever press
To that secluded ground.
Only at times a hound
Fierce in pursuit may pass
Amid the pits and moss
And from what lies within
In terror run to whine,
Beneath his master's hand
Still quivering. Unscanned
By man, each ancient reach
Is called in hunter's speech
'Jungle'.

       Thou'dst little wit,
Bruin, in this haunt safe,
To venture out of it.
What didst so far from home?
Did ripe oats draw thee
Or the honeycomb
Along the open ride
Where trees grow sparsely
By the forest's side?
The ranger saw thee there
And sent his spies abroad
To learn from them the lair
Where thou o' nights hast slept
And where thou'st fed. And now
Thy foes have crept
To bar thee every road
Back to the jungle
And thine own abode.

The hunters strained their ears;
As to a curious discourse hearkening,
They heard the forest's silence

Play for them, where the dogs
As loons swim undersea
In and out flickered. Guns
Trained on the woodside, eyes
Covered the Seneschal
Kneeling, ear to the ground,
In whose face, as in the face
Of a physician Hope
And Terror read, they read
His diagnosis. And this,
Rising subdued, he delivered:
'They have struck the trail.'

　　　　　　　　　　　He had heard
What they would hear: a single
Yelp (now they heard it),
Two now, and now twenty,
Now the concerted whine
Scattered at first, and now
Closed up. Not this
The baying which announces
Fox, hare or deer,
But a constant sharp
And broken yelp – the hounds
In sight of the quarry. Yet
The cry ceased, as the pack
Closed with the beast. Unseen
The attack was launched. And the brute
Defended himself, for the cries
Were punctuated often now and often
With the long death howl.

Guns at the ready, bent
Like a bow, each huntsman's head
Pointed. And they could wait
No longer, but they broke
Station, the Seneschal
Shouting unheeded, and moved
Crowding, as from horseback
He promised them all,
Gentle and simple, the lash.
No help for it – they'd see
And all see first. Came three
Shots, then a volley, then
Above the volley, shocking

The woodland echoes, a dreadful
Sound where pain, despair
And fury mixed, the bear's
Tormented roar. And ragged
Behind it, yelps,
Cries, and the horns of beaters
All on the move, and all
Except the Seneschal
Exultant.
          On the one side
They massed; but the beast turned back
To the open fields and the few
Who stayed, the Seneschal,
Tadéusz, the Count, with beaters
Where the wood thinned. A roaring
Within and the crackle of boughs
Came near and nearer.
             Out
Burst like a thunderbolt
From cloud, the bear!
Torn, with terror
And the dogs upon him,
He stopped, turned, reared
Erect, and with a roar
Quelled his assailants; stooped,
His forepaws scrabbling, tore
Roots from the earth and flung them
At dogs and men; uprooted
A tree he flailed like a club,
So turned and came on, rushing
Tadéusz and the Count,
Last of the line. Their muskets,
As lightning rods discharge
At a lowering cloud, discharged
And missed. Four hands together
Seize (the beast still bearing
Down on them) a pike
Planted between them,
Each way tugged at once.

So near to the bear
His double row of tusks
Gleamed on them from his red
Maw, and his claw descended

Upon them, thereupon turning
Through the sparse trees they doubled.

To claw the skull from their brains
As a hat uncovers a head,
The black paw reared. The Assessor
Appeared, and the Notary; Gerwazy
Showed up in front, and Robak
Behind him, running. As
At a command, together
Three shots rang out. Like a hare
Who, the hounds upon him, takes
To the air before them,
So leapt the bear,
Came down head foremost, hurled,
His four paws somersaulting,
His bloody bulk under the Count
And still would rise. The mastiffs
Each side closed upon him.

And now the Seneschal
Had seized his famous horn
That, mottled and involved,
Seemed a great snake. He bore it
To his lips, two-handed. His cheeks
Distended, and as his eyes
Were shot with blood, the lids
Half-veiled them. So he drew
From his pinched-in belly, breath,
And so expelled it. Cyclones
Of whirling air up-spiralled
To roll down and amaze the woods
With purity and volume. For he played
The original catch, the art
For which he was renowned
Of old through the forests: first
The morning call over the kennels,
Then yelps as the kennels were loosed,
The baying pack, and last
The volley sounded.

Here he broke off, but still
He held the horn;

It was the echo playing,
That seemed the Seneschal.

Again he sounded. You thought
The horn at his lips endured
Metamorphoses, swelling
And dwindling as it feigned
Now the bellow of bison
Cutting the wind; now, thickened,
The bear's throat roaring. It thinned
And a wolf's long howling
Came down wind.

Here he broke off, but still
He held the horn:
It was the echo playing,
That seemed the Seneschal.
Oaks to the oaks repeated it,
The beeches to the beeches.

Again he blew. The horn,
It was a hundred horns.
The wrath and terror
Of the men, the pack
And the quarry mingled. Last
The lifted horn pealed
Triumph skyward.

Here he broke off, but still
He held the horn:
It was the echo playing,
That seemed the Seneschal.
And all about the forest,
To every tree a horn.
Trees to the trees, as choirs
Take up from choirs, repeated
The note that broader, further
And fainter spread,
And in the extreme distance
At the sill of heaven expired.

But now his arms were thrown
Wide, and the horn
Fell, swung on a thong;

As, cruciform
And swollen-faced, his eyes
Lifted, still he tried
To catch the last and long
Long-drawn
Note from the skies,

As plaudits came to drown
The horn.

V   *The Quarrel*

Seneschal leaving the wood
Your hunt is over, but hers
In the empty house you return to
Hers is beginning.
Telimena sits without moving
Folding her arms; but her thoughts
Pursue from a view to a kill
At once, two quarries;
The Count, and Tadéusz.
(And so she gets up from the sofa.
Does she only seem to grow taller,
Parting her bodice, consulting
Sidelong the glass on the wall?)

'However their thoughts may wander
Young men are more constant at heart,
For conscience's sake, than their elders;
She who was first to impart
The sweets of love can expect
From their simple and maidenly feeling,
Long after, a grateful respect.
Youth welcomes and rises from love
As from a modestly planned
Meal that we eat with a friend,
Gaily. Consumed from within,
Only the old debauchee
Detests what he drowns himself in.'

Thus a woman of experience
Reflects on these matters,
Sensibly.

But white,
In a long white gown,
Turning about as a fountain
Turns among flowers,   ,
Zosia is feeding the fowl.
Over the wings and the heads
Pearl of a white hand, pearl
Of the hail of the barley
Scatters out, dense from the sieve.
Telimena, her guardian,
Summons. She deals them the rest,
Strikes on the sieve as a dancer
Will strike on a tabor, whirling
Striking a strict time. Swooping
Now she flies through the fowl
That scatter before her. Doves,
Doves go before her
As before Venus's car
As she goes, skimming.

Alas how unwise
To augment the advantage of girlhood
With a pitcher of water
Tipped into a basin of silver;
How much too indulgent
Unstoppering flasks from the Nevsky,
Pomade for corn-coloured hair
And scent too sweet for a rival;
Alas, and how rash
White open-work stockings from Warsaw
And white satin shoes,
And braids, the hair smooth on the temples.

In vain to importune a lover
Whose cheeks have paled for a youthful
Small head, once seen, now remembered;
In vain to attempt a diversion
And sharpen a jest on him standing,
Arm on a mantel,
Silent, apart, in a corner;
In vain, when all fail, to upbraid
Till he plunge, like a pike, for his freedom,
Dragging the iron and line.

His evil spirit has prompted;
He eavesdrops now on his rival
Engaging the diffident Zosia
With a private joke.
                              Digesting
The bitterness into his soul
And as, full-fed upon poison,
A snake will coil
Death on a garden alley,
So full in the path of the talk
Tadéusz coils, envenomed;

And so resentfully
His eyes accuse
The nervous Telimena:
Those roses in her face
– Is he or she betrayed? –
Are false. And whether laid
Too thin a pane
Upon a coarse complexion,
Or scratched (and at his hand),
Or else by her returning
From the assignation mended
In too much haste,
The moth's wing dust of carmine
Blabs. And by his eyes,
Those secret agents, learning
A single piece of treason,
The newly instructed youth
Finds gap-tooth now, and freckle
And crowsfoot – nowhere, truth!

Alas, how unwise
To observe too closely a beauty!
Alas, how unworthy
To spy out the mole in a mistress!
Alas, how unwholesome
To change about in affection!
Yet the heart, who can constrain?
In vain, where love is deficient,
To call for injunctions on duty!
In vain by the flame of her glance
To thaw the ice of the soul!
In vain, if that glance, like a moon,

Throw a bright but heatless reflection
Over a frozen terrain.

VI   *The Year 1812*

Year well remembered! Happy who beheld thee!
The commons knew thee as the year of yield,
But as the year of war, the soldiery.

Rumours and skyward prodigies revealed
The poet's dream, the tale on old men's lips,
The spring when kine preferred the barren field.

Short of the acres green with growing tips
They halted lowing, chewing the winter's cud;
The men awaited an apocalypse.

Languid the farmer sought his livelihood
And checked his team and gazed, as if enquiring
What marvels gathered westward while he stood.

He asked the stork, whose white returning wing
Already spread above its native pine
Had raised the early standard of the Spring.

From swallows gathering frozen mud to line
Their tiny homes, or in loud regiments
Ranged over water, he implored a sign.

The thickets hear each night as dusk descends
The woodcock's call. The forests hear the geese
Honk, and go down. The crane's voice never ends.

What storms have whirled them from what shaken seas,
The watchers ask, that they should come so soon?
Or in the feathered world, what mutinies?

For now fresh migrants of a brighter plume
Than finch or plover gleam above the hills,
Impend, descend, and on our meadows loom.

Cavalry! Troop after troop it spills
With strange insignia, strangely armed,
As snow in a spring thaw fills

The valley roads. From the forests long
Bright bayonets issue, as brigades of foot
Debouch like ants, form up, and densely throng;

All heading north as if the bird, the scout,
Had led men here from halcyon lands, impelled
By instincts too imperative to doubt.

War! the war! – a meaning that transpires
To the remotest corner. In the wood
Beyond whose bounds no rustic mind enquires,

Where in the sky the peasant understood
Only the wind's cry, and on earth the brute's
(And all his visitors the neighbourhood),

A sudden glare! A crash! A ball that shoots
Far from the field, makes its impeded way,
Rips through the branches and lays bare the roots.

The bearded bison trembles, and at bay
Heaves to his forelegs, ruffs his mane, and glares
At sudden sparks that glitter on the spray.

The stray bomb spins and hisses; as he stares,
Bursts. And the beast that never knew alarm
Blunders in panic to profounder lairs.

'Whither the battle?' – and the young men arm.
The women pray, 'God is Napoleon's shield,
Napoleon ours', as to the outcome calm.

Spring well remembered! Happy who saw thee then,
Spring of the war, Spring of the mighty yield,
That promised corn but ripened into men.

*   *   *

Out of the moist dark
Dawn without glow brings
Day without brightness.

Sunrise, a whiteness
In a thatch of mist,
Shows late to eastward.

Earth is as tardy;
Cows go to pasture,
Startle hares grazing.

Fog that had spared them
Dayspring's alarum
Dispels them with herds.

Groves where the damp birds
Brood are their havens
In the still woodland.

Storks clack from marshland;
Ravens on haycocks
Croak of wet weather.

Scythes ring together,
Clink of the sickle,
Hone, hammer, and dirge.

Fog at the field's verge
Strangles the echo
Of labour and song.

The bravery of its gentry,
The beauty of their women
Exalt Dobrzyn
Through Lithuania. Once
Six hundred gentry armed
Answered the summons,
The besom made of twigs;
But now no easy living
For gentry of Dobrzyn
In magnates' households,
In troops or at assemblies –
Like serfs they work their way,
Not clad like serfs, the men
In gowns black-striped on white,
In gloves their women spinning
Or leather-shod tending the herds.

All Bartlemies, Matthiases,
Of Polish stock,
Masovian still
In speech and usages,
Black-haired and aquiline,
Nicknamed to save confusion;
Their patriarch, Matthias,
'The Maciek of Macieks';
His house, although untended,
Their Capitol.

Mercury's vivid fringe,
Mullein and crocus bow
The thatch; and mosses tinge
The roof as green as tin.
The rabbit mines below
Windows where birds fly in.
Birdcage or warren now
The fortress of Dobrzyn.

Where once the gate would creak,
Swedes left a cannon ball.
Unhallowed crosses speak
Of sudden obsequies.
Specks swarm on every wall
And seem a rash of fleas;
In each there nests a ball
As in earth-burrows, bees.

Innocent every door
Of nail or hook or latch.
(The steel old swordsmen wore
Bit iron, and stood the test
Nor ever showed a notch.)
Above, Dobrzynski crests;
Cheeses the bearings smutch
And swallows blur with nests.

Four helms, once ornaments
Of martial brows, the dove,
Love's votary, frequents;
A corselet of chain mail
Hangs as a chute above
A horse's stall; a tail

Lopped from the charger of
The Ottoman cleans a pail.

Ceres has banished Mars;
Vertumnus and Pomona
And Flora heal the scars
On stable, house and barn.
Today shall they throw over
That distaff rule, and learn
Old habits to recover
To greet the god's return.

*   *   *

Fair weather, and the day breaking
Day of our Lady of Flowers;
The sky clear, hung over land
Like a sea curved forward and backward;
Pearls under its wave
Some few stars still, though paling;
White cloudlet alone
(Wing feathers fray out in the azure),
Spirit departing
Belated by prayers,
Fares fast to its heavenly fellows.

Pearls dim and go out in the deep.
Pallor on the sky's brow midmost
Spreads, and one temple is swarthy
Crumpled, pillowed on shadows,
The other ruddy. The distant
Horizon parts like a lid
On the white of an eye
Iris and pupil, and a ray circles
Dazzles, a gold shaft
Stuck through the heart of a cloud.

Fires cluster and dart
Cross over, light over light
Overarches the sky-round;
Drowsy, a broken
Light under lashes shaken
The eye of the sun rose up
Glittered, seven-tinted:

Sapphire by blood is to ruby
Ruby by yellow to topaz
Crystal, by lucent
To diamond, and by flame
Great moon or fitful star.
And the eye of the sun rose up
Alone across the unmeasured.

Strange manifestations expected
Bring piety in before sunrise;
Today come captains to worship.
Saints, the commanders of legions,
Gospel, the tale of their journeys,
Engagements, campaigns. A detachment
Thronged and surrounded convinces
The folk of their countrymen armed
Free, and on their lips Polish!

There, arm in a sling, stands
One who was lately a greenhorn,
A lancer now, Tadéusz;
And Zosia with him, explaining
Painfully how in his absence
Love was borne in on her,
Uncertainly recalling
The tear in his eye at parting,
Or, teased by her schoolfellows, finding
Her heart contract at his name.

Dombrowski said to Maciek:
'What about it, my friend?
Aren't you glad we're here?
What's on your mind?
Doesn't it do your heart good
To see the gold eagles and the silver eagles
And to hear the buglers
Sound Kosciusko's reveille?
Maciek, I thought you were more
Of a fighting man; if you won't
Take sabre and ride,
At least you will drink
Heartily, to
Napoleon and the hopes of Poland!'

'Aye', said Maciek, 'I've heard
Of the set-up all right
And I see it, too. A pair
Of eagles, is it? They don't nest together.
The high and mighty ride
Piebald. And the Emperor's
A hero, is he? The Pulawskis,
Old mates of mine, they used to say
The hero Poland wants
Is a Pole, no
Frenchman nor Eyetie neither, a
Piast, a Jan or a Josef
Or a Maciek, maybe. The army...
They call it Polish! All these
Grenadiers, engineers,
Cannoneers, fusiliers! I tell you
You hear more Jerry monikers in that crowd
Than ours, any day.
I reckon you've got Turks among you, Tartars,
Nonconformists, Christ knows what religion.
Haven't I seen them myself,
Setting on village women,
Beating up men in the street,
Mucking up churches?
The Emperor's off to Moscow!
It's a long haul that
For his most Imperial,
If he's got no God at his back.
And he don't hit it off
With the Padre, I understand...'

Thronged chapel spills into a meadow.
Lowered in worship the heads;
Field of ripe grain
The Lithuanian flaxen;
Girl's head with flowers adorned
Or as ribbons flow loose from a braid,
Cornflower in corn or a poppy;
And the heads sway down
As at a breath of the wind
Over the wheat ears
So to the bell on the wind.

Village girls brought to the altar
Spring's earliest tribute of green
Sheaves over altar and ikon
Belfry and galleries decked.
Zephyr of morning
Stirring out of the East
Throws down a garland
Fragrance as of a censer.

Epilogue

How many memories, what long sorrow
There where a man shall cleave to his master
As here no wife cleaves to her man;
There where a man grieves for loss of his weapons
Longer than here for who sired him;
And his tears fall more sincerely and faster
There for a hound than this people's for heroes.

My friends of those days made my speech come easy,
Each good for some singable idiom. Spring
Brought in the fable cranes of the wild island flying
Over the spellbound castle and the spellbound
Boy lamenting, who was loosed
By each pitying bird as it flew, one feather:
He flew out on those wings to his own people.

First published by the Marvell Press (Hessle, Yorkshire), 1959.

5   Polish Baroque

Five Centuries of Polish Poetry, 1450-1950, by Jerzy Peterkiewicz and Burns Singer. London: Secker & Warburg, 1960; Philadelphia: Dufour Editions, 1962.

The translation of poetry is not impossible, it is just very difficult. Unlike most assertions about poetry, this one can be verified. Let all who believe with Robert Graves that 'poetry is what gets left out in translation', take a look inside this book of versions from the Polish. Either poem after poem here is a wonderfully good translation, or else Burns Singer has surpassed himself as a poet on his own account and has perversely chosen not to take the credit for it:

> Who brightens the extinguished stars which play
> Like shy sharp fingers with the hackled snow?
> That fleece, what makes it? How do hailstones grow?
> And who has pinned upon the wind its wings?
> Or given this world so many different things?
> Who tells tonight that last night has gone by?
> Nor deviates though daylights multiply?
> What mind hacks minutes from slow centuries
> And documents with clocks what no man sees?
> As at a rollcall, the small seconds shout
> Their names and hours, and hours take turn about.
> And when Favonius chases lazy ice
> Far into Tartary, with his winged device,
> The melting snow beyond Hercynian shores
> Grumbles and crumbles almost as it snores;
> And youthful Spring unsheets her gentle bed
> And rubs her cheeks with dew till they shine red.

Are these lines by Burns Singer, thirty-two years old, American-born and Scottish-educated? Or should they be credited to Bartlomiej Zimorowicz, a bourgeois of Lvov, who died about 1680? At one level, who cares? These are memorable verses added to our language, and this is something that doesn't happen every day; why look a gift-horse in the mouth? But of course Jerzy Peterkiewicz will have something to say about that, very properly; and indeed one can see that the distinction of these verses even in isolation isn't at all a twentieth-century distinction, but something at once more naïve and more sophisticated: more naïve in their expansive openness that we may choose to call 'Slavic'; more sophisticated in their classicism. (They come from a collection called 'New Ruthenian Idylls', and one apprehends that Zimorowicz has the classicist's seriousness about *genre*.) The complexity of this double allegiance – on the one hand to the Slav spaces and the Slav folk, on the other to the Mediterranean inheritance – is something that we are told (I suspect wrongly) not to look for in Russian poetry before Pushkin. But in Polish, from Kochanowski on throughout the seventeenth and eighteenth centuries, poet after poet inherits the double allegiance as part of his Polishness. It is with two seventeenth-century poets of the same name, Andrzej and Zbigniew Morsztyn, that Burns Singer scores his most dazzling successes; and these will be acclaimed (it is to be hoped they will) as 'metaphysical'. The analogy is certainly helpful: George Herbert in sacred poetry, Carew or Marvell in secular – these so-called 'metaphysicals' seem without doubt the nearest English equivalents. But Jerzy Peterkiewicz does better when he speaks of these poets, and others like Zimorowic, as 'baroque'; for the Polish poets are nearer than the English ones to the European consciousness of that age, nearer because within the Latin Christendom of the Counter-Reformation. Surprisingly, much of Polish baroque architecture has survived; rather plainly these are the literary equivalents of those buildings, witnessing to the same civilization.

A tart remark by Burns Singer about Slowacki's 'Hymn' suggests, as his versions do, that he is more in sympathy with the earlier poets than with Romantics like Slowacki. And in general it is true that the versions become less appealing, the nearer we get to the present day. Of the later poets only Kasprowicz (1860-1926) comes through impressively; and I was particularly disappointed by the presentation of Cyprian Norwid (1821-1883), for whom the Poles nowadays make very large and very interesting claims. But it is the baroque Poland that we need to be told about, and one shudders to think what would have happened to these baroque poems in the hands of the cultivated amateurs who not so long ago had a monopoly of verse translation into English. Verse translation even more than verse composition is a job for professionals; and the fruits of this collaboration reflect great credit equally on the professional student of the foreign literature and on the professional poet in

English. We should hope that their partnership is not soon dissolved.

Postscript: Alas, it was dissolved by Singer's death in 1964. See Peterkiewicz in the slightly amplified second edition, with new poems translated in collaboration with Jon Stallworthy. London & New York: OUP, 1970.

6 Pushkin, Walter Scott, and Mickiewicz

THE CAPTAIN'S DAUGHTER:
PUSHKIN'S PROSE AND RUSSIAN REALISM

Pushkin's historical novel *The Captain's Daughter* is a story of the experiences of Pyotr Andreyitch Grinyov, son of a Russian country gentleman, inheriting a tradition of martial and loyalist service, in the period of the Cossack rebellion of Pugatchov in the 1770s. Grinyov, travelling to his first garrison, is helped by an anonymous Cossack to whom he makes in return a small gift. After an interview in Orenburg with his general, he is appointed to a small garrison in territory still not entirely conquered from the Bashkirs and Kirghiz. The commander of the garrison, Captain Mironov, is a simple old soldier, much under the thumb of his admirable and upright wife, and has a paternal attitude to the troops under his command. Grinyov gradually falls in love with the captain's daughter, and fights a duel on her behalf with the other junior officer, Shvabrin, an exiled rake. Grinyov is wounded, but recovers in time to see Pugatchov and the rebel Cossacks take the 'fortress'. Shvabrin turns traitor and the Mironovs are brutally executed, but Pugatchov, revealed as the anonymous Cossack of the earlier incident, allows Grinyov to escape, to help in the defence of Orenburg against the rebels. The captain's daughter, however, Marya Ivanovna, is left in the hands of Shvabrin, and Grinyov again enlists the aid of Pugatchov to release her. He rejoins the loyalist forces and is able to defend the paternal estate against the rebels under Shvabrin, but when the rising is finally quelled, he faces a court-martial because of his dealings with Pugatchov. He is saved by the personal intervention of the Empress, after Marya Ivanovna has enlisted her aid.

When Pushkin's English translator remarks[1], with reference to *The Captain's Daughter*: 'The realism so characteristic of Pushkin's writing is the key-note of Russian literature as a whole', no reader, I suppose, will account himself materially assisted. It is arguable that the novel is necessarily more realistic than other forms, as incapable

---

[1] Natalie Duddington, Introduction to Everyman edition.

of a high degree of abstraction; any category which includes, by implication, both Tolstoy and Dostoevsky, cannot easily mean anything more specific. Russian literature is richer in good novels than in good poems; that, it seems, is all that is implied in talk of 'Russian realism'. Still, Pushkin's influence was, when all due respect has been paid to Gogol and to Western Romantics, so considerable, that to examine what meaning can be allowed to 'realism' in relation to Pushkin's prose is likely to enlighten also an understanding of later Russian fiction.

The coarsest gloss on 'realism' will represent it as a photographic fidelity to appearance. And this, at any rate, cannot stand as just with reference to *The Captain's Daughter*:

> 'Well, lads', the Commandant said, 'now open the gates, beat the drum. Forward, children; come out, follow me!'
>
> The Commandant, Ivan Ignatyitch, and I were instantly beyond the rampart; but the garrison lost their nerve and did not move.
>
> 'Why do you stand still, children?' Ivan Kuzmitch shouted. 'If we must die, we must – it's all in the day's work!'
>
> At that moment the rebels ran up to us and rushed into the fortress. The drum stopped; the soldiers threw down their rifles; I was knocked down, but got up again and walked into the fortress together with the rebels.

The representation of action is here as stylized as the treatment of the direct speech. Very obviously, no attempt is made to render faithfully the sense of the hurly-burly, to bring before the mind's eye anything but a selective picture. 'The Commandant, Ivan Ignatyitch, and I were instantly beyond the rampart...' The effect is as unnatural as the rapidity and conclusiveness of movement in the early films. Movement, in fact, is not presented at all; only a sequence of tableaux. Of course, this method is a characteristic of the period. One finds it for instance in *The Last of the Mohicans* when the heroine's father leads a sally against the French beleaguering his fort, and hears in the mist his daughters trying to reach him – an episode hilariously criticized by Mark Twain. And of course, the acceptance of such conventions is not incompatible with realism. But in saying so, one is at once using that term in a special and limited sense.

If Pushkin is not realistic to the extent of observing a fidelity to appearance, still less is he concerned with probability. The intrigue depends upon a large initial coincidence, but probability is violated in other, more interesting, ways:

Suddenly the moon came out from behind the cloud and lighted a terrible sight. A gallows fixed to a raft was floating towards us. Three corpses were swinging on the cross-bar. A morbid curiosity possessed me. I wanted to look into the hanged men's faces. I told the oarsmen to hold the raft with a boat-hook, and my boat knocked against the floating gallows. I jumped out and found myself between the terrible posts. The full moon lighted the disfigured faces of the unfortunate creatures...

The episode is not included for its own sake. One of the hanged men is found by Grinyov, the narrator, to be one of his father's servants. And, as thus alarming Grinyov, the episode contributes smoothly enough to the main action. But the contribution is not a necessary contribution, and is in fact so slight that the passage, with its emphases – 'morbid curiosity', 'the full moon', 'disfigured faces' – will at first be taken as simply a horrific set-piece. But it is not that either. 'Morbid curiosity', in Pushkin's prose, can be allowed to carry full weight, to refer at once to the jaded ennui of his so-called Byronic characters, of which Eugene Onegin is only the best known. Shvabrin, the only 'Byronic' character in *The Captain's Daughter*, is only sketched (though fairly condemned). But the history of Grinyov's relations with him before the fall of the fortress takes up such a reference as the 'morbid curiosity' here, to suggest a capacity for moral compromise in Grinyov. And such a suggestion is integral to the total organization of the tale.

For Pushkin's concern in *The Captain's Daughter* is a moral concern. And his realism must be construed to include an interest which is ideological, which can, with whatever looseness, be called 'philosophical'. Here the ideological theme is at its most insistent:

'Listen,' Pugatchov said, with a kind of wild inspiration, 'I will tell you a fairy-tale which in my childhood an old Calmuck woman told me. The eagle asked the raven one day: "Tell me, raven-bird, why do you live in the world for three hundred years and I only for thirty-three?" – "Because, father-eagle, you drink living blood," the raven said, "and I feed on things that are dead." The eagle thought "I will try and feed as he does." Very well. The eagle and the raven flew along. They saw the carcass of a horse, came down and perched on it. The raven plucked and praised the food. The eagle took a peck or two, then waved his wing and said: "No, brother raven, rather than feed on dead flesh for three hundred years, I would have one drink of living blood – and leave the rest to God!" What do you think of the Calmuck tale?'

'It is clever,' I answered. 'But to live by murder and brigandage is, to my mind, just what plucking dead flesh means.'

The argument here is the argument of the whole tale. Pugatchov and his associates represent the impulsive appetite, an innate barbarian grandeur.[1] Grinyov is here made the spokesman of the opposing code, of order and tradition, a code represented more usually, however, by his father, by his general, and by Captain Mironov, his garrison-commander. The Russian military and patriotic tradition is here a moral symbol, precisely as the tradition of the British Merchant Service was a moral symbol for Conrad. Moreover the two codes, represented by Pugatchov on the one side and by Mironov on the other, could, it is plain, comprehensibly be described, in view of the period at which the tale was written, as 'Romantic' and 'Classical' respectively. In that light the passage is related to the general direction of all Pushkin's work, evident repeatedly at specific moments in his verse, where that takes up simultaneously the whole of two traditions, of Byron and Chénier on the one hand, of Parny and Voltaire on the other. And it is the consciousness in Pushkin of the two traditions, and of the necessity of judging between them, which invites the comparison with Goethe, and justifies the acknowledgement of Pushkin as a 'European artist'.

I do not mean to imply, however, that the passage about the Calmuck tale contains, in any usual sense, the 'moral' of *The Captain's Daughter*, a hard kernel of foreign matter at the centre. On the contrary, it represents only the most explicit phase of an argument which is the substance of the plot, and which is never, in fact, decided. For the sake of an early kindness, Pugatchov helps Grinyov to save the woman he loves, though both of them are connected with the loyalist forces opposing Pugatchov. Grinyov is forced, therefore, to feel, in some degree, a divided allegiance:

> 'And yet a strange feeling poisoned my joy: I could not help being troubled at the thought of the villain smeared with the blood of so many innocent victims and now awaiting his punishment. "Why didn't he fall on a bayonet: or get hit with a cannonball?" I thought with vexation. "He could not have done anything better." What will you have? I could not think of Pugatchov without remembering how he had spared me at one of the awful moments of my life and saved my betrothed from the vile Shvabrin's hands.'

But the explanation offered, in terms of the plot, does not exhaust

---

[1] 'I cannot describe how affected I was by this peasant song about the gallows, sung by men doomed to the gallows. Their menacing faces, their tuneful voices, the mournful expression they gave to the words expressive enough in themselves – it all thrilled me with a feeling akin to awe.'

Grinyov's feeling of guilt, of complicity, with regard to Pugatchov. This is certain. How otherwise explain Grinyov's foreshadowing dream, described while Pugatchov is still anonymous, and before Grinyov has contracted any obligations towards him?

'I was in that state of mind when reality gives way to dreams and merges into them in the shadowy visions of oncoming sleep. It seemed to me the storm was still raging and we were still wandering in the snowy desert.... Suddenly I saw a gateway and drove into the courtyard of our estate. My first thought was fear lest my father should be angry with me for my involuntary return and regard it as an intentional disobedience. Anxious, I jumped down from the chaise and saw my mother who came out to meet me on the steps, with an air of profound grief.

"Don't make any noise," she said. "Your father is ill; he is dying and wants to say good-bye to you."

Terror-stricken, I followed her to the bedroom. It was dimly lighted; people with sad-looking faces were standing by the bed. I approached the bed quietly; my mother lifted the bed-curtains and said: "Andrey Petrovitch! Petrusha has come; he returned when he heard of your illness; bless him." I knelt down and looked at the sick man. But what did I see? Instead of my father a black-bearded peasant lay on the bed looking at me merrily. I turned to my mother in perplexity and said to her: "What does it mean? This is not my father. And why should I ask this peasant's blessing?"... "Never mind, Petrusha," my mother answered, "he takes your father's place for the wedding; kiss his hand and he will bless you...." I would not do it. Then the peasant jumped off the bed, seized an axe from behind his back, and began waving it about. I wanted to run away and could not; the room was full of dead bodies; I stumbled against them and slipped in the pools of blood.... The terrible peasant called to me kindly, saying: "Don't be afraid, come and let me bless you." Terror and confusion possessed me...'

Now this passage cannot be a concession to 'atmosphere', a horrific indulgence. For the effect is not appalling, but profoundly disturbing, in a way which was to be characteristic of Russian fiction, and which depends upon the simultaneous presence of discordant elements. Grinyov's mother has 'an air of profound grief'; Grinyov is 'terror-stricken'. But the peasant 'lay on the bed looking at me *merrily*'. Grinyov 'slipped in the pools of blood'. But 'the terrible peasant called to me *kindly*'. So 'terror and confusion possessed me'. The incident perplexes and confuses the reader, as well as Grinyov.

And one must suppose that the nightmare is intended to carry full weight, to convey to the reader that, in some sense more radical than the coils of plot, the savage peasant is Grinyov's father, that Grinyov does require his blessing, and that when at the end Grinyov is brought to trial he is on trial almost like Kafka's 'K', ignorant of the cause he must plead, the offence with which he is charged. It does not much matter how the indebtedness is rationalized. One can imagine the Marxist critic, who would make an obvious case on the grounds that Pugatchov is a peasant and/or the representative of a racial minority. The quite special status of the Cossack on both these counts would, as a fact of history, require some manipulation. More important, such a crucial passage as the address of Grinyov's father to his repentant serfs is far too much in character to be taken as evidence:

> 'My father went out on the steps to talk to them. When the peasants saw him they knelt down. "Well, you silly fools," he said to them, "whatever did you rebel for?".'

And the same is true of the only passage which could be supposed relevant to the problem of minorities, Grinyov's pious retrospective complacency over the mutilation of the captive Bashkir:

> 'When I recall that this happened in my lifetime and that now I have lived to see the gentle reign of the Emperor Alexander, I cannot but marvel at the rapid progress of enlightenment and the diffusion of humane principles. Young man! If my notes ever fall into your hands, remember that the best and most permanent changes are those due to the softening of manners and morals and not to any violent upheavals.'

On the whole I do not think one can or should rationalize Grinyov's indebtedness to Pugatchov and the Cossacks, except in so far as the latter, on the evidence of the Calmuck tale and the gallows-song, seem to 'stand for' the life of passionate impulse and barbarian grandeur. The plot seems to imply that the quite different tradition of civility arises out of barbarian values and is nourished by them.

It will certainly be argued that if Grinyov's trial is a real trial, valid outside the terms of the plot, then his release by the *deus ex machina*, the Empress, is a gross shelving of the issues raised. The fairy-tale convention, though, is consistent from first to last. The intrigue starts with a coincidence which has all the air of 'once upon a time...' and the denouement, the interview with the Empress, has the casual abruptness of the fairy godmother's waving of the wand.

The whole tale, in short, is set firmly within a frame. It is highly conventional throughout. What remains within all the conventions, and in conjunction with the moral argument, is Pushkin's realism. And the nature of that realism it is now not hard to see. Grinyov is realistically drawn, is no Faustian or Promethean prototype, serving to symbolize in his own conflicts the extreme conflicts of mankind. He is, on the contrary, a Russian country gentleman of the eighteenth century, conducting his internal argument at no more than normal intensity, with no more than normal honesty and courage. As such, he may be allowed to embody an ideological conflict, but not to resolve the conflict, nor to push it to the limit. He is no more, in many ways, than David Copperfield, but seen with much less indulgence, much more seriously. Characteristically, Pushkin's apparent *naïveté* masks, in the end, an effect of extreme sophistication:

> The memoirs of Pyotr Andreyitch Grinyov end at this point. It is known from the family tradition that he was released from confinement at the end of 1774, at the express order of the Empress; that he was present at the execution of Pugatchov, who recognized him in the crowd and nodded to him a minute before his lifeless, bleeding head was held up before the people.

The Captain's Daughter is in no sense a difficult work. Except for the reader who has been invited to consider it as 'realistic', a description which is, in any other than a very special and limited sense, inappropriate, the tale insists upon being read with all the stresses and patterns which I have found it necessary here to draw out at some length. Once it is so read, even the minor episodes are seen to serve the purpose of an inclusive pattern. The allusion to *David Copperfield*, for example, recalls an episode which is superficially Dickensian. Yet a moment's thought suffices to emphasize that in Pushkin's scheme the episode serves a purpose which is far indeed from that of Dickens. I mean the description of Grinyov's first encounter with Zurin, the officer of Hussars, when Grinyov, the raw recruit travelling to his first garrison, is misled by Zurin into drinking too much and to losing money at billiards and at play. Where Dickens (at his usual level) would have used the episode to evoke a facile sympathy for the raw youth at large in the bewildering world, and probably would have 'played up' Zurin either into a melodramatic villain, or (more probably) into a 'fantastic', in Pushkin's hands the story advises the reader of the presence of a moral weakness in both characters. And as both characters represent that tradition which is offered by Pushkin as his 'moral positive', it further enlightens the reader that his author does not see the thing of which he approves through any rose tints, but critically, cautiously, and with reservations. Pugatchov, on the other hand, representing the other term in the moral problem, is seen with the same honesty. For he is almost at once presented in his worst light, at the bloody execution in the captured loyalist settlement. More complex than either is the delightful account of the council of war in Orenburg. Grinyov, as having personal experience of Pugatchov, is invited to attend the discussion held in Orenburg about the measures to be taken to meet the advancing rebels. He advises attack, an open engagement outside the walls. The cautious burghers prefer defence, caution and bribery. The general, being called upon to decide, admits his sympathy with the views of Grinyov, but submits to pressure and adopts the advice of the civilians. There is implicit criticism of the general, again the representative of what the reader is invited to approve. But more subtly (because Grinyov, the narrator, is obviously unaware of any moral compromise upon his part) there is criticism of Grinyov too. For the reader is not allowed to forget that it is in Grinyov's interest to advise the more dashing course of action, since the girl he loves is in the hands of his rival, behind the rebel lines.

The difficulties which face the English reader of Pushkin are very considerable. Pushkin was well-read in English literature, and the English reader continually comes across conventions from English writers, adopted by Pushkin, but modified by him, until they are almost (but not quite) unrecognizable. Here, in *The Captain's Daughter*, the conventions are those of Walter Scott. But Pushkin, through his rigorous economy in style and composition, has so far changed the methods he took from Scott that to the English reader the conventions governing the story seem something wholly strange. So, in *Eugene Onegin*, the English reader will discern the influences of Byron and, perhaps, of Sterne. So, in other parts of Pushkin's prose-writing, the English reader comes across conventions adopted from the tale of terror. But this discernment in the reader may prove to be more of a hindrance than a help. For in nearly every case Pushkin improves upon his models, using conventions which were originally arbitrary and frivolous, for the discussion of a serious moral problem. Is there, for instance, any novel by Scott in which the moral issue is seen so clearly, the literary instrument used so honestly, as in Pushkin's self-effacing 'romance'?

There is a patent connection between *The Captain's Daughter* and one of Scott's novels. When Pushkin's story was first translated into English,[1] George Saintsbury was quick to seize upon it, in order to damn with faint praise:

> These tales are really attractive enough, especially by reason of the odd simplicity which seems characteristic of Russian story. Except in manner, there is nothing very original about them; indeed, the last scene of the first and longest story, 'The Captain's Daughter', is, to use a very mild word, borrowed from Jeanie Deans' interview with Queen Caroline.[2]

Pushkin, writing for a Russian society which was avidly devouring the Waverley novels as they came out (and also the novels of Fenimore Cooper) was plainly and consciously challenging this comparison with *The Heart of Midlothian*.

The Heart of Midlothian is nowadays in better repute than any other of Scott's novels, and Robin Mayhead voices influential opinion when he is prepared to salvage this book alone from the body of Scott's *oeuvre*.[3] Even at that, he can really respect only the first half of the book, and in fact his case for a 'deeply pondered and carefully worked-out theme' – the nature of human justice – can't be endorsed even so. (The case could be better argued, surely, with *Redgauntlet*.) Joan Pittock, rejecting Mr Mayhead's case,[4] reveals how low Scott's reputation has sunk when she decides that nevertheless '*The Heart of Midlothian* emerges as Scott's best novel', simply because 'Scott's own national antiquarian and legal interests were called more constantly, more powerfully (but not, on the whole, more coherently and significantly) into play than elsewhere.'

If this is the best that can be done for Scott, we might as well forget about him altogether. In fact, however, though there may be more of Scott in this novel than in any other, it is far from being his best.

In the first place the narration is insufferably orotund:

> The careful father was absent in his well-stocked byre, foddering those useful and patient animals on whose produce his living

[1]   *A Russian Romance*, translated by Mrs J. Buchan Telfer (*née* Mouravieff), 1873.
[2]   *The Academy*, 29 May 1875.
[3]   Robin Mayhead, '*The Heart of Midlothian*: Scott as Artist', *Essays in Criticism*, Vol. VI, No.3. July 1956.
[4]   Joan H. Pittock, in 'The Critical Forum', *Essays in Criticism*, Vol. VII, No.4. October 1957.

depended, and the summer evening was beginning to close in, when Jeanie Deans began to be very anxious for the appearance of her sister, and to fear that she would not reach home before her father returned from the labour of the evening...

(Chapter X)

Or again:

Some weeks intervened before Mr Middleburgh, agreeably to his benevolent resolution, found an opportunity of taking a walk towards St Leonard's, in order to discover whether it might be possible to obtain the evidence hinted at in the anonymous letter respecting Effie Deans.

(Chapter XVIII)

Of course this sort of thing is always to be feared in Scott, but here it runs to an extreme. 'In order to discover whether it might be possible to obtain' (i.e. 'to see if he could get') – a little of this (and these are salient but fair examples of the narrative prose as a whole) does a lot of damage. One begins to suspect that Pushkin worked at *The Heart of Midlothian* in a spirit not far short of parody. For Pushkin, however imperfect his command of English, wasn't likely to respect an author who wrote 'those useful and patient animals on whose produce his living depended', when what he meant was 'his cows'. It is the less likely because what marks Pushkin's work as a whole, in verse and prose alike, is its extreme economy, the stripped severity of outline. There is a striking example of this in precisely the parallel which is too conspicuous to be missed, the similarity between Marya Ivanovna's interview with the Empress, and Jeanie Deans' interview with Queen Caroline. The two scenes have too much in common to leave it in doubt that the Scott episode was Pushkin's model in an unusually deliberate and immediate way. And this throws into relief the one large change that Pushkin introduces, the absence from his story of any intermediary such as John, Duke of Argyle, in the novel by Scott. By thus removing the one element needed for plausibility and verisimilitude, Pushkin makes the whole matter of the royal interview like something in a fairy-story or a dream; and the Empress stands forth unashamedly as a *dea ex machina*. The ruthless elimination of superfluities is Pushkin's controlling principle alike in the framing of plot and in the framing of sentences – as can be detected even when we read translations.

To see how far Scott is from any such rigour in style, one need go no further than to a passage which Mr Mayhead picks out for particular approval:

In former times, England had her Tyburn, to which the devoted victims of justice were conducted in solemn procession up what is now called Oxford Road. In Edinburgh, a large open street, or rather oblong square, surrounded by high houses, called the Grassmarket, was used for the same melancholy purpose, It was not ill-chosen for such a scene, being of considerable extent, and therefore fit to accommodate a greater number of spectators, such as were usually assembled by this melancholy spectacle. On the other hand, few of the houses which surround it were, even in early times, inhabited by persons of fashion; so that those likely to be offended or over deeply affected by such unpleasant exhib-itions were not in the way of having their quiet disturbed by them. The houses in the Grassmarket are, generally speaking, of a mean description; yet the place is not without some features of grandeur, being overhung by the southern side of the huge rock on which the castle stands, and by the moss-grown battlements and turreted walls of that ancient fortress.

Mr Mayhead observes, 'One cannot miss the irony of that phrase, "the devoted victims of justice".' But there can be little doubt that Scott missed it, since 'devoted' means what it meant for Milton, not what it means today, and it is regularly used by Scott (and by Fenimore Cooper) as an inert makeweight, one of the heedless Latinisms which pepper their staple styles, and have no more func-tion there than just to impart a hollow dignity. In this passage 'melan-choly purpose', slackly echoed by 'melancholy spectacle' at the end of the next sentence, is proof of how far Scott was from inviting the sort of attention which Mr Mayhead exhorts us to give it. 'Melancholy' is used twice, and yet in neither case is it doing enough work to be used once. To anyone who still believes that 'the essential technique in an art that works by using words is the way in which words are used'[1] it may as well be said at once that Scott in his prose never uses words so as to invite attention of Mr Mayhead's sort. Still, Scott's style in *The Heart of Midlothian* is exceptionally slack. And so it is likely that such of Scott as contributed substantially to *The Captain's Daughter* came from other novels where the style is incomparably cleaner and firmer.

And not just the style, but the narrative structure also. For the plot of *The Heart of Midlothian* is a tissue of improbabilities and coincidences. So is the plot of Pushkin. But Pushkin makes no bones about it; rather, he deliberately heightens the unreality so as to establish firmly a frame of convention for us to enter into, the convention of the fairy-story or folk-tale. This, as we have seen,

---

[1]   Q.D. Leavis, *Fiction and the Reading Public*, p.233.

is the effect of not providing any figure to correspond to Scott's Duke of Argyle. Scott on the other hand tries to paper over the implausibilities, and conceal them. It is Scott, not Pushkin, who is the 'realist'. And so the implausibilities infect what is or should have been the central action. As in better novels by Scott, the central action in *The Heart of Midlothian* is tied to a turning-point in history, the revolutionary change from Scotland before the Union to Scotland after it. But whereas in *The Captain's Daughter* one person, the central character (made susceptible and wavering for the purpose) is torn between this past and this future, in *The Heart of Midlothian* it is a family that is thus torn apart, not a person but a group of persons. And since one of these persons, Jeanie Deans, has to be 'strong', her sister Effie has to be not just 'weak' but, to counterbalance her sister, so extremely weak that her weakness cannot be motivated nor accounted for by any features of temperament or environment. And in fact Scott never even attempts to justify or explain this weakness, not by analysis nor (and this is more damaging) by any direct presentation. Effie's susceptibility, on which the whole action turns, is not even defined, not even described, let alone analysed or accounted for.

And yet of course there are distinguished things in Scott's novel, and things which have a direct bearing on Pushkin. A recent critic has remarked:

> It is one of the ironies of literature that Scott should have been taken for a pioneer of romanticism – indeed, should have actually been one, on the Continent especially. For touch his mind at any point and set it against any of the basic trends of true romanticism, and the two will at once appear to be in flat opposition. The cult of wild Nature? – he said himself that he had no eye for the picturesque in scenery. Human beings came first for him; rocks, mountains, trees and waterfalls were very bad seconds. The cult of the ego? – he despised the autobiographical, what he called the age's 'desire, or rather rage, for literary anecdote and private history'; and although he liked Byron and admired his verse, he deplored and hated the Byronic exhibitionism. The cult of the unconscious? – he was a man of common sense, of the conscious and controlling will. The cult of sentiment, of the Man of Feeling? – 'of all sorts of parade', he wrote to Maria Edgeworth, 'I think the parade of feeling and sentiment the most disgusting'. The cult of the individualist genius, the law unto himself? – again and again he asserts that the writer should be and live like other men, accept their responsibilities and live by their standard. He was no romantic; he was an Augustan, who brought to bear on romantic

materials a mind humorous and worldly-wise, extrovert and sane.[1]

It will suffice for the moment to choose just one tendency of Romanticism which seems to me more 'basic' than any of those here listed, and to set Scott against it. This is the Romanticism of Wordsworth's tract on the Convention of Cintra:

> The instincts of natural and social man; the deeper emotions; the simpler feelings; the spacious range of the disinterested imagination; the pride in country for country's sake, when to serve has not been a formal profession – and the mind is therefore left in a state of dignity only to be surpassed by having served nobly and generously; the instantaneous accomplishment in which they start up who, upon a searching call, stir for the land which they love – not from personal motives, but for a reward which is undefined and cannot be missed; the solemn fraternity which a great Nation composes – gathered together, in a stormy season, under the shade of ancestral feeling; the delicacy of moral honour which pervades the minds of a people, when despair has been suddenly thrown off and expectations are lofty; the apprehensiveness to a touch unkindly or irreverent, where sympathy is at once exacted as a tribute and welcomed as a gift; the power of injustice and inordinate calamity to transmute, to invigorate, and to govern – to sweep away the barriers of opinion – to reduce under submission passions purely evil – to exalt the nature of indifferent qualities, and to render them fit companions for the absolute virtues with which they are summoned to associate – to consecrate passions which, if not bad in themselves, are of such temper that, in the calm of ordinary life, they are rightly deemed so – to correct and embody these passions – and, without weakening them (nay, with tenfold addition to their strength), to make them worthy of taking their place as the advanced guard of hope, when a sublime movement of deliverance is to be originated; – these arrangements and resources of nature, these ways and means of society, have so little connection with those others upon which a ruling minister of a long-established government is accustomed to depend; these – elements as it were of a universe, functions of a living body – are so opposite, in their mode of action, to the formal machine which it has been his pride to manage; – that he has but a faint perception of their immediate efficacy; knows not the facility with which they assimilate with other powers; nor

[1]   Patrick Cruttwell, 'Walter Scott', in *From Blake to Byron* (Pelican Guide to English Literature, Vol.5), pp.110-11.

the property by which such of them – as, from necessity of nature, must change or pass away – will, under wise and fearless management, surely generate lawful successors to fill their place when their appropriate work is performed.

It is a far call from this oratorical splendour to Scott in Chapter XXVIII of his novel, defending his countrymen against the imputation of clannishness. And yet Scott is surely appealing to and defining the same values:

> The eagerness with which Scottish people meet, communicate, and, to the extent of their power, assist each other, although it is often objected to us as a prejudice and narrowness of sentiment, seems, on the contrary, to arise from a most justifiable and honourable feeling of patriotism, combined with a conviction which, if undeserved, would long since have been confuted by experience, that the habits and principles of the nation are a sort of guarantee for the character of the individual. At any rate, if the extensive influence of this national partiality be considered as an additional tie, binding man to man, and calling forth the good offices of such as can render them to the countryman who happens to need them, we think it must be found to exceed, as an active and efficient motive to generosity, that more impartial and wider principle of general benevolence, which we have sometimes seen pleaded as an excuse for assisting no individual whatever.

This shows Scott explicitly preferring to the 'Augustan' tenet of rational benevolence the unwritten and irrational laws of usage, custom and habit. And it shows him thoroughly in tune with at least one of 'the basic trends of true romanticism', a trend which is as apparent in Wordsworth's 'Old Cumberland Beggar' as in the Miltonic eloquence of his tract on the Convention of Cintra – 'the solemn fraternity which a great Nation composes – gathered together, in a stormy season, under the shade of ancestral feeling...' (The nation that Wordsworth has particularly in view is not of course the English but the Spanish nation.) This is not a 'cult' of this nor a 'cult' of that, but a perception that the central fact of politics, and the guiding principle of all public and much private morality, is the fact of community considered as a state of being or a state of feeling. The name of Burke and the title of a work so strictly and deliberately parochial as 'The Old Cumberland Beggar' – these may suffice to distinguish this wisdom from the nationalistic chauvinism which is its perversion. And this is a wisdom rediscovered by the Romantic movement, which both Pushkin and Mickiewicz appreciated in Scott, which made him – thanks to them and to others, and through no 'irony of literature' – 'a pioneer of romanticism... on the Continent especially'.

This is indeed implied in everything Scott writes, an assumption so basic that it is seldom explicit; and it gives value and energy to *The Heart of Midlothian* as to much that is inferior to that. For the sake of it, even his poorest novels repay the reading. Those who talk of Scott's 'humanity' say too little by asserting too much; but this sense of what the community is, a feeling of and for the community, is a major constituent if it is not indeed the definitive distinction of what we apprehend too loosely as his 'humanity'. For Pushkin and Mickiewicz, because of the chronically bad relations between Poland and Russia, it was far more difficult, and at times it proved impossible, to prevent this feeling from being debased into chauvinism, its parody. Yet certainly this conviction that all are brothers, that the national community and even larger communities are at least potentially fraternities, is part of what lies behind Grinyov's dream about his peasant-father, as behind the elder Grinyov's address to his penitent serfs. It is part of the effect of the passage about the dream, however little we may be aware of it. And so one knows from *The Captain's Daughter* alone, and from that even in translation, that it is a travesty of Pushkin to say 'The brotherhood of man would have appealed to Pushkin, if he had thought about it at all, as an excellent subject for a satiric poem'.[1] This is a far worse perversion than that of those Stalinist critics who would make Pushkin seem to be saying this at times when he isn't. Pushkin shared with Scott the sense for what community is, and the conviction of its value; and this is enough to prove that *The Captain's Daughter* isn't after all a parody of Scott, however conscious Pushkin may have been, and doubtless was, of making a terse elegance out of what in Scott was turgid, muffled and untidy.

Yet there is more to *The Captain's Daughter* than this, and in particular there is more to Grinyov's dream than this. To find it we shall need to look further into Scott than *The Heart of Midlothian*.

---

[1]   E.J. Simmons. *Pushkin* (Oxford University Press, 1937), p.5: 'one must not search for a moral in his works; his muse is truly on the side of both good and evil. There is no tendentiousness, no social teaching, no moral pathos. Although a sincere patriot, he was never a Slavophile, for intellectually he felt as much at home in the culture of Europe as in that of his own country. He opposed evil, but he never preached a crusade against it.... The brotherhood of man would have appealed to Pushkin, if he had thought about it at all, as an excellent subject for a satiric poem. As for purpose in art – he summed it all up in one phrase: the purpose of poetry is poetry.'

It is a long time now since anyone coupled the name of Scott, as
Hazlitt and Ruskin did, with the name of Shakespeare. Yet to
Pushkin and Mickiewicz this coupling would have been natural, and
Pushkin in fact explicitly made the comparison. Writing in 1830, he
declared:

> The principal charm of Walter Scott's novels lies in the fact
> that we are introduced to the past not through the *enflure* of French
> tragedies, not through the primness of sentimental novels, not
> through the *dignité* of history, but in a contemporary domestic
> manner . . . *ce qui nous charme dans le roman historique – c'est ce qui
> est historique est absolument ce que nous voyons* – Shakespeare,
> Goethe, Walter Scott have no servile predilection for kings and
> heroes. . . .

And as for the name of Goethe in this connection, it is interesting
that within a couple of years of Pushkin's making this connection,
Mickiewicz, his one-time friend, was in his *Pan Tadeusz* combining
the procedures of Goethe in *Hermann und Dorothea* with the procedures
of Scott's *Waverley*. All this of course, and Pushkin's tribute to Scott,
are couched in very general terms. I hope I may in a short while
make the point with more particularity. And at least I venture to
hope that, if we no longer listen to Hazlitt and Ruskin on Scott, we
may listen to Mickiewicz and Pushkin.

Now, to be sure, reading what critics have to say of these Slavic
writers, one would not readily imagine that either author held a
high opinion of Scott, or drew on him to much purpose in their
own writing. Prince Mirsky, for instance, writing of Pushkin's first
attempt at the novel, *The Negro of Peter the Great*, which he left
unfinished in 1828, applauds the first chapter as 'reminiscent of the
French novelists of the eighteenth century rather than of Scott'.
'But', he goes on, 'the following chapters are over-encumbered with
historical colour and all the antiquarianism dear to the heart of Sir
Walter.' And he decides there is good reason to suppose that Pushkin
abandoned the story precisely because he admired Scott as little as
apparently Prince Mirsky does. Similarly, when he treats of Pushkin's completed novel *The Captain's Daughter*, having to note the
very close affinity between the heroine's interview with the Empress
and Jeanie Deans' interview with Queen Caroline at the end of *The
Heart of Midlothian*, he hastens to remove the implied slur by declaring of Pushkin's story that nevertheless 'It is quite free from all
antiquarianism, description, and bric-à-brac'. Prince Mirsky's
attitude to Scott is clear, and it is one that is shared in the English-

speaking countries: Scott clutters up his stories with antiquarian information and stagey properties which have no relation to his themes, those themes in fact being quite perfunctory, no more than convenient clothes-rails on which to hang the author's idiosyncratic hobbies. Rather similarly, Czesław Miłosz, writing in the magazine *Encounter* about G.R. Noyes's version of *Pan Tadeusz*, decides '...all that remains of that extraordinary "novel in verse", whose characters move like the figures in a ballet, is the sort of plot one might find in Sir Walter Scott...' And here too we gather quite clearly that this is very little to be left with. The critic of Mickiewicz is at one with the critic of Pushkin in thinking they know better than either poet about the author the poets had chosen in some degree (and on this showing, how unfortunately) to imitate.

Scott, in the General Preface to the edition of 1829, tells how 'about the year 1805, I threw together about one third of the first volume of *Waverley*'. The MS. was shown to a friend who reported adversely upon it, and it was then abandoned for, it seems, about seven years. Scott was then induced to take it up again partly by accident (he recalls finding the forgotten MS. when searching for fishing-tackle in an attic), but partly by design, in an attempt to emulate Maria Edgeworth:

> I felt that something might be attempted for my own country, of the same kind with that which Miss Edgeworth so fortunately achieved for Ireland – something which might introduce her natives to those of the sister kingdom, in a more favourable light than they had been placed in hitherto, and tend to procure sympathy for their virtues and indulgence for their foibles.

So far as Scott could remember, the portion completed in 1805 comprised only the first seven chapters. And if we re-read these with this in mind, the difference between these and those that follow is very obvious. It is a difference of kind, not of degree. The writing of these chapters is as accomplished as in the rest, but in a different convention. It is stiff and weighty, and Augustan; it is within measurable distance of, for instance, Jane Austen's *Mansfield Park*:

> His resolution of marriage had been adopted in a fit of indignation; the labour of courtship did not quite suit the dignified indolence of his habits; he had but just escaped the risk of marrying a woman who could never love him, and his pride could not be greatly flattered by the termination of his amour, even if his heart had not suffered.

At other times we are reminded not so much of *Mansfield Park* as of Fielding's *Amelia*; but at all events the writer of these earlier chapters is what the late eighteenth century called 'a moral writer'. His intention is not 'to procure sympathy' (that came later, as we have seen, from Miss Edgeworth) but to judge and discriminate. This is especially apparent in the treatment of the hero; the first seven chapters (especially Chapter III, 'Education', where, Scott tells us, he is describing his own boyhood through Waverley's) seem prepared to judge Waverley quite harshly, whereas in the novel as a whole the question of how far we respect the hero just does not arise. In fact, it is precisely in thus inducing the reader to suspend judgement that Scott's momentous innovation consists; the value of this effect, and the means of achieving it, were I believe precisely what Pushkin and Mickiewicz seized upon. This is something different from for instance Fielding's treatment of *Tom Jones*. We are invited to be indulgent to Fielding's hero. But we are asked to feel that this indulgence is right and natural; and Tom is finally held up for admiration, judged and gloriously acquitted. Pushkin's Grinyov and Mickiewicz's Tadeusz are, like Edward Waverley, obscurely likeable young men of no particular distinction, whom we neither judge nor wish to judge. And if Scott had in fact any predecessors in this, I don't think we need look further than where he points us, to the Irish novelist Maria Edgeworth, who made the discovery in *Castle Rackrent* but chose never to develop it. And this is one reason for dwelling on the gap in the writing of *Waverley*, because between the writing before the intermission and after it we can see the discovery being made.

Again, Chapter I is a humorous disquisition, rather ponderous but effective enough, on the implications of Scott's subtitle, *'Tis Sixty Years Since*, and on the sort of novel *Waverley* might have been, had it been subtitled differently. It might have been *Waverley, a Tale of other Days* (that is, a Gothic novel like Mrs Radcliffe's *Udolpho*, the favourite reading of Pushkin's heroine in *Dubrovsky*); or it might have been *Waverley, a Romance from the German* (that is, a tale of terror, like that fictitious one in which one of Mickiewicz's characters is proud to have figured, *The Count, or the Mysteries of the Castle of Birbante-Rocca*); or it might have been, Scott says, a 'Sentimental Tale'; or, finally, 'A Tale of the Times'. Scott maintains that, by casting his story sixty years earlier, he forfeits on the one hand the appeal of the topical, on the other hand the appeal of the antique and the remote. And he claims to make the best of this by writing a novel not of manners but of men:

> Considering the disadvantages inseparable from this part of my subject, I must be understood to have resolved to avoid them as far as possible, by throwing the force of my narrative upon

the characters and passions of the actors; – those passions common to men in all stages of society, and which have alike agitated the human heart, whether it throbbed under the steel corselet of the fifteenth century, the brocaded coat of the eighteenth, or the blue frock and white dimity waistcoat of the present day. Upon these passions it is no doubt true that the state of manners and laws casts a necessary colouring; but the bearings, to use the language of heraldry, remain the same, though the tincture may be not only different, but opposed in strong contradistinction.

This constitutes a plea for the thoroughly neo-classical principle that the business of the artist is with 'nature', meaning by that the constant elements in human nature to be detected beneath the adventitious distinctions of period, race and trade. And certainly this profession fits well enough the first seven chapters; if it fits the rest, it does so much less plainly. At any rate one must say, using Scott's metaphor, that in the rest of the book far more attention is given to the 'tincture' than is apparent at the start. And it is, I suppose, one of the most serious questions that can be asked of the whole *Waverley* series, whether in these novels Scott believes in a constant 'nature' in this sense, or not. Mr Duncan Forbes believes he does; Professor Trevelyan declared he does not.

At any rate, the clearest indication that Scott resumed his novel with a different intention is the fact that some of the features derided in Chapter I, as stock properties of the kind of novel he did not intend to write, in fact appear in the novel he *did* write. Thus 'the jocularity of a clownish but faithful valet' is adduced as one of the few features of light relief permissible to the Gothic novel; yet the later chapters of *Waverley* present more than one such figure. And similarly the 'Sentimental Tale', according to Scott, requires 'a heroine with a profusion of auburn hair, and a harp, the soft solace of her solitary hours, which she fortunately finds always the means of transporting from castle to cottage'; in *Waverley* Flora MacIvor has dark hair, but apart from that this business with the harp appears with all solemnity in the sentimental tableau of Chapter XXII, 'Highland Minstrelsy'. This chapter is an Ossianic indulgence on Scott's part, and a weakness in the book though not an important one. Neither Mickiewicz's Telimena nor the heroine of Pushkin's *Dubrovsky* are harpists, but they are permitted to take up romantically interesting postures in the open air, and it is notable that both authors make them far more aware of what they are doing than Scott does with his Flora, and both Pushkin and Mickiewicz are ironically detached and wary about this decorative femininity as Scott is not. As for the 'clownish but faithful valet', this tradition dies hard. Pushkin's version of this figure is Savelyich in *The Captain's Daughter*, a character who habitually gets from the critics far more attention than he deserves from his relatively marginal function in the economy of the story as a whole. But the worst case of the clownish valet is Andrew Fairservice in *Rob Roy*.

As for *Waverley*, one important and unexpected feature of this novel is the way it profits from the seven years' gap in Scott's writing of it. For although the difference between the writing of 1805 and the rest stands out very plainly when we know to look for it, it does not jar on the reader who knows nothing about it. On the contrary it has a powerful effect on him without his noticing it. For as it happens Scott broke off the first writing at just the point where Waverley moves out of English into Scottish society; and the change in attitude and style thus corresponds with the change of social milieu, contributing at once something to the different atmosphere that Scott at this point needs to create. The formality and sedateness of the style of the first chapters reflects just those qualities in English society; something fantastic and craggy in the writing when Scott resumes it (one thinks of Sterne now rather than Fielding) corresponds no less aptly to a quality he wants to bring out in the society of the Scots. One example of this will be enough.

Maria Edgeworth, responding to Scott's tribute in the Epilogue to *Waverley*, found only one criticism to make in the course of a full and elaborate examination:

> 'We were so possessed with the belief that the whole story and every character in it was real, that we could not endure the occasional addresses from the author to the reader. They are like Fielding: but for that reason we cannot bear them, we cannot bear that an author of such high powers, of such original genius, should for a moment stoop to imitation...'[1]

This objection is such as will appeal in quarters where it is still fashionable to dislike Thackeray for 'breathing down our necks'; and of course, coming from Miss Edgeworth, it carries weight. But I am not sure that it is fair:

> 'The ingenious licentiate, Francisco de Ubeda, when he commenced his history of La Picara Justina Diez, – which, by the way, is one of the most rare books of Spanish literature, – complained of his pen having caught up a hair, and forthwith begins, with more eloquence than common sense, an affectionate expostulation with that useful implement, upbraiding it with being the

---

[1] *Life and Letters of Maria Edgeworth*, ed. A.J.C. Hare, Vol. I, pp.226–31.

quill of a goose, – a bird inconstant by nature, as frequenting the three elements of water, earth, and air, indifferently, and being, of course, "to one thing constant never". Now I protest to thee, gentle reader, that I entirely dissent from Francisco de Ubeda in this matter, and hold it the most useful quality of my pen, that it can speedily change from grave to gay, and from description and dialogue to narrative and character. So that if my quill display no other properties of its mother-goose than her mutability, truly I shall be well pleased; and I conceive that you, my worthy friend, will have no occasion for discontent. From the jargon, therefore, of the Highland gillies, I pass to the character of their Chief. It is an important examination, and therefore, like Dogberry, we must spare no wisdom.'

This, in its sprightliness, is more like Sterne than Fielding. It is surprising when it comes in the book, and as we read it we take it to be only an embarrassed apology that we could do without. Yet in fact, as we read on, we see that it sets the tone admirably for what follows, our first introduction to the personality and situation of the Highland chieftain, Fergus MacIvor. Everything that is volatile, arbitrary, quaint, even exotic (the Spanish reference) is thoroughly in keeping with the situation and the personality of MacIvor and of others like him. Chapter XXIV begins in a similar way, and can also be justified, I think, though on different grounds.

It is plain, as I have said, that in 1814 Scott was prepared to regard such a character as Edward Waverley's far more leniently than when he first envisaged him in 1805. On the other hand, he is still recognizably the same person at the end of the book as at the beginning. And if Scott's attitude towards him has changed, he does not make the reader's attitude change at the turn of a page. The change of attitude to the hero is gradual and insidious; it is a drift through the whole book, not an abrupt change of front. In Chapter XXV, for instance, the flaws in Waverley's character are still insisted upon, as here, where he is contrasted with the Highland chieftain Fergus MacIvor:

> ...the bold and prompt habits of thinking, acting, and speaking, which distinguished this young Chieftain, had given him a considerable ascendancy over the mind of Waverley. Endowed with at least equal powers of understanding, and with much finer genius, Edward yet stooped to the bold and decisive activity of an intellect which was sharpened by the habit of acting on a preconceived and regular system, as well as by extensive knowledge of the world.

After this, Waverley's character is seen by the reader exclusively as it strikes off from, and appears in contrast to, Fergus MacIvor's. Each is the foil to the other. And by a management of great art, our attitude to Waverley changes as his attitude changes towards Fergus. As Waverley is gradually disillusioned with MacIvor, so we find more to esteem in Waverley. And, even more effectively, the development of our attitude towards him reflects the course of the whole rebellion which is fomented, breaks out and is quelled as the book draws on. In the first weeks of the insurrection, all our sympathies are with the intrepid Fergus, and Waverley seems only his inconstant shadow; on the march to Derby, as the Jacobite impetus gradually falls away, we esteem Waverley more and Fergus less. For, from the standpoint of 1745, Waverley represents the future and Fergus the past.

This is the meaning of the book, at its deepest and most affecting level. It shows the victory of the un-heroic (the English Waverley) over the heroic (the Scottish MacIvor); it shows that this was inevitable and on the whole welcome, yet also sad. This complex balanced attitude towards the historical turning-point is maintained, above all, by the fine stroke (in a sense the clue to the whole book) of making both the representative of the heroic attitude, and his counterpart, the representative of the un-heroic, flawed characters. The Baron Bradwardine is a more estimable representative of Scottish heroism than MacIvor is; Colonel Talbot is a more admirable representative of the unheroic English than Waverley is. Yet MacIvor and Waverley are in the centre of the picture; Talbot and the Baron support only the two main figures.

'Heroic' and 'un-heroic' may both be misunderstood, unless we admit that for 'heroic' we may substitute 'barbarian', for 'un-heroic', 'civilized'. The second pair of terms tilts the scales of approval towards the English, as the first pair towards the Scots; the novelist's achievement is in tilting neither way, but holding the balance scrupulously steady. Certainly by calling Waverley and Talbot 'un-heroic' we do not mean that they are anything but brave; both *are* brave, as Scott is at some pains to insist. The real distinction perhaps is that for MacIvor and Bradwardine the principle governing all conduct is the barbarian heroic principle of 'honour'; for Waverley and Talbot it is something else, reasonableness, public spirit, justice, or 'the greatest happiness of the greatest number'. Of all the characters Colonel Philip Talbot is presented as the most nearly perfect; yet he is made to justify the punitive measures after Culloden, and on grounds only speciously 'moral', really utilitarian, to excuse the quite random justice that pardoned Bradwardine and beheaded poor Evan Dhu. The question at issue is brought to a head very well when Talbot reports on his intercession on behalf of the Baron:

'Thus you see *my* prince can be as generous as *yours*. I do not pretend, indeed, that he conveys a favour with all the foreign graces and compliments of your Chevalier errant; but he has a plain English manner, and the evident reluctance with which he grants your request, indicates the sacrifice which he makes of his own inclination to your wishes.'

(Is it going beyond our brief to point out that in thus acceding the Elector abandoned his own honour, no less than both Talbot's and Waverley's? No principle governs his actions, which are entirely arbitrary, like the acts of a despot. He does what he believes to be unjust, and makes the intercessors share the guilt and the responsibility.)

Inevitably Scott feels nostalgia for the heroism that the passing of time has destroyed. And this nostalgia, when it comes to overt expression, is all the more just and affecting because the author has shown himself, in treating of MacIvor, well aware of the dangerous and discreditable aspects of the heroic attitude. Here is the Baron Bradwardine after the rebellion is over and he has been pardoned, but is still homeless:

A natural sigh closed the sentence; but the quiet equanimity with which the Baron endured his misfortunes, had something in it venerable, and even sublime. There was no fruitless repining, no turbid melancholy; he bore his lot, and the hardships which it involved, with a good-humoured, though serious composure, and used no violent language against the prevailing party.

'I did what I thought my duty', said the good old man, 'and questionless they are doing what they think theirs. It grieves me sometimes to look upon these blackened walls of the house of my ancestors; but doubtless officers cannot always keep the soldier's hand from depredation and spuilzie; and Gustavus Adolphus himself as ye may read in Colonel Munro his Expedition with the worthy Scotch regiment called Mackay's regiment, did often permit it. – Indeed I have myself seen as sad sights as Tully-Veolan now is, when I served with the Marechal Duke of Berwick. To be sure we may say with Virgilius Maro, *Fuimus Troes* – and there's an end of an auld sang. But houses and families and men have a' stood lang eneuch when they have stood till they fall with honour; and now I hae gotten a house that is not unlike a *domus ultima*' – they were now standing below a steep rock. 'We poor Jacobites', continued the Baron, looking up, 'are now like the conies in Holy Scripture (which the great traveller Pococke called Jerboa), a feeble people, that make our abode in the rocks. So, fare you well, my good lad, till we meet at Janet's in the even;

for I must get into my Patmos, which is no easy matter for my auld stiff limbs.'

The noble poignancy here ('houses and families and men have a' stood lang eneuch when they have stood till they fall with honour') depends upon the pedantry that stands around it. This pedantry is in character; but its purpose is at this point no longer just to make the figure of the Baron picturesque and individual. It is what makes this passage elegiac, rather than nostalgic. The references, scriptural, military, classical, build up a picture not just of one man's spiritual world, but of a whole society. The same ranges of reference come together in a Presbyterian poet like Alexander Hume in the sixteenth century; they belong to a Scottish cultural tradition, transcending distinctions of political or religious allegiance, which was destroyed in 1745. The reference to Virgil is particularly pregnant. The Baron is always translating Latin tags, as here with 'there's the end of an aud sang', into the racy and colloquial Scots language of his time; and in consequence the society he laments is seen to be Augustan in the strict sense, that is to say, appealing to the Rome of Augustus as a model of civilization, every bit as earnestly as the more notori- ously Augustan society of London under Queen Anne. 'There's the end of an auld sang' is a translation of 'Fuimus Troes' only in the specially free sense in which Pope's *Imitations of Horace* are transla- tions of Horace. All this, by giving the nostalgic feeling something precise and articulated on which to work, takes the passage out of the realm of the nostalgic as commonly understood, and makes it elegiac, something of a stately ritual, clear-sighted, composed, and sad rather than melancholy – like the state of mind of the Baron himself.

Nothing less and nothing different, I think, should be said of some passages from Mickiewicz's *Pan Tadeusz*, such as this:

> The Lithuanian judge
> Offers by way of reproof
> To the young Pan Tadeusz
> Decorum, the difficult science,
> No matter of graceful posture
> Or ease at the affable counter,
> But bearing of old Poland;
> Courtesy, being extended
> To all, not without distinction
> But in the mode most proper,
> As to master with man, or to children
> With parents, or each to each
> In public husband and wife.

'Discourse in noble mansions
Was then a persistent history,
And talk among the gentry
The annals of their provinces;
Gentlemen watched their step,
Knowing such pains were taken
To judge of their deserving;
But neither name nor stock,
Associates nor achievements,
Are now enquired after,
And each goes where he pleases
Short of the known informer
And the scrounger by profession.
Vespasian never questioned
Out of what hands his riches
Came to him, having decided
Money was "not to be sniffed at".
So men approve a title
And value their connections
By current estimates,
As if to strike up a friendship
Were also a transaction.
But a sense of personal worth
Is arrived at only by weighing;
The beam is only plumb
With a counterpoise in the pan,
A worthiness in another.'

If we recall the accent of living speech and dialectal modification in the passage from Scott, we doubtless get some idea of what we have lost in translation. But the Judge's allusion to Vespasian seems to function in just the same way as Bradwardine's reference to Virgil – except that, as always, there is an added edge to the Polish specimen, that comes of Poland's being, and feeling herself to be down the centuries, on the embattled frontier of Christendom and the Latin world. This affinity once recognized, the points of comparison multiply. Scott's Scotland, like Mickiewicz's Lithuania, is the seat of a provincial culture which has, so each writer persuades us, all the virtues of the provincial – a slow and steady tempo as against the whirl of fad and fashion in the metropolis, St Petersburg or London; social communities bound together organically by usage and unwritten law as against blue-print regimentation from above; personal idiosyncrasies allowed to flower into eccentricities or harmless obsessions instead of being ironed out or else aggravated into perversions. These provinces escape, on the other hand, the vices of the provincial, being 'out of touch', parochial or complacent, only in indifferent matters, having in essential things a direct channel clear and running, back to the well springs of European culture. Mickiewicz's judge is a lawyer of sorts, but his pedantry has not a specifically legal flavour, any more than Bradwardine's. However Scott, himself a lawyer, is fond of introducing characters like Bartoline Saddletree in *The Heart of Midlothian* or Peter Peebles in *Redgauntlet*, who are pedants of the law; and in *Pan Tadeusz* Mickiewicz, the son of a lawyer, has at least one such character, the Apparitor. What is more, at his best (which is to say, in *Redgauntlet* rather than *The Heart of Midlothian*), this pedantry in Scott throws an oblique light on the central theme, which is precisely the question of the rule of law in a society where loyalties are legitimately divided. And this is a main concern of *Pan Tadeusz*, too, in all that is related to its subtitle, the *Last Foray in Lithuania*. Mickiewicz's treatment is comic, where Scott's at least in *Redgauntlet*, which is one of his most sombre books, is tragic in feeling. Indeed, when one comes to think of it, everything in Mickiewicz's poem which concern the Foray and the vengeful intrigues of the old squire Gerwazy is an exact parallel to the Jacobitism of *Waverley*, in that it represents the barbaric principle of honour surviving from feudal society into an era which demands rather the rule of law; and between the two bodies of sentiment Mickiewicz's feelings appear to be divided as equally as Scott's. The balance is held just as steadily, though perhaps the use of the comic mode makes this impartiality rather easier for Mickiewicz than for Scott.

There are many other elements which *Pan Tadeusz* and *Waverley* have in common, and of course we mustn't lose sight of the possibility that some of these derive from a common source in what one can only call 'the spirit of the age'. But there is one other common element which cannot be allowed to pass unremarked. This is 'the man of feeling'. In *Waverley*, one is made to realize how irretrievably the old Scotland has disappeared, by the master-stroke of giving the dedication of the work at the end – 'To our Scottish Addison, Henry Mackenzie'. Mackenzie, author of the novel called *The Man of Feeling*, was or seemed to be the author of much more, of a new type of individual and a new moral paragon, the man who prided himself most on his susceptibility, more on his tender heart than his level head. And Scott is quite sincere of course – he really esteems the new Scottish culture (though it is Anglo-Scottish by this time), which has come to replace the old and is represented by 'the man of feeling' in Boswell's *Hypochondriack* and Burns's letters no less than in Mackenzie himself. In this new Scotland of Henry Mackenzie the criterion of behaviour is no longer objective at all, neither barbaric honour nor the greatest happiness of the greatest number, but subjective, the intensity of one's own emotional reactions.

If anyone thinks that this is to read too much into Scott's story, they would do well to read Chapter LII, and Flora MacIvor's prophecy of what Waverley will become in later life:

> I will tell you where he will be at home, my dear, and in his place, – in the quiet circle of domestic happiness, lettered indolence, and elegant enjoyments, of Waverley-Honour. And he will refit the old library in the most exquisite Gothic taste, and garnish its shelves with the rarest and most valuable volumes; and he will draw plans and landscapes, and write verses, and rear temples, and dig grottoes; – and he will stand in a clear summer night in the colonnade before the hall, and gaze on the deer as they stray in the moonlight, or lie shadowed by the boughs of the huge old fantastic oaks; – and he will repeat verses to his beautiful wife, who will hang upon his arm; – and he will be a happy man.

Here is the man of feeling already – in 1745! Scott takes pains to show that Miss MacIvor is an exceptionally intelligent woman, but she must needs be extraordinary indeed to divine that the taste of the next half-century was to be 'exquisite Gothic'. For Waverley in 1745 is the man of the future. The 'man of feeling' was just emerging on to the stage of history (Shenstone perhaps was the prototype) but it was a full generation later, in the time of Uvedale Price, that he became common. Scott, by catching the type at its very first appearance, envisages the future and throws it into dramatic contrast with Vich Ian Vohr, Fergus MacIvor, the belated representative of the past, artificially preserved in the special atmospheres of St. Germains and Glennaquoich.

Scott suggests, in *Waverley*, that the man of feeling, and the whole cult of 'sensibility', were originally English phenomena which could make no way in Scotland until older indigenous habits of thought and feeling were destroyed at Culloden, for Scottish Whigs and Scottish Jacobites alike. If so, the Scots learnt fast. For the English prophets of the movement, Richardson and Sterne, had to be bowdlerized before they could fit the requirements of the cult; whereas by 1770 the Athens of the North was supplying London, through Mackenzie and Macpherson, Beattie and Logan, Boswell and (soon after) Burns, with all the literature characteristic of the new vogue. As late as 1814, it seems, this era appeared to the Scots a great cultural achievement on the part of their countrymen; and Scott's dedication shows that, despite all the affection he felt for an older Scotland, he too regarded Mackenzie, and all that he stood for, as something to be applauded.

Indeed, we must go further. Among those 'rarest and most valuable volumes' with which Edward Waverley was to garnish the library of Waverley Honour might we not expect to find *La Picara Justina Diez* – 'which, by the way, is one of the most rare books of Spanish literature'? At any rate, the Sternian pen that 'can speedily change from grave to gay, and from description and dialogue to narrative and character' was never so much valued as by those who catered for the cult of 'sensibility'. Among the men of feeling we have to list the author of *Waverley* himself.

Whether Walter Scott and 'the author of *Waverley*' are at all points one and the same person is another matter. In view of the author's jealously guarded anonymity, it would be possible to argue that when Scott wrote *Waverley*, he was writing in an assumed character, as Sterne wrote in the character of Yorick. But at any rate, if we think that Scott was in some sort a 'man of feeling' himself, it throws light on his avowed object, 'to procure sympathy'. Of that aspect of Scott's intention and achievement (and by his own account it is the most important aspect), I have said nothing at all, because there is no way of saying it. I have, after all, considered *Waverley* as a work of discrimination and judgement, as if the whole book were written in the style of the first seven chapters. But it is written to procure our sympathies, and it is on that count that it stands or falls. Here every reader can only judge for himself whether his sympathies are engaged, and how strongly. For my own part I am moved continually and powerfully, and it is because I am so moved that I consider *Waverley* one of the greatest novels in the language. The most an essay of this kind can do is to show that if our sympathies are engaged, they are not engaged indiscriminately but to some purpose. That cannot be said of all Scott's books; but it can be said of this one.

IV   *PAN TADEUSZ*

Mickiewicz's man of feeling is the young Count, who plays in *Pan Tadeusz* the fourth hand necessary to make up a double triangle with the hero and his two women, Zosia and Telimena. The Count has all the features of the type, down to the sketching pencil in the pocket and the taste for the Gothic in literature, architecture and manners. Mickiewicz treats him with an affectionate indulgence, making comedy out of his inability to distinguish between the ideally imagined and the actual; and it is this no doubt which leads the critics to call him Quixotic and invoke the name of Cervantes. All the same it does not strike me as a useful identification. Or rather, it is once again a case which is clarified by Scott's heraldic metaphor of 'the bearings' and 'the tincture'. The Quixotic is perhaps an undying recurrent type, and to this extent the bearings of Cervantes remain the same in Mickiewicz; but the tincture is unmistakably that of the period, of the man of feeling. Scott appears to have no qualms about the man of feeling. But it was a type which had already deteriorated. By Byron's day the epicure of the feelings, continually probing his own emotions to induce new and more exotic feelings, was suffering already from a jaded palate, having enjoyed all the available tastes before he was past his youth, and therefore the prey of ennui and *le mal du siècle*. His later history is well known, and it was Russian authors who traced it most closely, from the Onegin of Pushkin through the Pechorin of Lermontov to the Stavrogin of Dostoevsky. Mickiewicz acknowledges these darker potentialities of the type only once, I think, when the Count realizes how his imagination has obscured the reality of the heroine, Zosia:

> His soul like the earth after sundown
> Darkened and chilled; his abstraction
> Brought him bad dreams; he awakened
> In anger that sought its occasion.

But in the poem as a whole Mickiewicz treats this figure with humorous indulgence, with none of Scott's sense that this type is the man of the future. And he is farther still from entertaining any of Pushkin's much darker forebodings about characters of this type.

In any case, however, *Waverley* is related to both *Pan Tadeusz* and *The Captain's Daughter* in a far more obvious way, by virtue of its unheroic hero. Czesław Miłosz observes this in *Pan Tadeusz* when he says of Mickiewicz that 'The humour with which he sets his limited and mediocre heroes in motion is without malice.' My information doesn't extend so far as to know whether Polish critics earlier than Mr Miłosz have made heavier weather of this 'weakness' in Mickiewicz's Tadeusz. But the Russian critics have censured Pushkin for his 'limited and mediocre' Grinyov in just the same way as the English critics have objected to Scott's Edward Waverley. Belinsky, no less, writing in 1846 on *The Captain's Daughter*, decided 'The insignificant, colourless character of the hero of the story and his beloved Marya Ivanovna . . . belong to its striking shortcomings'. And we have to wait for Leontiev before finding it acknowledged that, as Professor Lednicki has said, 'the average character of the narrator' is 'the finest, the unique device of Pushkin the historian'. I wish to suggest that Scott had something to do with Pushkin's discovery of this 'device', as with Mickiewicz's discovery of it about the same time.

Thackeray, when he subtitled *Vanity Fair* 'a novel without a hero', meant by that something very interesting but quite different from what it may mean as applied to *Waverley*. The formula fits the Scott novel just as neatly. And the enormous advantage of the Scott method in this particular is that it makes of the central character a sounding-board for historical reverberations, or else, to change the metaphor, a weathervane responding to every shift in the winds of history which blow around it. This device, and this alone, of a weak hero poised and vacillating between opposites, allows the historian to hold the balance absolutely firm and impartial, giving credit everywhere it is due. If the central figure is exempted from judgement, this is not from any moral laxity in the story-teller; but is designed to permit judgement of the parties, the ideologies, the alternative societies which contend for his allegiance. Thus, just as Scott's hero is poised between MacIvor and Talbot, between Scottish and English, between Jacobite and Hanoverian, between past and future, so Pushkin's Grinyov is poised between the peasant rebel and pretender Pugatchov and the true Tsar represented by his own father and the father of his sweetheart; and so Mickiewicz's Tadeusz is poised between Zosia and Telimena, between a healthy provincialism centred on Vilno and a superficially more sophisticated but really more damaging provincialism which looks to St Petersburg.

According to David Daiches, this holding of the balance between phases of history is the true theme of all Scott's good novels, the true 'plot' to which what Mr Daiches calls 'the external plot' is irrelevant. That this is the true theme I would agree. But I do not think that the question of Scott's plots can be dismissed quite so easily. For if the apparent plot bears no relation to the true theme, this is surely a major flaw in the writing. Yet this, or something like it, is the best that another of Scott's modern apologists, Edwin Muir, can do for him:

> Scott was a very great story-teller, as well as a very bad one. *The Antiquary* certainly contains one of his worst plots. But his particular kind of story-telling did not depend on plot, and was often good in spite of it, the story being excellent even where the plot was mediocre or bad.[1]

This, I'm afraid, strikes me as playing with words. Of course, the whole notion of 'plot' in literature is one that has been in bad odour for a long time, ever since Henry James declared exultantly of a novel

---

[1]   Edwin Muir, *Essays on Literature and Society* (1944).

by Turgenev, 'And never a patch of plot, to draw blood!' And certainly, if the only questions to be asked of plot are 'Does it keep us wondering what is coming next?' and 'Is this the way things happen in daily life?' – if these are the only criteria to be applied to plot (and they are the only questions commonly asked), then indeed 'plot' is an irrelevance, a mere conventional machine. But lately we have begun to wonder again what Aristotle meant when he laid down the principle of unity of action in drama, and to wonder if this has not some bearing on questions of plot in narrative as well. If we follow this line of thought, we find ourselves deciding that a plot is no worse for being totally unlike what happens in daily life, as in the case of fairy stories or *Oedipus Rex*; and none the worse either if we know throughout all that is coming next, as in the case of *Oedipus Rex* again. What is required is that, whatever the elaborations of the plot, all of these should be firmly related to a central action which is banally simple and a sort of symbolic pivot for the theme. As Mr Daiches points out, Edward Waverley's proposal of marriage to Rose Bradwardine rather than Flora MacIvor is just such a symbolic action, which justifies all the rest, and makes the plot of *Waverley* a very good one indeed. For where the central action is so firmly related to the theme, it can be embellished with sub-plots which, however fantastic and implausible in themselves, do not damage the form.

Considering plots in this way, we soon find ourselves thinking in terms of the twelve or thirty-two or however-many-it-is 'basic plots'. And from this it is only a step to the territory of archetypes and depth-psychology, which is a landscape that I must confess I don't much like the look of. But we may, and indeed we must, penetrate a little way into this jungle. For *Waverley* and *The Captain's Daughter* and *Pan Tadeusz* (to which we may add another of Scott's best novels, *Redgauntlet*) all make play with one of the hoariest of all archetypal plots, the plot of the lost father, a situation which occurs rarely in daily life but frequently in literature. In *Waverley* this fairy-tale element is sketched in so lightly, and accommodated so scrupulously to the demands of everyday likelihood, that it is easily overlooked. But in fact Edward Waverley has a mildly unnatural father, a time-serving politician, who is so intent on making a career in London that he leaves his son to be brought up in the family home by an uncle with Jacobite sympathies and connections. Thus Waverley's involvement with the Jacobites and his gradual extrication from them, throughout the book, represent his search for the real father, the Hanoverian Whig, behind the figure of the substitute father, the Tory uncle. And sure enough, it is the father's influence with the prevailing party which finally procures Waverley a pardon.

Mickiewicz's Tadeusz is similarly brought up by an uncle, the Judge, and discovers his true father only at the end of the story; and, since the true father is an agitator on behalf of the advancing Napoleonic armies, he represents the future with which Tadeusz allies himself when at the end he joins the army of liberation. But it was a short future, for the Napoleonic liberation was short-lived; and so the end of *Pan Tadeusz*, a conclusion tragic in feeling after so much smilingly indulgent comedy, is far more complex and affecting than anything in Scott. And one is left with the impression that the false father, the uncle, is ultimately the true father after all, in the sense that he represents the innate strength of Lithuanian Poland, and this is the only basis on which to build; whereas the true father has pinned his hopes on the French, who have betrayed the Poles hardly less than the Russians have.

In terms of artistic strategy, Mickiewicz is much the boldest of the three writers: by having the true father hover continually in disguise about the developing action, he risks the fairy-tale far more, and challenges daily plausibility far more defiantly than either Scott or Pushkin. Pushkin is by far the most deft and economical in his handling of the lost-father element. In keeping with the whole of *The Captain's Daughter*, a novel resolutely stripped of all superfluities, in which every word is made to count, this whole symbolic dimension of the story is opened up only once, in the dream Grinyov has after his first meeting with Pugatchov, at a time when he still does not know who Pugatchov is. I must be permitted to quote from this afresh:

> I had a dream which I could never since forget and in which I still see a kind of prophecy when I reflect upon the strange vicissitudes of my life. The reader will forgive me, probably knowing from experience how natural it is for man to indulge in superstition, however great his contempt for all vain imaginings may be.

He dreams that he returns to the home which he has lately left to join his regiment, and that his mother meets him, telling him his father is dying:

> Terror-stricken, I followed her to the bedroom. It was dimly lighted; people with sad-looking faces were standing by the bed. I approached the bed quietly; my mother lifted the bed-curtains and said: 'Andrey Petrovitch! Petrusha has come; he returned when he heard of your illness; bless him.' I knelt down and looked at the sick man. But what did I see? Instead of my father a black-bearded peasant lay on the bed looking at me merrily. I turned to my mother in perplexity, and said to her: 'What does it mean?

This is not my father. And why should I ask this peasant's blessing?'
– 'Never mind, Petrusha,' my mother answered, 'he takes your
father's place for the wedding; kiss his hand and let him bless
you....' I would not do it. Then the peasant jumped off the bed,
seized an axe from behind his back, and began waving it about. I
wanted to run away and could not; the room was full of dead bodies;
I stumbled against them and slipped in the pools of blood....
The terrible peasant called to me kindly, saying: 'Don't be afraid,
come and let me bless you.' Terror and confusion possessed me...
At that moment I woke up.

By the end of the book, when Grinyov has been helped to his bride
by the peasant-pretender Pugatchov, when he has seen Pugatchov
hang his friends before his eyes, when he has seen Pugatchov executed in his turn, there is hardly an item of this dream – not the
wedding, the pools of blood, the obdurate 'I would not' – that lacks
symbolic resonance, of the compelling sort that continually asks to
be reduced to allegory but in the end always escapes that reduction.
And meanwhile verisimilitude is scrupulously preserved. For this is
what dreams are like; the characteristically Dostoevskyan vertigo
which comes of a forcing together of incompatible feelings is from
this point of view very exactly, almost clinically, 'realistic'. And the
more one looks at this passage, the harder it is to deny to the Soviet
critics at least part of their case that Pushkin, writing under
immediate personal censorship from the tsar, yet contrived by
sheerly artistic means to express rabidly subversive sentiments.

Now, one must guard against the ludicrous idea (which, ludicrous
as it is, is not uncommon) that the writer has only to tap the archetype, which will thereupon write his masterpiece for him. The lost-
father archetype is of no artistic value whatever, until it is placed in
a context in which its symbolic overtones are meaningful, in which
the search for the father can become the search for the birthright,
for the source of true authority to which allegiance can rightfully
be given. The archetype is profitable for Scott, for Mickiewicz, for
Pushkin, only because all three authors have established the ranges
of choice that are open, the different allegiances which present themselves in all their baffling incompatible plausibility at a given moment
of history, And meanwhile we may note that the hero in the lost-
father fable *has to be* what Scott and the others have made him –
wavering (there is a sort of pun with 'Waverley'), inconstant,
mediocre, weak. How else should he behave, since, not knowing
his father, he does not know who he is, nor where his allegiance lies?
There is another basic plot or archetypal fable in *Waverley* and in
Pan Tadeusz – what may be called the Romeo-and-Juliet plot, of the

youth and the maiden born to warring houses, who fall in love with each other. This does not occur in *The Captain's Daughter*, though it is the basic fable of Pushkin's earlier and unfinished novel *Dubrovsky*. It is also the basic fable of *The Bride of Lammermoor*, and accordingly critics have found in that novel by Scott the source or one source for Pushkin's story. This attribution does not recommend itself to me, for these basic fables are by definition widely available, and nothing else in *Dubrovsky* reminds me of *The Bride of Lammermoor*. What is more interesting than anything else which emerges from these comparisons is the striking contrast between Pushkin and Mickiewicz in their procedures. Pushkin's abstemiousness – his allocation of one fable to one story – is in line with his constant practice in all kinds of writing, his classical severity, his concern above all to have only one line of interest and action running clean and unfettered. I am not so sure whether it is typical of Mickiewicz to do the other thing, though I think it is. As to *Pan Tadeusz*, there can be no doubt: where Pushkin strips his story to the bone, Mickiewicz accumulates and elaborates. The lost-father theme at its most challengingly implausible is pointed up by Mickiewicz and brought out of the discreet shadow where Scott had left it; the Romeo-and-Juliet plot is planted firmly on top of it; not content with the triangle situation which thereupon emerges, Mickiewicz introduces a fourth young man to make a double triangle; the Lithuanian Montagues and Capulets are brought face to face in a pitched battle; and below and behind these numerous actions, all in some degree private, surges always the public drama of the Napoleonic invasion of Russia. And no one of these lines of action is allowed to run so smoothly that it cannot loiter into digressions, lyrical invocations, set-pieces of genre-painting, vignettes from a comedy of manners. If Pushkin's manner is classical, Mickiewicz's is exuberantly Gothic; and if *Pan Tadeusz* is a novel-in-verse, then *The Captain's Daughter* is a poem in prose. For this is the astonishing thing; we are accustomed to allow that prose is more cumulative in effect than poetry, and so to allow to prose far more liberty to elaborate and discursively accumulate than we allow to poetry. Yet in this case it is the poem, Mickiewicz's, which is leisurely, digressive, cumulative, and the novel, Pushkin's, which has all the severity and rapidity.

It is our conviction or prejudice about the simplicity of plot in poetry which makes us suspicious of the whole genre of the novel-in-verse. In any case, we have in English no generally acknowledged masterpieces in this kind. The nearest we can come to it in modern times is Byron's *Don Juan* or Wordsworth's *Excursion* (and of course it is no accident that both these works belong to the Romantic period, as does *Pan Tadeusz*), but everyone will admit that in the end these poems are something else again; and so we are left with Elizabeth Barrett Browning's *Aurora Leigh* as the best example of a genre which that curious work has not served to make respectable among us. Confessing so much, we are often asked to relate *Pan Tadeusz* to an accepted masterpiece in this kind, Pushkin's *Eugene Onegin*. But in fact this is worse than useless, for in that work, despite the digressions and vignettes which remind us of *Pan Tadeusz* as of Byron's *Don Juan*, Pushkin's narrative leanness is carried to a splendid extreme. For the plot can be reduced as Professor Lednicki has said, to the formula: A loved B, but B does not love A; B falls in love with A when A can no longer love B. In the massive simplicity of this there is nothing that can lull our disquiets about the complexities of plot in *Pan Tadeusz*. And indeed I do not know how to lull them, except by pointing out that they immediately go to sleep of themselves as soon as we begin to read. And this means, I think, that we accept the elaboration of the action because it is all of a piece with everything else. It is not that the plot is elaborated at the expense of anything else. On the contrary, the same exuberant inventiveness which is continually throwing out new complications in the story is at the same time inexhaustibly devouring the commonplace, elevating and idealizing it at every turn with apt and beautiful metaphor. And if Mickiewicz falls foul of our preconceptions about the simplicity of plot proper to poetry, he falls in with a set of preconceptions far less ancient but far more powerful – our admiration for the particular and the concrete in poetry, especially when these go along with creative metaphor. An example is his evocation of the Lithuanian sky:

> Blue, that Italian sky
> Clear, as is frozen water;
> But in this country
> As the wind or the storm passes,
> What images, what actions
> The sportive wrack composes:
> Shower-logged, sluggish in Spring
> Clouds like tortoises labour
> Over a sky where tresses
> Of the long rain sway earthward;
> The bowling hailstorm crosses
> The heavens by balloon
> Blue, but with yellow flashes;
> And then, what metamorphoses
> Pursue the white quotidian
> Clouds that like a gaggle

Of swans or geese the falcon
Wind hard presses;
Harried, they multiply
Prodigies, and crested
With sudden manes as serried
Legs bud beneath them, coursers
Over the steppes of the sky,
Necks arched, they gallop.

This stream of images, clouds in wind becoming tortoises, locks of hair, balloons, swans and geese and falcons, and galloping horses – all in rapid succession as if by cutting in the cinema – this is the sort of thing we are very ready to admire. After all, it is the Shakespearean thing; and we respond to it very readily, far more readily (it is worth pointing out) than to anything in Pushkin, whose imagination works in a quite different and far less translatable way. Moreover, there is one very important element in *Pan Tadeusz* – an element rather of character than plot – which is treated throughout in the poet's way, not the novelist's way. This is the figure of the heroine Zosia, the unformed and vulnerable Juliet to the Romeo of the young Tadeusz. Zosia is on the stage far less than her thematic importance would seem to require. When she *is* on stage, she is hardly ever in the centre of it, but a fugitive apparition glimpsed obliquely and entrancingly as she disappears into the wings. And even a translation can reveal that if this figure none the less pulls its weight, it is because of the *quality* which inheres in her brief appearances, a quality of intensity in language which I think we have to call lyrical, and a quality which by its intensity, counterbalances the far more cumulative, particularized and even analytical treatment given to her more mature rival, her aunt Telimena. If we compare this treatment of Zosia with Pushkin's treatment of a similar figure, Tatiana in *Eugene Onegin*, I think we have to say that in this particular it is Pushkin who is more the novelist-in-verse, Mickiewicz who is more the poet. This is the point at which to acknowledge that of course there *is* a novel-in-verse in English which is an acknowledged masterpiece, Chaucer's *Troilus and Criseyde*. Criseyde is treated with the novelist's hand as much as Pushkin's Tatiana is, or Mickiewicz's Telimena. And I should be happy if someone would draw the conclusion that such terms as I have been using, like singleness of action, are still or may be as relevant to the discussion of poems as of novels and dramas – as of course they were always supposed to be by neo-classical critics.

Yet to give the flavour of Mickiewicz's incomparable poem to those who do not know it, one needs to point, not to a piece of static description, but to what is far more remarkable, the sustained passages describing tumultuous and fluctuating action. And more remarkable than either are the gradations and transitions of tone as of matter by which the poet slides in and out of his digressions and his set-pieces. It was precisely this feature of Pushkin's *Eugene Onegin* which Mickiewicz drew attention to when he lectured on the poem in Paris, remarking that 'the reader does not even notice how from the key of an ode the poem descends to an epigram and, rising again, passes imperceptibly into a fragment told with almost epic gravity.'[1]

It need not be pretended that these aspects of Mickiewicz's art can be paralleled in Walter Scott, or that they have any relation to what Mickiewicz may have learned from Scott – beyond this: that *Pan Tadeusz* can carry the weight of inventiveness at the level of diction as at the level of plot, only because the plot, for all its elaboration, is at bottom, as the neo-classic theorists used to say, *a single action*, and a single action on the model of Scott's central action in *Waverley*, made symbolic and central by just the means that Scott employed there and elsewhere. And so it is no surprise that Mickiewicz himself, even as he wrote *Pan Tadeusz*, described the poem as nearest in genre to a Scott novel.[2]

To turn to Pushkin is to enter a world in human terms very similar but utterly different in terms of artistic strategies. Pushkin's novels and short stories, except perhaps for the *Queen of Spades*, reveal their narrative structures with unparalleled nakedness. And just for that reason one feels that *The Captain's Daughter* is hardly a novel at all, just as Pushkin's stories are hardly stories. *The Captain's Daughter* is like the Platonic idea of the perfect novel; it is the idea, the incomparable symmetry and economy in the fitting of means to ends, which remain with us from the reading and which we suppose, perhaps unfairly, is what most interested the novelist in the writing. By the same token it is the bare hard impersonality of style, its inexorable movement from subject through verb to object, which is truly poetic prose – not the yearning cadences and jewelled imagery of the prose of W.B. Yeats, but everything sacrificed to concentration and rapidity. I fall among paradoxes. But this at least must be said: that Pushkin in prose is a virtuoso, interested above all in the technical problems of a strange and new medium. (For Russian narrative prose in any serviceable mode was all to make when Pushkin began writing; and Pushkin duly made it, for himself and for others.) This virtuosity reaches its peak in Pushkin's short stories, the *Tales of Belkin*, but the same brilliance is apparent in only slightly less

---

[1]   Quoted by Waclaw Lednicki, *Bits of Table Talk on Pushkin, Mickiewicz, Goethe, Turgenev and Sienkiewicz* (The Hague, 1956), p.24.

[2]   Weintraub, *The Poetry of Adam Mickiewicz*, p.223.

degree in *The Captain's Daughter*. I have already remarked on the singleness of the symbolic action in the novel, a principle learned I suspect from Scott, but here applied with a rigour quite alien to Scott's temper of mind; and this is the central and most important case of virtuosity in the work. But I will remark briefly on two others, devices which once again Pushkin may have found in Scott, but only in a rudimentary form. I mean the device of the framed narrator, and the device of the epigraph.

Pushkin's early unfinished novels, *Dubrovsky* and *The Negro of Peter the Great* are both written *in propria persona*: that is to say, the voice that we hear telling the tale is that of the omniscient narrator, quite uninvolved in the action he recounts. But in *The Captain's Daughter* as also in the *Tales of Belkin* the man who tells the story is himself part of the story, and we see it all through the none too perceptive or clear-sighted eyes of Grinyov in one case, Belkin in the other. Scott, in novels later than *Waverley*, had made perfunctory gestures in this direction, grouping his stories as 'Tales of my Land-lord', and sometimes placing between the reader and the story the shadowy figure of an imaginary narrator, Jedediah Cleishbotham; but Scott never made anything of the device, and indeed, most of the time in *The Heart of Midlothian*, for instance, we forget about Cleishbotham altogether as I'm sure Scott did too.[1] But this one simple device of the framed narrator, as developed particularly by Turgenev, was handed on by Turgenev to James, and thence to Joseph Conrad and Ford Madox Ford, issuing at last in the elaborations of the Henry James prefaces, with their theory of 'the limited point of view', in the intricacies of Conrad's *Chance*, where the framed narrator reconstructs a scene described to him by another character who herself has only a report of it from yet another, and in the tour-de-force of Ford's *The Good Soldier*. It is hardly too much to say that the whole cycle of this development was foreseen and followed through by Pushkin in the capsulated form of the *Tales of Belkin*, as in a sort of controlled experiment.

Once the novelist agrees to tell a story through the limited sensibility of a framed narrator, his problem of course is how to transcend these self-sought limitations in order to light up the narrative from an angle that the fictitious narrator cannot perceive. Turgenev and James, Conrad and Ford, all had their own ways of getting

---

[1] Mickiewicz used something like this device in *Grazyna* but not I think in *Pan Tadeusz*; though Professor Weintraub claims that there too the voice which tells the story is not that of the poet but of a framed narrator, a sort of village gossip. This view has been challenged, and in any case it seems that if there is a framed narrator in *Pan Tadeusz*, he is present only vestigially.

round this difficulty. Pushkin's device to this end was another one which he could have found in Scott; I mean, the epigraph. Scott's use of this device is already quite sophisticated, in such a case for instance as the epigraphs from Massinger's *New Way to Pay Old Debts* at the head of chapters in *The Bride of Lammermoor*. But here again Pushkin carried the device to an extreme of ingenuity; if one is to believe the brilliant Soviet scholar Viktor Shklovsky, Pushkin's epigraphs to the chapters of *The Captain's Daughter* carry, as it were in code, a reading of history directly opposed to the blamelessly conservative sentiments overtly professed by the narrator Grinyov.

Whatever we may think of Shklovsky's ingenious thesis as a whole, there is at least enough truth in it to make me guard against the impression I may have given, by my talk of 'virtuosity', that Pushkin was not intimately interested in the *subject* of *The Captain's Daughter*. He was of course avidly interested, and personally involved. The easiest way to establish this is to read, along with *The Captain's Daughter*, the unfinished *Negro of Peter the Great*, which is an exception to all I have said, in that it shows no virtuosity but is the torso of a novel straightforwardly on Scott's plan and designed on a massive scale. There could have been no classic severity of outline here. In the few chapters which are completed we can see pre-Petrine Russia aligned against the Russia of Peter the Great, a closed Russia against a Russia open to the West, and a Russia administered by the traditional classes of the boyars and minor gentry against a Russia administered by a specially created cadre of bureaucrats, many of them foreigners. With a patriarchal boyar household on the one hand (and a heroine springing from it), and with on the other no less than three foreigners, the negro himself, a Swedish prisoner-of-war, and a Frenchified young aristocrat appalled by the Tsar's bourgeois and Germanic entourage, the tapestry already has as many threads as Scott at his most ambitious would hardly try to weave together; and there is, over and above this, since the basic fable is the Romeo-and-Juliet one, a distracting and irrelevant question of the colour-bar. Altogether there was every reason why Pushkin abandoned the story, fascinating as it is so far as it goes. But when we read this fragment, and when we recall also that Pushkin was descended on his mother's side from in fact a negro favourite of Peter's, and on his father's side from precisely one of the gentle families whose hereditary functions had been usurped by these foreign favourites and paid administrators, we realize that the issue in *The Captain's Daughter* is not at all between Tsarist autocracy on the one side and peasant democracy on the other. On the contrary, the conflict is between a patriarchal society on the one hand, and on the other an antagonist present only in innuendo and epigraph and the ambiguous figure of the German-Russian general Andrey Kar-lovich, that is to say, the Tsarist bureaucracy. In short, Shklovsky is certainly so far right that there is more in this story than meets the eye; and though Pugatchov certainly stands for a way of life (heroic and barbarian like Scott's Vich Ian Vohr), so far as he is a peasant Pugatchov poses the question only whether the peasants fare better under the unjust patriarchal rule of the hereditary gentry, or under a remote autocracy operating through bureaucrats with no stake in the country and no organic ties with the peasants under them.

And so we come round once again to 'the solemn fraternity which a great nation composes – gathered together, in a stormy season, under the shade of ancestral feeling'. It appears when one has decoded the signals of the epigraphs to the chapters, that this is not just one of many feelings inspired by *The Captain's Daughter* and inspiring it, but the single strain of feeling which governs the whole. The same may be said of *Pan Tadeusz*, more certainly and more emphat-ically. For Mickiewicz's poem, celebrating the awakening of the Lithuanian nation to its nationhood and the chance of vindicating it, may be said to be presenting, in one massive and internally com-plicated image, just what Wordsworth is talking about – 'the power of injustice and inordinate calamity to transmute, to invigorate, and to govern – to sweep away the barriers of opinion – to reduce under submission passions purely evil – to exalt the nature of indifferent qualities, and to render them fit companions for the absolute virtues with which they are summoned to associate – to consecrate passions which, if not bad in themselves, are of such temper that, in the calm of ordinary life, they are rightly deemed so – to correct and embody these passions – and, without weakening them (nay, with tenfold addition to their strength), to make them worthy of taking their place as the advanced guard of hope, when a sublime movement of deliverance is to be originated; . . .' The same necessity which pro-duces Wordsworth's intricately exciting and accumulative syntax produces in Mickiewicz's poem the wealth of digression, illustra-tion, and incident; and the catalogues of minutiae like the listing of the varieties of mushrooms. What operates in both writers and deter-mines their procedures is the same conviction of how natural laws of communal feeling operate surely yet with unmasterable subtlety of ramification and cross-reference. It is for this reason that a novel – or at least a novel with this theme – has to be, in the word of Ortega y Gasset, 'sluggish', has to proceed at a snail's pace, by accumulating minutiae. Only in this way can justice be done to the weavings and interweavings and mutual transmutations by which a community becomes and remains more than the sum of the individuals who compose it. And it is for this reason that, however grateful we may be for Pushkin's terseness and elegance, yet what he does in *The Captain's Daughter* is somehow eccentric, is not what the novel is by its very nature. And it is for this reason that *Pan Tadeusz*, though a poem, is more of a novel or else a better novel than *The Captain's Daughter* is.

From *The Heyday of Sir Walter Scott*. London: Routledge & Kegan Paul, 1961; New York: Barnes & Noble, 1961.

7   *The Poems of Doctor Zhivago*

I   INTRODUCTION

At the end of Pasternak's *Doctor Zhivago*, translated by Max Hayward and Manya Harari, there appear, in the British edition, twenty-five pieces under the heading, 'Zhivago's Poems'. The reader does not know what to do with these pages; we are given no indication of how they are connected with the 464 pages of prose narrative which precede them, and as soon as we begin to read this enigmatic appendix we find it as wearisome as reading verse in prose translation usually is.

I have set out to discover what function Pasternak intended these pages to serve, how he intended us to read them, and how they are connected with what goes before them. I believe I have found that unless we read these poems in the right way we have failed to read *Doctor Zhivago* at all; that, contrary to appearances, *Doctor Zhivago* is not a novel with an appendix of poems, but one whole thing, intricately interlocking, in which prose supports poetry and vice versa; that the many discussions whether *Doctor Zhivago* is a good novel, or a true novel, are all beside the point so long as Zhivago's poems are considered an optional appendix, or bonus, to something which can stand without them.

The first requirement was to translate Zhivago's poems afresh; and the translations which follow are the versions I made. That is to say, they are working translations: the whole point in making them was to cleave very closely and faithfully to the original, to bring over all the sense of the Russian, and to introduce nothing that the Russian gives no warrant for. There could be no question in this case of imitation, adaptation, paraphrase, so-called 'free' translation. (To this there is one exception, the ninth poem in the sequence; see my note to that poem.) Nevertheless, these are *verse*-translations, as they have to be if faithfulness is what we are after. To quote D.G. Rossetti:

> The life-blood of rhythmical translation is this commandment: that a good poem shall not be turned into a bad one. The only motive of putting poetry into a fresh language must be to endow a fresh nation, if possible, with one more possession of beauty.

'If possible...' And of course it is not possible always, nor even very often; yet this must always be the objective that is aimed at.

I should like to be more specific. For it is commonly believed that a translation, if it is close, cannot be poetic; or if it is poetic, cannot be close. Yet why be surprised if it is poets who offer the closest translations? It is their business and also their passion to know what poetry is, wherein it consists. It is for instance the professional poet who knows that in the end rhyme and metre (though certainly not rhythm) are normally expendable; that neither the substance of poetry nor the *form* of poetry are to be found in these features – that on the contrary the essential form is the track of the poet's feeling, from first to last through his poem. There are exceptions; poems in which rhyme for instance plays an unusually vital role. The third of Zhivago's poems is such an exception, and I have given it exceptional treatment. But in general the verse-translator who is a professional poet will realize that in translating rhymed verse the rhyme is the first thing to go, and metre the second; whereas the amateur, wretched sceptic that he is, cannot be sure of having poetry at all unless he has these external features of it.

I have supplied notes to each poem; and these are designed to hang together in a continuous commentary on the form and significance of *Doctor Zhivago* as a whole, as this has emerged for me through translating the poems and re-reading the prose. Here I will briefly state in advance the conclusions I have reached.

The poems are faithful to a psychological reality, the psychological reality of poetic composition in the act of dredging up, transforming, and juxtaposing memories. One of the pleasures which they provide is of the kind that we get from J. Livingstone Lowes's book about Coleridge, *The Road to Xanadu*; we see the poet (Zhivago, not Pasternak) dealing magisterially with the images which we have seen him accumulate throughout his life. The sixteen chapters of prose narrative present us with the life; the seventeenth chapter, of poems (for this is the arrangement in the Russian edition), presents the art which came out of that life, its crown and its justification. If we try to justify Zhivago's life without taking his poems into account, we shall fail. For the justifications which we shall then find will not be those which Pasternak intended, or would accept. Many of the poems draw for images on widely separated and logically unconnected parts of Zhivago's life as we know it from the novel; and conversely many passages of the prose have no function, and no place in the economy of the whole, except that they can be seen to present Zhivago with images which later get into one of his poems.

From this point of view, the best hint on how to read the poems is early in the novel, in the first section of Chapter Three, which tells how Zhivago's mother-in-law contracted the illness which was to prove fatal. She slipped when assisting the handyman to install an antique wardrobe.

> Anna did not like the wardrobe. Its shape and size reminded her of a catafalque or a royal tomb and filled her with a superstitious dread. She nicknamed it the tomb of Askold; she meant the horse of Prince Oleg, which had caused its master's death. Owing to her unsystematic reading her association of ideas was odd.
> After this incident Anna developed a pulmonary weakness.

One shudders to think of the symbol-hunting critic (some have been at work on *Doctor Zhivago* already) who will take note of this, and will notice also that, twenty pages later, when Anna's coffin is being carried out of her room, the handyman 'got stuck in the bedroom where the wreaths had been piled up, because the bedroom door was blocked by that of the wardrobe on the landing, which had swung open' (the 16th section of Chapter Three). The same wardrobe! What allegories one would be meant to read into this, if *Doctor Zhivago* had been written by Hawthorne! But in Pasternak's novel I take it that, if there is anything to this incident beyond the pathos and the irony which chance introduces into all our lives, it represents as it were a poem offered to Zhivago which he never got round to writing. 'Owing to her unsystematic reading her association of ideas was odd' – so is Zhivago's, so is everyone's; and of absorbing interest to Pasternak is this oddity, and the logic which lies hidden in and behind it.

I do not intend, by thus stressing the psychological interest in *Doctor Zhivago*, to deny or minimize the metaphysical and religious interests which Pasternak seems to pursue. He truly does pursue them; and if the metaphysical references can be translated into psychological terms (Jesus the Redeemer being scaled down into Zhivago the Poet), so the psychological interests are metaphysical also, and the Poet truly is the Redeemer. For what Pasternak knows about the poet's mind and how it works creatively is not just part of what he knows about the human mind; it is also part of what he knows about purpose in the universe, and about the mind of God. Thus, when John Strachey, in his interesting and valuable essay, 'The Strangled Cry', says that Pasternak in *Doctor Zhivago* sets up three ultimate values, Love, Art and Christ, what needs to be said is that these three values are for Pasternak not distinct. These are three aspects of one reality, which can be approached through experience of God, through experience of woman, or through experience of art – the experience of creating art, not (I think) the experience of appreciating it.

The approach we follow in *Doctor Zhivago* is the experience of creating art. Far more than it is a love-story, *Doctor Zhivago* is the story of an artistic vocation. On top of the experience of appreciating art which *Doctor Zhivago* offers since it is itself a work of art, we get from it also the experience of creating art – vicarious experience certainly, but perhaps none the worse for that.

If I see the book in this way, I cannot easily find a parallel to it. It has been many times observed that if an author introduces into his book a character who is alleged to be brilliantly witty, he is under the necessity of constantly finding brilliantly witty things for that character to say; and similarly the trouble with a fictional character who is alleged to be a greatly endowed artist is that we are inevitably required to take his great gifts on trust – that which gives significance to his life is precisely the one thing about him which cannot be shown, which we can only be told about. This is the trouble with Thomas Mann's *Doctor Faustus*. After all the exertions which Mann takes to establish Adrian Leverkuhn as a great composer of music, in the end we have to take this on trust. Nothing could *prove* this contention short of Mann's providing us with the scores of Leverkuhn's alleged compositions; and for these to match what Mann claims for Leverkuhn, the scores would have to reveal in Mann as great a composer as Arnold Schoenberg – which is absurd. Only in the one art of literature can this difficulty be overcome; and Pasternak, so far as I am aware, is the one writer to have realized this and acted accordingly. It is essential to the meaning of *Doctor Zhivago* that Zhivago should be a great poet. Very well; instead of merely telling us that this is so, Pasternak *proves* it – in the only way possible, that is, by giving to Zhivago great poems. They are not poems by Pasternak which he merely donates to Zhivago, but truly Zhivago's poems in that they can be seen to derive from Yury Zhivago's experience, not from Boris Pasternak's.

II   THE POEMS TRANSLATED INTO ENGLISH VERSE

1

Hamlet

The buzz abates. I have issued upon the boards
And I hang on the jamb of a door
To flush from recession of echoes
What the times intend shall occur.

Down all of a thousand opera-glasses'
Axes focused, dark of the night impales me.
Abba, my father, let this cup
Pass from me, if it may be.

I love your stubborn shaping of a theme.
I have agreed to play this character.
But now a different drama is in train.
Leave me this once an unscripted actor.

But the scenes' sequence was thought out beforehand,
Not to be evaded is the end they move to.
I am alone, all sinks to the Pharisee.
Living a life is not a field we pass through.

2
March

The sun works up to a lather,
To a thresh in stupefied lowlands.
Like the chores of a strapping cow-girl,
Spring's busy-ness seethes through the hands.

Snow sinks, anaemia saps it
Along weak, blue, twig-like veins.
But life smokes up from the cowhouse;
Hale, it darts out from the tines of pitchforks.

All these nights, these days and nights!
Thud of the thaw at noon, the spatter
Of icicles dripping from roof-tops,
The sleepless culverts' chatter...

Open it all lies, stable and cowshed.
Pigeons peck oat-ears out of snow.
Off the all-blameable, all-engendering
Dunghill the air blows freshly.

3
In Holy Week

Still all around night's murk in the air.
Still in the world so soon astir,
Stars in the sky more than any man knew
And each of them, like day, shone true,
And had earth chosen what to do
She would have slept all Easter through
To the sound of the Psalter.

Still all around night's murk in the air.
Life so betimes is come
That, all eternity, the Square
Corner to cross-roads spread out there,
And thence to dawn and warmer air
Stretched a millennium.

The earth is all a barebones yet
And o' nights has never a tatter
To swing on a bell-rope in, and set
Chimes to the chorister.

And from ·Maundy Thursday
Through to Easter Sunday
Water bores the bank away
Drills in the eddy.

Forests uncover and divest themselves
And at Christ's Passion-tide
Congregated pinestems guide
Order of worship, steadfast.

But in the town the space is straiter
For a poor gathering
Of trees that at the church's grating
Stand stark and peering.

Aghast they gaze. And they have cause,
As may be understood:
No fence holds in the gardens' force,
Earth trembles now through all her course;
They sepulchre a God.
Through the Tsars' Gate they see the light

And the black shroud, and the candles' order,
The faces streaming-eyed –
And abruptly towards them the cross and banners
And the blessed grave-cloth ride,
And the two birches at the gateway
Must stir and stand aside.

Round the slow procession paces
Almost in the street,
And back to its courts out of public places
Brings Spring, Spring's gossip, and the traces
Of the Host still tasted in the air's spaces,
And a Spring smell, heady and sweet.

And March spills snow in a sudden scurry
On the church-porch huddle of the maimed
As if there were someone came
And brought and opened a reliquary
And gave away each last straw.

And singing lasts until the dawn
When, tears all spent, more calm
And softlier, from withindoors drawn,
Sounds, over lamplit barrens borne,
The gospel-chant or psalm.

But, mute at midnight, flesh and fur
Hear the Spring's prediction
Murmured, how the seasons stir
And Death may have a vanquisher
By might of Resurrection.

4

White Night

Before me a far-off time arises,
A house in the Petersburg quarter.
Daughter of modest gentry from the Steppes
Is what you are; Kursk-born, attending courses.

You are attractive, boys pursue you.
This white night, we two are
Looking out from your window sill
In a skyscraper, down at the view.

The street-lamps are like butterflies made of gas
Which the morning has touched to a first tremor.
This which I tell you quietly
Is in accord with distances in slumber.

We are caught up in the same confidences
Safeguarded with apprehension,
As in the widespread panorama
Petersburg is, behind Neva's boundless expanses.

There in the distance, in the tangled brakes
On this white spring night
Worshipful thunder of the nightingale
Is released by limits of woodland.

The lunatic trills unroll,
The voice of the small unnoticeable bird
Excites elation and turmoil
In the depths of spellbound thickets.

Towards that place the bare-footed vagrant, Night,
Worms his way, inching along by fences;
Behind him from the window sill runs out
A trail of talk, of overheard exchanges.

Within earshot of talk that is shared,
In the garden, in the fenced enclosures
The apple-bearing branches and the cherries
Change into blossom-white dresses.

And the spectral trees debouch,
A white throng in the highway,
As if to speed with a gesture
White night that has seen so much.

5

Foul Ways in Springtime

The fires of sunset burning out, by foul
Footing on quickset forest track,
To a homestead deep in the Urals
Toiled one on horseback.

Jar of his mount's loud teeth upon the bit,
And hard upon the shock-waves of the horse's
Shod hooves spattering, all the way pursuit
Echoed, of springs sluicing down watercourses.

Or when his hold on the reins slackened
And he slowed to a walking pace,
The floods swept by, and followed near at hand,
Grinding and deafening, the water-race.

Someone laughed, someone wept.
Stone crumbled, dashed on stone,
And down the cascades, whirling, swept
Stumps torn out of root-lock, and pitched down.

But on the burnt-out premises of sundown
And charred black branchy distances, prevail
Like the sullen bell of the tocsin
Fulminations of the nightingale.

Where the widowed willow dips her veil,
Inclined aslant the gully,
There, like the ancient Robber-Nightingale,
He fluted on his sevenfold oak-tree whistle.

What calamity or paramour
Was object of this love?
Whom was that small-shot meant for,
Sprayed from redoubtable barrels across thickets?

It seemed that, look! wood-goblin, he confronted,
Come from the bivouac of the wanted man,
The mounted or else unmounted levies
Of the local Partisan.

Earth and sky, forest and fallow–plot,
Caught that discontinuous strain,
Those portionings out by lot
Of trials, glee, fatuities, and pain.

6
Explanation

Life has come back with as little reason
As once it was strangely interrupted.
I am in the same old-fashioned thoroughfare
Now as then, in the selfsame summer season.

People the same, with the same troubles,
And the fire of sunset no cooler
Since that which death of an afternoon
Nailed up on the Manège's gables.

In the cheap cottons that they always wore
Women still go slopping by at night-time.
After a while, under the iron roofs
The attics crucify them as before.

Here is a tired one, taking the going hard,
Slowly comes out on a doorstep
And, climbing up from a basement,
Goes slanting across the yard.

Once again I get ready excuses
And again I couldn't care less.
And the neighbour goes round by the alley
And leaves us without intrusions.

Don't cry, don't primp into pleats and knit
Your swollen lips in puckers.
You will pick the dried scab open
Over spring's fever-fit.

Take the flat of your hand off my chest.
We are wires, the current through us
– Watch out for it! – has no reason
That again it throws us abreast.

Years will pass, you'll be married before you know it,
You'll forget these maladjustments.
It's a great step to take, to be woman;
To unhinge us is quite an exploit.

For me, in fealty I shall bow
Before the miracle of hands or throat,
Shoulder or arm or spine of woman
At every age as now.

And yet however night and my cravings may
Weld hoops around me, there's a stronger pull
Still in the world; the Passionate draft pulls
Out for the breakaway.

7
Summer in the City

Muted exchanges and
With a fervid haste
The hair is gathered up,
A whole shock swept from the nape.

From under the heavy comb
Looks out a woman helmed
The head falling
Backward among braids.

Along the street the night
Is close, promising storm
And a break-up comes, a shuffle,
Walkers dispersing homeward.

Abruptly thunder is heard
And its rejoinder, edgy,
And the wind swings
The window-curtain.

Ensues a hush.
As before, closeness.
As before, lightnings
Grope, grope in the heavens.

And when, with the breaking light
The morning, again torrid,
Dries puddled avenues
After nocturnal downpour,

There comes a look that is
Cross-grained from lack of sleep
About the centuries-old,
Fragrant, unfading limes.

8

Wind

This is my end, but you live on.
And the wind, complaining and lamenting,
Agitates forest and country lodge.
Not the pine trees one by one
But a consensus of all trees
And the boundless distances, on and on,
Like hulls that are stripped of canvas
In a haven satin for squadrons.
And this not out of audacity
Nor from a fury without occasion,
But in anguish to find you
Words for a cradle-song.

9

Barley-mow

Under the broom here, ivy-clad,
The squall sends us to cover.
We hunch our shoulders under the plaid,
My hands on you ivying over.

I've slipped up. What these thickets grow
All wreathed with isn't ivy-creepers.
Come now, it's the barley-mow.
Best spread that plaid beneath us!

10

Indian Summer

The leaf of the currant is coarse in weave.
The house shouts laughter, glasses ring.
Indoors they salt, and pepper, and cleave up
And cloves are dealt out for preserving.

Derisively a wood pelts down
Its steep declivities all these sounds,
To where the burnt-up hazel stands
Consumed in sunlight, all a bonfire brown.

Here is a way down to the sunk place,
Here for old sticks that parch and shrink
And for ragman Autumn it's a hard case,
Sweeping everything down this sink;

Hard, that the world's way is shorter
And simpler than sharp ones pretend,
That the grove sinks down as in water
And each thing waits for its end;

That when all you are looking at goes
To ash, and the white soot of Autumn
Hauls gossamer over windows,
The look of it all is mindless.

A path breaks through a garden fence
And is lost among birches. There, indoors,
Laughter sounds, and the buzz of household chores.
That buzz and laughing also come from the distance.

11

Wedding

Cutting over into the yard
The guests for the wedding-wake
Have moved in for the night at the bride's house,
Come with a concertina.

Behind the doors with felt on them
Of the man whose place it is,
From one in the morning till seven
There's not much noise of talking.

But as dawn comes up, in the depths of dream
When you're set to keep on sleeping,
The accordion cuts loose again
Lighting out from the wedding.

And he's spread it around, the accordionist
Making again with the squeeze-box
Spatter of clap-hands, bead-strings' glitter,
Whooping it up at a party.

And once more, once more, once again
The beat of the *chastushka*
Through to the sleepers together in bed
Has burst in out of the hubbub.

And there she goes, as white as snow
Riding it out, wolf-whistles, ting-a-ling,
Smooth into that peacock-step again,
Swung hips parading,

With a head to the beat rocked,
Right hand pulsing
In a peacock's stalk on the board-walk,
Peacock, a peacock dancing.

And the yard, the having fun,
The tread of the set-to-partners,
Are gone to hell out of it suddenly,
All washed up like water.

And it's come awake, the buzzing yard.
An echo of business deals
Has cut in on the talking
And the laughing spells.

Into the sky, unlimited, up
In an upswirl of dove-motes
Pigeons in a flock have spurted
Towering out of dove-cotes.

As if to be minded of these
In a wedding's wake were to stir
Well-wishings for many a year
Sent out to overtake them.

Life right enough is likewise only an instant
Only a loosening out
Of ourselves among all others
As it might be a thing we gave them,

Only a wedding, blue deeps of a window
That it irrupts through upward,
Only a song that is sung, a dream,
Only a dove-blue pigeon.

12
Autumn

I gave up my people to go their several ways.
All that were near me long ago went asunder.
Now a loneliness I am used to
Fills all my heart and all the natural order.

And here I am with you, in an out-station
In a forest uninhabited and untrodden.
As it says in the song, the bridle-track
Is all to seek, the choked ride half-forgotten.

Now we are by ourselves, in a bad way,
And the walls of hewn logs scrutinize us blankly.
To take in our stride was never in the contract.
What we have to do is ride for our fall frankly.

We shall sit down at one in the morning, and at three
I shall let my book, and you your sewing, drop.
When day comes we shall not know
What made the kissing stop.

Ever more grandly, ever less guardedly, come
Into your clamours, uncover your seed-pods, leafage.
Let yesterday's cup, with its taste of sourness, brim
Over again with asperities of today.

Predispositions, latchings-on, allurements!
Let these be loose in alarums of September...
Install yourself in the lisping Autumn! Either
Forget yourself, or else fade out, dismember!

You disembarrass yourself of clothes
As the spinney disembarrasses
Itself of leaves, when you fall
Into my arms in your wrap with the silk tassels.

You are the windfall of the false step taken
When to live is nausea worse than illness causes;
But beauty is intrepid in the making;
And this it is that, each to the other, draws us.

13

Fairy Story

In days of old
Through a fabled land
Rode he amain
Over hill and hollow.

He sped to the fray.
On the dusty plain
Rose up afar
A dark wood in the way.

A keen pang
At the heart griped him:
'Ware of the well-water,
Draw the girth tighter.

Nothing list the rider
But made his steed to bound
And flew he amain
To the woody mound.

Turned he at the barrow,
Came into the dry fosse,
Passed he through the glade
And the mount he has crossed.

And strayed by the hollow dell
Come by the dark way
Found he the beasts' trace
And water of the well.

And deaf to the summons sent
No heed to ill bode,
Down to the brink he rode,
Gave to his horse to drink.

———————————

By the stream a cave's mouth,
Before the cave a ford.
As it were brimstone burning
Flamed in the opening.

Smoke billowed dun-red
His gaze baffled:
With a cry far sped
Sounded the forest.

Thereat upon the cleft
The horseman, ware,
Stepped soft-foot straightly
To whence the voice calling.

Saw then the horseman,
Tightened his lance-hold,
Head of the dragon,
Scales, and the tail coiled.

Ardent from maw spilt
Light showed plain
Three boughtes a damsel round
Wound he her spine.

Body of the serpent
As a whip's lash folds her,
His swayed the neck there
On hers the shoulder.

By that land's usage
Was paid in fee
To the monster of the wood
A captive comely.

Folk of the land
Huts that were theirs
Ransomed by rent paid
Thus to the serpent.

Serpent it was that bound
Hands fast, enwound her,
Took into throes of
The scapegoat the offering.

Looked in supplication
To high heaven the horseman.
Couched for altercation
Clasped he the lance then.

———————————

Sealed close the eye's lids.
Heights. And the cloud's climb.
Rivers. River-fords. Waters.
The years, the spans of time...

Rider, the helm brast,
Brought down in combat,
True steed with hoof-spurn
Tramples the serpent.

Charger next dragon's corse
Heaped on the sandbar,
In a swound the rider,
The damsel stounded.

Sheen of the noon's arch
Azure, dulcet.
What's she? A tsar's child?
Slip of earth? Earl's blood?

Abounding gladness
Flows now in tripled tears,
Now to a dead trance
Lie they in durance.

Charged to new hardihood
Now, and now listless,
Life in the spent blood,
Unstrung the sinews.

Beat still the hearts of them.
Dame first, then man
Strives against cumber,
Fails into slumber.

Sealed close the eye's lid.
Heights. And the cloud's climb.
Rivers. River-fords. Waters.
The years, the spans of time...

14
August

As good as its word, not to deceive,
The sun thrust through in the early morning
As a slant-wise stripe of a saffron colour
Athwart the sofa from between the curtains.

It overlaid with a hot ochre
The vicinity of woods, the village homesteads,
My bed, the pillow moistened,
And the reach of wall behind the bookshelf.

I have remembered what the reason is
That my pillow is damp a little:
The dream I had was that you saw me off,
One by one threading the woodland.

You went in a bunch, singly and in couples.
What day this was, was borne
Suddenly home to someone; sixth of August
Old style, and Our Lord's Transfiguration.

As a rule, this day, light without heat of burning
Issues out of Mount Tabor,
And Autumn, clear as a signal given,
Holds all eyes riveted.

And you were going through the penniless, paltry
Stark, shivering alder-brush
To the red-as-ginger grove that marked the graveyard
Burning up like a morsel of gingerbread.

The quietness of its tree-tops
Had the portentous heavens for neighbour,
And with the tongues of roosters
Distances held protracted colloquy.

In the grove, like a ministry surveyor,
Stood Death amidst the graveyard,
His eyes on the face of my mortality
Sizing me up for a grave-pit.

Remarked by all, calmly arose
A corporeal voice. From near at hand
Rang out the voice of the seer I was,
Intact and uncorrupted:

'Farewell the azure of Transfiguration
And the gold of Saviour's Day the second.
In my fateful hour let the bitter brew
Be allayed by a last ministration of woman.'

'Farewell years that went uncalendared!
Woman I part from, an abyss,
A world of indignities you have dared!
I am the acres you have fought across.'

'Farewell to the swept wing, sleek and planing;
Intentness in flight as the will travels;
Image of the world, a presence in language;
And Authorship; and the working wonders.'

15

Winter Night

The snow, the snow all over the earth
From end to end swirling.
And the candle burning on the table,
The candle burning.

As in a summer swarm the midges
Fly to the flame,
Flew the flakes from without
To the windowframe.

The snowstorm moulded on the pane
Arrows and rings.
And the candle burning on the table,
The candle burning.

On the illumined ceiling
The shadows massed
Of crossed hands, crossed legs,
Fates that crossed.

With a thud on the floor a pair
Of shoes fell down.
The wax from the nightlight wept
On to a gown.

And everything lost in a murk of snow
Greying, whitening.
And the candle burning on the table,
The candle burning.

On the candle a gust from the corner.
Temptation's lick
Of flame grew lifted arms,
Cross-like, angelic.

Snow all the month of February.
And intermittently
The candle burning on the table,
The candle burning.

16
The Breach

At the door he starts to doubt
If the house is his. Her going
Was nothing short of a rout.
Everywhere, signs of ruin.

All through the rooms, chaos.
Particulars escape him,
What with tears in his eyes
And his head aching.

In his head since morning an unaccountable noise.
He remembers, or is he dreaming?
And why should thoughts of the sea
Through his head be streaming?

When through rime on windows
No sight to be seen of Creation,
The corneredness of yearning is
Doubly like wastes of ocean.

She was as dear to him
In her every feature
As the sea is near to a coastline
In each wave breaking ashore.

As the inundation of reed-banks
By chopped seas after a storm,
Ebbed over the floor of his soul
Her features and her form.

From the years hard-driven, unthinkable
Ruses for getting by,
A wave of fate from the sea-floor washed her
Up to him, high and dry.

Amid snags past reckoning,
Perilous straits to be passed,
The one wave bore her, bore her
Home, and secured her fast.

And now here she has flitted,
Perhaps much to her sorrow.
The breach devours them both.
Emptiness eats in the marrow.

And the man looks all about him.
At the moment of her exit
She cleared the chest of drawers
Topsy-turvey of all that was in it.

He prowls around, in the darkness
He slams back all the scattered
Odds and ends into drawers
Along with the sample cut-out,

And finds a needle stuck
Still in a piece of sewing,
And it brings her all back, and his tears
Are suddenly, covertly flowing.

17

Rendezvous

The road lies buried in snow,
The burdened gables bend.
I go out walking;
Behind the door you stand.

Alone, in an autumn outfit,
You struggle for self-command;
Hat and overshoes wanting;
Gulping snow from your hand.

The darkening distance muffles
The shapes of fence and tree.
Alone in the snow falling
At the corner you confront me.

Streams fill from your scarf the cuffs
Of the sleeves of your coat. The air
In flecks of dew, condensing,
Sparkles about your hair.

A lock of pale hair, lifted,
Lights face, and scarf at throat,
Brightens the moulded figure,
Lights up the shabby coat.

Snow is wet on the lashes;
Pain at your eyes looks out;
Your whole aspect in keeping,
All of a piece throughout.

As if, under my rib,
Antimony-tipped
There grooved an iron nib,
Scoring my heart to imprint you;

And there in those same features
Humility dwelt apart
For ever, and so no matter
The world's unpitying heart.

And so it appears twice over,
This whole wide night of snow;
And fixing frontiers between us
Is more than I can do.

Who are we, though, where sprung from,
When out of all those years
Hearsay remains, but of us two, nothing
Under the sun appears?

18
Christmas Star

The winter held.
Blew the wind over the steppe.
In the burrow under the hill-slope
Cold for the child.

Snugly the breath of the ox lapped him.
Beasts of the steading crave
Standing room in the cave.
Hazing the crib warm currents of air wrapped him.

Shaking their sheepskins free of the trash and hay,
The loose bed-straw,
The blear-eyed shepherds saw
Midnight stretch out from the rock-ledge where they lay.

Far in a field of snow a graveyard was,
And hurdles, epitaphs,
Wagons snowed to the shafts,
And over the burial-ground a welkin full of stars.

But right at hand, though never heard tell till then,
More faltering than the glow
Out of a watchman's window,
Glimmered the star that fared for Bethlehem.

It flared like a rick, like a thing no more
The sky's, or God's, a fired stack,
Incendiary's work,
Like a farm on fire, and blaze on a threshing-floor.

It stood up like a stack, a glare
Of hay and straw on fire
Burning on the entire
World's frame unnerved at the new star in the air.

The glow upon it throve still ruddier.
Something was meant thereby.
Three scanners of the sky
Sped, summoned by such fires as never were.

Behind them were carried on camel-back gifts.
And asses in harness, some smaller than others, lifted
Neat delicate hooves, stepping down from among the cliffs.

And in a strange glamour of the coming era
Were stablished afar all later transpirings,
All the ages would think of, orbed stillnesses, cherished aspirings;
All that would be of museums and art-collections;
All misdemeanours of fairies, all wizardly transactions;
All of the bright world's fir-trees, all the dreams of youngsters.

All the quiver of candle-light, all festoons,
All the noble artifice of coloured crepe...
...All meanlier, all nippingly, blew the wind over the steppe...
...All the apples, all the gold balloons.

One part of the pond obscured among the alders,
Part could be noted well athwart the trammels
Of rookeries and the tree-tops, by sheep-herders.
From where they stood they made out asses, camels
Clearly along the verge of the pond meander.
– Go we with the rest, and worship we the marvel –
They told each other, shrugging wraps on shoulders.

Trudging the rough snow thawed them out in the end.
Across the sheeted snow-field, mica-bright,
Led round a hut the prints of naked feet.
About these prints, as to flame of a candle-end,
Padded and shifted sheep-dogs in the starlight.

The frosty night took shapes of faery-lore.
Someone out of the snow driven and mounded
Walked all the time invisibly with them banded.
The dogs plunged on, something they peered about for
Dogging the shepherd-boy, and ill hap apprehended.

By this same road, through the self-same parish,
Went some few angels where the throng most tended.
Invisibly fared they the way there, fleshless,
But where they had passed were steps imprinted.

Come to the rock, they thronged, a press of people.
Brightness came up. The stems could be seen of cedars.
– Who are you out there? – asked Mary.
– Of shepherds and legates of heaven our breed is,
For the lifting of lauds to you both are we come here. –
– Together you may not. Tarry there in the entry. –

In the murk of before-dawn, the grey as of ashes,
Trampled the drovers, the sheep-breeders,
Talkers wrangled with riders,
At the hollowed-out drinking-trough
Braying of camels, the kicking legs of asses.

Brightness came up. Dawn the last stars swept
Like grits of ashes clear of the sky-vault.
Only the Magi out of that countless rout
Did Mary receive through the rock-cleft.

He slept, all a shining, in a crib made oaken,
As the moon beams in on a trenched-out hollow.
For him was the office of fleeces taken
By lips of the ass and the ox's nostril.

They stood in the dusk of a shippon, in the shade
Whispering, summoning only the barest word.
Of a sudden, slightly, one in the darkness stirred,
A Magus moved left of the crib by someone's hand,
And the someone gazed in: from the doorstep straight at the Maid
Like a guest that calls, the Christmas star looked in.

19

Daybreak

You meant my entire destiny.
Then came the war, the break-down.
For a long, long time to me
No sight vouchsafed, no sign shown.

Over the many years, still
Your voice brings its warning sound.
All night I have read your will;
As if I had fainted and came round.

It comes upon me to feel
For the people whose morning comes
Alive in them, renewed. I'd shake piecemeal
And to their knees the lot of them.

And I run downstairs as though
For the first time ever my way
Lay by these streets under snow
And the derelict causeway.

They shrug awake, and lights come up,
A house-fug, drinking tea. And in the space
They take to get to the tram-stop,
Town looks a different place.

Snowgust over the gates knits up
Close mesh of the falling flakes; and geared
To keep to time, the cup
Is left half-full, the dish is left half-cleared.

I feel for them, the whole concourse,
As if I had been in their skin;
Myself I thaw as the snow thaws,
My brow lours like the morning.

In me are folk un-named, and trees,
Children, home-keeping kin.
I am won over by these;
This only is where I win.

20

The Miracle

He fared from Bethany to Jerusalem,
Foreshadowings of affliction weighing on him.

Burrs of brushwood scorched on the steep bluffs' oven,
Over the hovel nearby no blown smoke stirred;
Hot breath of the air, and the reedbeds there unmoving,
And on the Dead Sea repose immovably anchored.

With sourness at heart that vied with the sour sea-water
He fared, while behind a few clouds raggedly followed,
Along the dust-choked road to some man's shelter,
Fared to the town, where some He instructed gathered.

And so far sank He, self-absorbed and brooding,
A wormwood smell came up as the field saddened.
All stilled. Alone He midway along was standing,
And the terrain stretched, sheeted in unfeeling.
All swam and merged: the balmy air and the barrens,
The lizards, the gushing springs, the waters running.

A fig-tree rising no great distance off,
Utterly bare of fruit, nothing but leaves and wood,
He said to it: 'Do you do me any good?
Is your stockstillness anything to be glad of?'

'I hunger and thirst, and you – you barrenly flower.
Encountering you is comfortless as granite.
What a trial you are, and how devoid of talent!
Stay as you are to the world's last hour.'

Throughout the tree ran the quake of condemnation,
As the levin-flash along a lightning-rod
Flashed on the fig-tree sudden incineration.

Had leaf and branch and root and stem been granted
One moment's freedom, then the laws of Nature
Had made all haste, and doom been intercepted.
But a miracle is a miracle, a miracle is God.
When we are all at odds it comes upon us
Instantaneous, and when least expected.

21

Earth

The Muscovite's house in town
Spring tumbles upside-down.
The moth from the clothes-press fumbles
The milliner's summer creations,
Mink is stowed into hold-alls.

On the mezzanine storey's timbers
The pots are aromatic
With stock and wallflower. Chambers
Breathe spaces, dust remembers
A pollen smell in the attic.

And the street is in collusion
With the myopic window,
The river breeds confusion
Of white night and the sundown.

April along the ranges
Of the corridors divulges
What life the outdoors is leading.
She knows a thousand instances
Of mankind's dooms and dangers;

She chills, by chance exchanges
With the snow-thaw, darkling fences
Dwelling on these proceedings.

The one half-afire, half-fearful tension
Out there at large, and lapped about, domestic.
All round the very air is not itself.

All one the willow's grille of twigs,
And the white buds' distention,
On the window sill, at the crossroads,
In the street, and at the work-bench.

Then why does the distance weep in mist,
And the humus reek so sourly?
It is here you find me in earnest;
I am called on to interest spaces lest
Past city boundaries the oppressed
Earth left to itself be lonely.

My friends and I foregathering
For this in early Spring
Make evenings of farewells
And feasts out of making wills,
That the hidden rill of suffering
Warm what exists and chills.

22
The Bad Days

When in the very last week
He entered Jerusalem,
Hosannahs pealed, and the people broke
Branches off, to attend him.

But the days closed in on him, tough.
Scornfully the brows knit.
No heart touched by love.
Epilogue here, an end to it.

Skies as heavy as lead
Settled between the blocks.
Proofs the Pharisees wanted;
They played him along, the foxes.

In the temple obscure forces
Had skid-row apprehend him;
And the same inflamed consensus
That rooted for him, damned him.

The crowd from that part of town
Gawped at the gateway,
Jostled, waiting for the show-down,
Surged forward, surged away.

And a whisper threaded the quarter,
Everywhere the tip-off ventured.
The run to Egypt came into his thought,
And his childhood, as if he dreamt it.

And he remembered the bad land,
The scarp there, and that mountain
Where having the world to command
Was what he was lured with by Satan.

And at Cana the wedding breakfast,
The miracle leaving the table guessing,
And the sea like dry land that he crossed
In the fog, step by step, to the vessel.

And the down-and-out bunch in a hut,
And the candle lit at the top
Of the cellar stairs, that went out
For fear, as the risen stood up...

23

Magdalene I

Hardly night falls when there my devil is,
What I owe to my past, a mortgage.
There they come, they suck the heart from my side,
The memories of foul things I did

When, slave to the idiosyncrasies
Of the male, crazy, in a sort of rage,
I had the street for orphanage.

There are still a few minutes to go,
Then the quiet comes, quiet of the tomb.
But first, before these come,
My life gone to the limit
Like an alabaster casket
I am breaking up before you.

Oh now where should I be,
Schoolmaster to me and Redeemer,
If at the table Eternity
Weren't the new one waiting to be
Netted in the game by me,
Night after night my customer?

Straighten this out – what does sin amount to,
Death, Hell, burning sulphur, when
Here I am, for all the world to see
Knit in with you, like a graft to the tree it's spliced in,
By my own miseries past the telling over?

Jesus, your feet locked fast
In my knees, I am learning to clasp
The quadrilateral shaft
Of a cross perhaps. I am raped
Of feeling as into my body
I hold you strained, and primed for the grave already.

24

Magdalene II

Folk set themselves to rights for a party.
Keeping clear of this lot,
I wash down with balm from a bucket
Your feet without spot.

I can't even find the sandals.
Crying, I can't see.
My hair's come down, hanks of it
Hanging over my eyes caul me.

I've grabbed your legs into my skirt,
I've sluiced them with tears, and there
I've the beads from my neck for a cord around them, Jesus.
I've smothered them in a burnous of hair.

I see what happens now, each item of it
As if you'd had the whole thing grind to a stop.
Just now I'm so good at predictions
I can see through things, I'm a sybil.

Tomorrow the screen comes down in the temple,
We shall be bunched together at one side
And the earth wobbles under our feet.
I reckon it's sorry for me.

The escort will form up again in column.
They'll make a start to the movement away of horses.
Like a waterspout in a cyclone, over our heads
The sky will be torn open, round that cross.

I'll hurl to the ground at the foot of the crucifixion.
I'll be out of my mind, I'll gnaw my lips.
You'd clasp too many, hands that on the cross's
Arms stretch out to the tips.

Who is it for in the world, so much bounty,
So much hurt, such a capacity?
Is there so much of being and life in the world?
So much of colony, of river-run and spinney?

But they'll wear by, three times sun-up to sundown,
And ram such vacancy that through
All that terrific intermission
It's Resurrection I'll be thriving to.

25

Gethsemane

With an indifferent flicker of distant stars
Was the turning in the road illumined.
The road went round about the Mount of Olives,
Beneath it flowed the Kedron.

The plot of grass sheared off halfway across.
The Milky Way went on from there.
The grey and silver of the olive trees
Drove themselves into distance, treading air.

In the end there was someone's garden or allotment.
Parting from the disciples at the wall
He said, 'My soul is sorrowful unto death':
'Tarry ye here, and watch with me' he said.

He abdicated there without contention,
As if from things that he had borrowed once,
From his Omnipotence and wonder-working,
And now he was a mortal, and like us.

The night's remoteness seemed a region now
Of the annihilated and the null.
Space through all the frame of things lay empty.
The garden alone was place for living in.

And gazing down those murky intervals,
Alleyways that went nowhere out of nowhere,
For the cup of this death to pass from him
In a sweat of blood he pleaded with the Father.

Easing by prayer these mortal slackenings,
He went out through the paling. On the ground
Lay the disciples, overborne and drowsing
On the road's verges, sprawling among tussocks.

He roused them then: 'You has the Lord appointed
To live my days, yet like the clay you crumble.
The hour of the Son of Man is come.
To the hands of sinners he betrays himself.'

No sooner said than bursting in from nowhere
Appears a rout of serfs and tinker rabble
With fire and sword and in the forefront Judas
With all the treacherous kissing in his lips.

Peter at the sword's point held them off.
He smote an ear from off the head of one
Only to hear: 'Resolve no feud with steel.
Man, put up your sword into its place.'

Could not a myriad of wingèd legions
Dispatched here by the Father reinforce me?
Then, with no hair of mine so much as touched,
Should all my foes with never a trace be scattered.'

'The book of life turns over to the page
Which is a dearer relique than them all.
Now must that which was written come to pass,
So be it, and fulfilment. And amen.'

'See how the times turn allegorical,
How they catch fire in very course of turning.
In the name of the terror of their potency
I seek the tomb in voluntary pains.'

'I seek the tomb and on the third day rise,
And as the rafts come floating down the river,
To me for judgment like a string of barges
The centuries shall drift up from the dark.'

III   THE COMMENTARY

'Hamlet'

The best commentary on this poem is by Nils Åke Nilsson, his essay 'Life as Ecstasy and Sacrifice', in *Scando-Slavica* (Copenhagen) for 1959. In particular Nilsson shows how for the understanding of this poem, alone in the whole sequence, it is essential to go for clues elsewhere than just to the sixteen chapters of prose narrative which in *Doctor Zhivago* precede the seventeenth chapter given to the poems. The other document by Pasternak which has to be called upon is an essay he published just after the war, on his translations from Shakespeare. Here Pasternak defines his own understanding of Shakespeare's *Hamlet*:

> From the moment that the ghost appears Hamlet denies himself in order to do the will of him who sent him. Hamlet is not a drama of a weak-willed character but of duty and self-abnegation. When it is discovered that appearances and reality are irreconcilable, that there is a gulf between them, it is of no moment that the reminder of the falseness of the world comes in a supernatural form, and that the Ghost calls for revenge. It is far more important that chance has so willed it that Hamlet is chosen as the judge of his own time and the servant of a more distant time. Hamlet is a play of the high destiny, the drama of a vocation.[1]

In view of the scriptural allusion in the seventh and eighth lines, which bind this first poem of Zhivago's sequence with the last, 'Gethsemane', even more striking are some of Pasternak's comments on Hamlet's soliloquy, 'To be or not to be...':

> These are the most heartfelt and frenzied lines ever written on the anguish of the unknown at the gates of death, in strength of feeling they rise to the bitterness of Gethsemane.

The prose narrative does, however, offer to throw light on this poem. In the 11th section of Chapter Fifteen we are given what purport to be notes by Zhivago, found among his papers:

> ...cities are the only source of inspiration for a truly modern, contemporary art.

> The seemingly incongruous and arbitrary jumble of things and ideas in the work of the symbolists (Blok, Verhaeren, Whitman) is not a stylistic fancy. This new juxtaposition of impressions is taken directly from life.

> Just as they hurry their succession of images through the lines of their poems, so the street in a busy town hurries past us with its crowds and its broughams and carriages at the end of the last century, or its trams, buses and electric trains at the beginning of ours.

> Where, in such a life, is pastoral simplicity in art to come from? Where it is attempted, its pseudo-artlessness is a literary fraud, not inspired by the countryside but taken from academic bookshelves. The living language of our times is urban...

> ...The incessant rumbling by day and night in the street outside our walls is as much connected with our thoughts as the opening

---

[1]   *Soviet Literature* 1946: 9, p.51. Quoted by Nilsson, loc. cit.

bars of an overture with the curtain, as yet dark and secret, but already beginning to crimson in the glow of the footlights. The incessant, uninterrupted rustle and movement of the town outside our doors and windows is a huge, immeasurable overture to life for each of us. It is in these terms that I should like to write about the town.

And this section of the notes ends with a significant comment by the supposed narrator: 'There are no such poems in what has been preserved of Zhivago's work. Perhaps "Hamlet" belonged to such a series.'

It must be said that without this explicit indication no one would have associated this section of the prose with the poem. Hence the contrivance strikes me as cumbrous, and not altogether fair. For the single image of the binoculars is not enough to make 'Hamlet' a poem of urban experience such as the prose envisages. The point of the prose passage seems to be, by the use of the same theatrical metaphor as in the poem, to establish that the 'echoes' of line 3 are those of the audience's movements and chatter dying down as the curtain rises. This puts the speaker of the poem, the actor, in the same physical relation to his fellow-citizens as the poet behind the walls of his city apartment.

Without this the speaker of the poem, who is established as an actor playing Hamlet, as Hamlet himself, and as Christ, would not have been established as himself a poet. As the actor is to Shakespeare, so Hamlet was to his father's ghost, so Christ was to his Father, so we are to that same Father or to destiny. Thus the voice, whose remote echo we have to hunt from to know our time or our times, is in the first place Shakespeare, in the second place King Hamlet's ghost, in the third place God the Father, in the fourth place (if you are a Marxist, as in some sense Pasternak was) it is 'the logic of history'. But in the fifth place – so the crucial prose-passage informs us – it is the voice of his anonymous fellows coming through to the poet, who will express their times for them.

The last line is proverbial, and will carry a lot of weight. Nilsson for instance says admirably:

> Both Hamlet and Christ were set tasks by their fathers. What, then, is the task of the poet? Has he come to save mankind or to set the time in joint again? The poem says nothing about this. The poet is certainly surrounded by falsehood just as Hamlet was, but nothing is said to intimate that his task and duty is to fight it. What the poem has to say about the poet's task one has to look for in the last line with its tone of contemplation and gravity: 'Living life is no easy matter.' Life is the poet's task.

And for Pasternak, who saw Shakespeare's *Hamlet* as 'the drama of a vocation', life is not a field of experience to be crossed, but the path of a destiny to be found and followed. His *Doctor Zhivago* is the story of such a finding and following.

'March'

In Chapter Four (the 2nd section) Lara is installed in the studio of an absent artist:

> ... near Smolensky Market. The flat was at the top of an elderly-looking two-storey house. There were draymen living in the other part of it and a warehouse on the ground floor. The cobbled yard was always littered with spilt oats and hay. Pigeons strutted about cooing and fluttered up noisily to the level of Lara's window; sometimes a drove of rats swarmed down the stone gutter.

This town-scape is clearly the source of the rural imagery in the last stanza of 'March'. This is also the scene for Lara's and Pasha's wedding, and for 'Wedding', the poem which treats of this, where the pigeons reappear. I cannot see any other place in the prose narrative from which are derived, specifically, the images in this poem. But a passage of the prose which should surely be remembered in relation to 'March' is one of those quoted in the notes to 'Hamlet' – that excerpt given in the 11th section of Chapter Fifteen from notes supposedly found among Zhivago's papers, in which the latter derides 'pastoral simplicity in art', condemns its 'pseudo-artlessness' as 'a literary fraud', and declares that 'the living language of our time is urban'. This should suffice to instruct the reader of 'March' (as of that later nature-poem, 'The Earth', which significantly takes up the image of dung) to see more than the description, 'nature-poem', suggests. Certainly 'March' is no charming water-colour of natural scenes; and 'Hamlet', which precedes it, should have prepared us to see, for instance, behind the image of 'dung', the tragic and Christian paradox of the man who loses his life that he may save it.

'In Holy Week'

F.D. Reeve (*Kenyon Review*, Winter 1960) observes that the third line 're-phrases and re-locates the meaning of a famous line by Lomonosov'.

I have taken pains to be faithful to rhyme, both in its placing and its quality, and to the fluctuating metrical shape of the stanzas, so as to bring over the very intricate and original structure in which a liquid and richly chiming melody, repeatedly disrupted by deliberate dissonance, is never wholly lost.

The source of this poem is in the first five sections of Chapter Ten, 'The Highway', which take us to the Siberian town of Krestovozdvizhensk, grouped round its monastery in territory held by Admiral Kolchak and the Whites. We are told (Section 2): 'It was Holy Week, the end of Lent; winter was almost over.' That is to say, it was the week before Easter Sunday. Most of the images that are to get into the poem are present here in the prose. For instance, lines 14 to 17, and 18 to 21, plainly derive from this paragraph:

> At the seventh hour by the Church's reckoning and at one in the morning by the clock, a dark low sweet humming drifted from the deepest of the monastery bells, which hardly stirred. It mixed with the dark drizzle in the air. It drifted from the bell, sinking and dissolving in the air, as a clump of earth, torn from the river bank, sinks and dissolves in the water of the spring floods.

The order of the images is the same, though the prose makes a connection between the bell-ringing and the water undermining, whereas in the verse, very interestingly, the two images are simply juxtaposed. Again, lines 38 to 43 are clearer if one has noted from the 2nd section some of the topography of the town. The religious procession making the circuit of the precincts is 'almost in the street' (literally, 'along the edge of the sidewalk'), because the main road 'skirted the monastery grounds..., for the green-painted icon door of the monastery gave on to the main square'.

But here is a difficulty. For we are given no reason to think that Zhivago was ever in Krestovozdvizhensk, in Holy Week or at any other time; and, since he has at this point been captured by the Reds, whereas this town is held by the Whites, there is every reason to suppose that he was not. The difficulty is the greater when we find some parts of the poem deriving from the scenes as experienced by a person Zhivago never met, Galuzina, the grocer's wife, who in the 3rd section leaves the service when it has barely begun, and wanders through the streets in the early hours. Lines 10 to 13 for instance derive from this passage about Galuzina:

> The stormy sadness of her thoughts oppressed her. Had she tried to think them all out aloud, one by one, she would not have had sufficient words or time enough till dawn. But out here, in the street, these comfortless reflections flew at her in clusters, and she could deal with all of them together, in the short while it took her to walk a few times from the monastery gate to the corner of the square and back.

And the two quatrains (ll. 22 to 25, and 26 to 29), with their strongly marked contrast between the forest trees and the town trees, may owe something to Galuzina's reflections, in the 4th section, on country as against town.

How can Zhivago know a time and a place of which he has no experience, and know them moreover through the mind of a woman he never met? The answer is given in one way by the 2nd section of Chapter Eleven, where Zhivago, in another Siberian town, happens across Tyagunova, a woman he had known in the train from Moscow three years before, who had escaped from the train with the boy-conscript Vassya Brykin. It turns out that Tyagunova is Galuzina's sister, and she tells Zhivago about Krestovozdvizhensk and about her sister's troubles there. We are surely meant to think that this sketchy information, together with the evocative and ecclesiastical name (Krestovozdvizhensk means 'town of the Exaltation of the Cross'), is enough to give Zhivago his poem.

And after all, how could we think otherwise? We do not suppose that Boris Pasternak, in order to enter into the feelings of a commonplace woman in a Siberian town in Holy Week, during the Civil War, had to have been there at just that time, or had to have known just such a woman. And Yury Zhivago is to be supposed at least as good a poet as Boris Pasternak, with imagination and human sympathies just as acute.

What is interesting is that Pasternak should pose the problem and make us work out the solution. (I cannot see that the 2nd section of Chapter Eleven has any other function than just to supply it.) Evidently it was important to him to establish in this way how much a poet like Zhivago can make out of only a couple of bare hints. And it was (we may suppose) even more important to establish that Zhivago, who has already in the poem 'Hamlet' made such sophisticated not to say blasphemous use of Christian references, and who is to treat them with even more sophistication in later poems of the sequence, is able at this point to sympathize with the traditional barely formulated Christianity of Old Russia. That Christianity, as Zhivago imagines it in someone like Galuzina, and indeed as he contrives to feel it himself, is full of feeling for fertility ritual. Nevertheless what the poem presents is an urbanized and vulgarized version of that ancient Christian-pagan compound; and this prevents the poem from dissolving into a nostalgia for the archaic and the rooted.

'White Night'

I am in danger of reading too much into this poem, but it seems a case where it is better to read too much than too little.

Some translators have rendered 'far-off time' in the first line by 'a distant past', and then have gone so far as to change every present tense into past, to support this reading. But it is an unsatisfactory reading in any case; for the daughter of a landowner from the steppes of Kursk does not figure in Zhivago's past, at least as we know it from the prose narrative.

A time may be distant in the future no less than in the past. And this may seem much to the point in view of some excellent remarks by F.D. Reeve in *The Kenyon Review* for Winter 1960. For Reeve acutely sends us, for a gloss on this poem, not to any happening that is recorded from Zhivago's life-time, but to an occasion twenty years after Zhivago is dead. This is recorded at the end of the Epilogue, in the very last paragraphs of the whole narrative:

> On a quiet summer evening in Moscow, . . . Gordon and Dudorov were again together, sitting by a window high above the immense city spreading away into the dusk. They were turning the pages of a book of Yury's writings which Yevgraf had compiled, a book they had read more than once and almost knew by heart. In the intervals of reading, they exchanged reflections and followed their own thoughts. It grew dark so that they could no longer make out the print and had to put on the light.
>
> Moscow below them and reaching into the distance – Moscow, the author's native town and the half of all that had befallen him – now appeared to them, not as the place where all these things had happened, but as the heroine of a long tale of which that evening, book in hand, they were reaching the end.
>
> Although the enlightenment and liberation which had been expected to come after the war had not come with victory, a presage of freedom was in the air throughout these post-war years, and it was their only historical meaning.
>
> To the two ageing friends sitting by the window it seemed that this freedom of the spirit was there, that on that very evening the future had become almost tangible in the streets below, and that they had themselves entered that future and would, from now on, be part of it. They felt a peaceful joy for this holy city and for the whole land and for the survivors among those who had played a part in this story and for their children, and the silent music of happiness filled them and enveloped them and spread far and wide. And it seemed that the book in their hands knew what they were feeling and gave them its support and confirmation.

At first sight this brings us no nearer than Hayward's and Harari's reading, to identifying the daughter of the gentry from Kursk. On the other hand some other puzzling features of the poem make more sense if it is regarded as Zhivago's prevision of some such occasion as this, than if it is his recollection of some unrecorded incident from his past. In the fourth quatrain the line *Orobeloyu vernost'yu tainye*, which I translate as 'Confidences safeguarded with apprehension', seems to be a direct reference to the ever-present fear of informers under the Stalinist regime; that is to say, to the police-state which was re-imposed or continued unalleviated after 1945, thus disappointing the hopes of Gordon and Dudorov that victory would lead to 'enlightenment and liberation'. Only a little less certainly, in the 7th stanza the sinister colouring of the image of Night as a barefoot wanderer, with its reference to 'conversation overheard', seems to re-create the same police-state atmosphere, playing upon the same apprehensions.

The odd thing of course is that the prose insists how the conversation between Gordon and Dudorov takes place in Moscow, whereas the poem locates its conversation no less emphatically in Petersburg. But the very paragraph which insists on Moscow also identifies the young lady from Kursk. 'Moscow... now appeared to them, not as the place where all these things had happened, but as the heroine of a long tale of which that evening, book in hand, they were reaching the end.' By this insistence, right at the end of the story, on how completely Zhivago is a Muscovite, and how entirely his story is a Muscovite story, Pasternak goes out of his way to make us notice how the second city of Russia, Petersburg or Leningrad, plays no part at all and is the locale of not a single incident in the whole book. There could hardly be a clearer directive to the reader; when he turns a few pages and comes to a poem which insists on how it is a poem of Petersburg, what is he to think? Surely he is meant to realize that this is a poem not to be read literally. It is to be read allegorically or symbolically – in a way which permits the heroine of the poem to be, not any human young woman, but for instance Moscow or Muscovite Russia personified. The Muscovite moves in imagination away from Moscow (to Petersburg), so as to see Moscow, and his own allegiance to her, more truly because in perspective.

Before dismissing this interpretation as far-fetched, one must take into account the accumulated resonance, for the Russian literary imagination, of these two names, 'Moscow' and 'Petersburg'. The very title of the poem is resonant in this way, and prepares the reader to listen for the resonance in what follows it. 'White Night' – merely the phrase itself, in isolation, sets up echoes of Pushkin, of Gogol, of Dostoevsky, of Blok; and of other writers who have treated this meteorological phenomenon peculiar to the Neva estuary, so as to re-create – not just as a locality but as one powerful element in the Russian imagination and Russian destiny – Petersburg, the fabricated city of Peter the Great, created by forced labour and an imperious act of will. As every schoolboy learns, Peter, the great westernizer, created this city to be Russia's window on the west; created it by fiat, all at once, on the model of such western cities as Venice and Stockholm. To Zhivago the Muscovite, Petersburg is indeed a window; but he looks out of that window *eastwards*, to Moscow and the steppes beyond. Moscow is not Kursk, and it is a long way from the steppes; it is only when they are looked at from Petersburg that Moscow and Kursk and the steppes seem to hang together, standing for all that in Russia which is not western. Zhivago is writing very deliberately in the tradition of Pushkin, Dostoevsky and Blok, when he sets up organically dishevelled Moscow against inorganically symmetrical Petersburg; Christian Moscow against Petersburg of the rationalist Enlightenment; village Moscow against civic Petersburg; homely and earthy Moscow against the unnatural dream-like beauty of the Petersburg waterfront. 'Skyscraper' in the second quatrain carries in Russian, as in English, all the converging significance of the modern, the inorganically symmetrical, and the humanly presumptuous.[1] The girl from Kursk is Moscow and the Muscovite temper; addressed in Petersburg and from Petersburg where she is an alien, she becomes Russia, or the soul of Russia, or that in Russia which is brought to the West, not borrowed from it.[2]

If the girl is not literally a girl but indigenous Russia personified, and if Petersburg in the poem is not literally a locality but rather a state of mind or (precisely) a viewpoint, are the nightingales literally nightingales, or the trees literally trees? Surely they are not. If the low-voiced conversation is taking place high up in a skyscraper, its echoes will not reach to any garden literally at the foot of the building, nor among any trees that literally stand there. And in any case no trees burst into blossom in an instant, as they do in the poem, nor do trees uproot themselves and come crowding out into roads. These episodes at the end of the poem we must in any case read as hyperbole; they cease to be fanciful or whimsical, they become imaginative, only when we have taken the allegorical meaning of springtime and daybreak. For Gordon and Dudorov conversed at nightfall – 'It grew dark so that they could no longer make out the print'; and in summer – 'on a quiet summer evening in Moscow'.

[1] Dr Monica Partridge points out to me the perhaps significant oddity of the post-Revolutionary word for 'skyscraper' in conjunction with the pre-Revolutionary name, Petersburg.

[2] On the 'stylization' of Petersburg in this tradition of Russian writing, see Waclaw Lednicki, *Russia, Poland and the West* (1954), *passim*.

Why then do the talkers in the poem converse at daybreak, and in spring? Surely it is to endorse what the prose affirms – that 'a presage of freedom was in the air throughout those post-war years, and it was their only historical meaning'. The day which breaks is the day of 'enlightenment', the spring is the springtime of 'liberation'.

It is illuminating at this point to compare Blok's treatment of the Petersburg theme in his unfinished poem, 'Retribution'. Because of what we know about Pasternak's peculiarly close feeling for Blok (see the notes to 'Christmas Star'), it is not surprising if, out of all the great Russian writers who had treated of Petersburg before Pasternak, it is Blok's treatment which is nearest to Zhivago's. And at the end of the second chapter of 'Retribution' (a novel in verse), Blok askes the reader if, 'going out on a white night', he has not heard, or dreamed that he heard, a sound from the sea; and if he has not seen, in dream or vision, a phantom fleet blockading the mouth of the Neva, with the figure of Peter the Great himself standing on a frigate's deck. But then, changing from those who thus dream to others who are awake, Blok speaks of those who watch through the night, who can see another fleet and another dawn, the Tsarist fleet returning humiliated, mutinous, and vengeful from defeat by the Japanese, and the bloody dawn of Revolution reddening already over Port Arthur and Tsushima, the scenes of those defeats. Zhivago's poem is about those who watch through another night, and addressed to others who thus watch; it assures them, as Blok's poem does, that the dawn is indeed coming – but the dawn in Zhivago's poem will not be bloody. I find it quite conceivable that Pasternak intended the reader to pick up these allusions to the poem by Blok.

It is not that we need imagine Zhivago's poem as set on some night still further in the future than that on which Gordon and Dudorov sit and talk. For on that selfsame evening the ageing friends of the dead Zhivago were carried into the future. It seemed to them 'that on that very evening the future had become almost tangible in the streets below, and that they had themselves entered that future and would, from now on, be part of it'. What brings this about in the poem is the singing of nightingales; what brings it about in the prose is the reading of Zhivago's book. In the poem it is the nightingales which give voice to the Russian hinterland; in the Epilogue that voice is the voice of a dead poet. For 'nightingale' we may read 'inspired poet' throughout – 'inspired' because the nightingales' singing is called 'crazy' (as it might be, 'possessed'), but also because what Gordon and Dudorov read is 'a book of Yury's writings *which Yevgraf had compiled*'; and the figure of Yevgraf, as we know from considering other poems, stands for poetic inspiration conceived of as full sympathy with living tradition.

Thus 'White Night' is of all Zhivago's poems the one which answers most exactly to Pasternak's saying: 'all art describes its own birth...' The trees which crowd into the road to wave good-bye do so, not as some loosely-anchored whimsical hyperbole about 'Nature' or 'Young Love', but according to the strict logic of symbolist poetry. These trees exist in the poem and nowhere else; it is the poem which determines their coming and their going, their planting, blossoming and fruiting. Since they are trees-in-a-poem, they need not and cannot observe the natural laws which govern trees-outside-of-poems. They wave good-bye because their end has come; and their end has come because an end has come to the poem which was the only world they existed in. What is astonishing, about this poem as about others in Zhivago's sequence, is that this extreme and militant aestheticism behind the poem does not in the least prevent it from dealing with issues as concrete and momentous as the Stalinist regime, and with others as sweeping and (in the Russian perspective) as 'classic' as the dialogue between Petersburg and Moscow.

I have used the word 'allegorical'. But with this poem, as with others of the sequence, an allegorical reading breaks down just as a literal reading does, though not quite so soon. Gordon talks with Dudorov; but the dead poet talks with them both, out of the pages of his book which lies between them; and inside the book the poet talks with his Muse in the shape of a young lady from Kursk. The one-to-one equivalences of allegory break down at the point where we ask which of these several dialogues is the dialogue in the poem. The poem is all of these dialogues at once, no one of them exclusively; for the poem *is* what it is 'about'. We have moved from the world of allegory to the world of symbolism, where the dialogue inside the book is indistinguishable from the dialogue of poet with reader. For the reader too is 'inside the book', in the sense that the book which Gordon and Dudorov read surely includes this poem, 'White Night' – a poem which is about Gordon's and Dudorov's reading of it. Thus when Zhivago in the third quatrain speaks of 'This which I tell you quietly', he is speaking to the young lady from Kursk who is his Muse, he is speaking also to Muscovite Russia behind her, he is speaking also to Gordon and Dudorov who read him, and he is speaking also to those other readers, ourselves. What is more, he speaks of himself as speaking ('All art describes its own birth'); not just the narration he speaks about, but the narration he speaks – that is, the whole poem – is addressed to us, to all of us at once. We are all of us inside this poem, so comprehensive as it is.

It is only by proving itself so comprehensive as this, by gradually engulfing into itself every inch of available reality even to the several identities of its readers, that the poem can justify the claims which it makes for itself. F.D. Reeve says finely, of *Doctor Zhivago* as a whole, 'Zhivago, who sets out to reform the world and to minister to it, gradually gives himself over to transforming it'. And in this poem the transformation is so complete that it ought to prove to Gordon and Dudorov, and to us, how right Zhivago was to make this choice; since the only sure pledge of enlightenment and liberty to come is the human capacity for transforming experience into poetry.

'Foul Ways in Springtime'

'Spring Floods', a title which some translators have given to this poem, is inaccurate but not altogether misleading if it recalls the springtime floods which Zhivago saw on his train-journey from Moscow. Certainly among the images which nourished the poem must be, for instance, these, which had come from the time of that journey (the 19th section of Chapter Seven):

> There was plenty of room for the water to play. It flung itself down the rocks, filled every pool to overflowing and spread. It roared and smoked and steamed in the forest. It streaked through the woods, sinking into the snow which hindered its movement; hissing on level ground or hurtling down and scattering into dusty spray. The earth was saturated. Ancient pine-trees, perched on dizzy heights, drank moisture almost from the clouds and it foamed and dried a rusty white at their roots like beer-foam on a moustache.

But that last brilliant and jovial image is quite out of key with the poem, where the tone is ominous throughout. And the ominousness is foreshadowed in a quite different passage, which supplies the images of riding and of the nightingale, to be compounded with the images of violently loosened waters. This is the account, in the 15th section of Chapter Nine, of how Zhivago, having attempted to break with Lara, rides out from Yuryatin to his family at Varykino ('a homestead deep in the Urals'):

> As the sun went down, the forest was filled with cold and darkness. It smelled of damp leaves. Swarms of gnats hung in the air as still as floats, humming sadly on a constant, high-pitched note. They settled on his face and neck and he kept swatting them, his noisy slaps keeping time with the sounds of riding – the creaking of the saddle, the heavy thud of hooves on the squelching mud and the dry salvoes bursting from the horse's guts. In the distance, where the sun was refusing to go down, a nightingale began to sing.

'Wake up! Wake up!' it called entreatingly; it sounded almost like the summons on the eve of Easter Sunday: 'Awake, O my soul, why dost thou slumber'.

Whether Zhivago obeys this solemn injunction, or disobeys it, is left carefully unclear; for what it prompts him to is regret for having broken with Lara, a conviction that this was premature, and a determination to go back on it. In other words the image of Lara pursues him as, in the poem, he feels that the waters do; and in fact later poems in the sequence, which repeatedly associate Lara with images of water, will abundantly confirm Edmund Wilson's guess that Lara's name ('Larissa' – the sea) has allegorical significance.

Just as the poem concludes with a reference to the partisans, so this episode in Chapter Nine closes when Zhivago, still riding home, is confronted by three Red partisans on horseback who carry him off to serve with their forces in the forest.

But these are only some of the associations which accumulate through the novel to enrich the meaning of this poem. Earlier in Chapter Nine (the 8th section) Zhivago has committed to his diary some observations on the nightingale's song:

> Once again I wondered at the difference between their song and that of all other birds, at the wide gulf left unbridged by nature between the others and the wealth and singularity of theirs. Such variety and power and resonance! Turgenev talks about it somewhere – that whistling, as if the demon of the woods were playing his flute. There were two phrases that stood out particularly. One was a luxurious, greedily repetitive 'tiokh-tiokh-tiokh'. At the sound of it, the thicket, all covered with dew, shivered as though with pleasure. The other was grave, imploring, an appeal or a warning: 'Wake up! Wake up!'

This indicates one of the literary allusions in Zhivago's poem; for Turgenev's wood-demon or wood-goblin gets into the last stanza. But two more principal allusions are identified in an earlier part of the same entry in the diary:

> Chapter 7 of *Eugene Onegin* describes the spring, Onegin's house deserted in his absence, Lensky's grave by the stream at the foot of the hill.
>
> > The nightingale, spring's lover,
> > Sings all night. The wild rose blooms.
>
> Why 'lover'? Well, it's a natural thing to say, it's fitting. 'Lover' is right. And then, he needed it for the rhyme. – Or was he really thinking of Nightingale the Robber, the one in the ballad? 'Robber Nightingale, the son of Odimantiy'.

At his nightingale whistle,
At his wild forest call,
The grass is all a-tremble,
The flowers shed their petals,
The dark forest bows down to the ground,
And all good people fall down dead.

In colloquial usage, a man with a fine voice is called 'a nightingale'.
And in the folk-poems called *byliny* the legendary hero *Soloveiraz-
boinik* '(Robber Nightingale') is able to knock down his opponents
merely by whistling. This provides Zhivago with a sort of oxymoron,
holding together the two potentialities, alternately baleful and
beneficent, of the season of spring and of spring phenomena like
loosened waters and nightingale's singing. Certainly the other allusion, to Pushkin, works in this way. For the lines which Zhivago
quotes are from the 6th stanza of Chapter Seven of *Eugene Onegin*.
In Babette Deutsch's translation:

Within the hill-encircled valley
Come seek the stream that slowly goes
Through meadowland and linden alley,
On down to where the river flows.
The nightingale, this season's lover,
There sings all night; wild roses cover
The bank; one hears a gentle spring;
And where two pines their shadows fling
A gravestone tells its mournful story.
The passer-by may read it clear:
'Vladimir Lensky slumbers here,
Who early found both death and glory,
In such a year, at such an age;
Take rest, young poet, as thy wage.'

But more instructive are the second and third stanzas.

Ah, spring, fair spring, the lovers' season,
How sad I find you! How you flood
My soul with dreams that challenge reason,
And with strange languor fill my blood!
My stricken heart cries out and fails me
When once the breath of spring assails me,
Although its touch be soft as fleece,
While I lie lapped in rural peace!
Is it that I was born to languish,
And all that sparkles, triumphs, sings,
Is alien to my breast, and brings

No gift but weariness and anguish
To one whose soul has perished, and
Who sees the dark on every hand?

Or is it that we fail to cherish
The tender leaves, but in the spring
Mourn those that autumn doomed to perish,
The while we hear the woodland sing?
Or are our thoughts in truth so cruel
That nature's season of renewal
But brings to mind our fading years
That no hope of renewal cheers?
Or it may be that we are taken
In our poetic reverie
Far back to a lost spring, and we,
By dreams of a far country shaken,
Recall with pain the vanished boon:
A night of magic, and a moon...

Obviously T.S. Eliot in *The Waste Land* was not the first to hear a voice saying:

April is the cruellest month, breeding
Lilacs out of the dead land, mixing
Memory and desire, stirring
Dull roots with spring rain...

And just as plainly Zhivago hears spring's nightingales 'fulminate', not out of any modish wish to reverse normal expectations, but from taking to heart the most classic poem in Russian literature.

He takes it to heart because it corroborates his own experience. For indeed, the cruel ambiguity of the spring is so nearly the central theme of the whole of *Doctor Zhivago* that in discussing it at all apart from the wealth of illustration which that work brings to it, we run the risk of dissolving it away into commonplaces and cloudy abstractions. We find ourselves saying that the season of life is by that token the season also of death – and this is an observation so portentously general that it engages with nothing in particular that we have experienced. Yet something like this is just about what the sum of Zhivago's experiences means to him; and the perception may regain some of its edge if we consider two in particular of Zhivago's experiences, which seem to point this way. One is the experience of writing poems, the other is the experience of assisting at a burial. The burial is that of Zhivago's mother-in-law, in the 17th section of Chapter Three: 'That day the hard frost had broken. It was a still, heavy day,

a day of ended frost and of departed life, a day meant for a funeral.'
How far Pasternak is from resting inertly on stereotyped responses
to the fact of spring may be seen from the ambiguity, here, of
'departed life': human life has indeed departed, but natural life has
returned. And the stock responses are to the fixity of frozen winter
as apt for death, the setting in of the thaw as a symbol for life;
Pasternak reverses the equations. And yet it is not just a case of
arguing that black is white. For, ten sentences later:

> Yura walked on alone, ahead of the others, stopping occasionally
> to let them catch up with him. In answer to the challenge of the
> desolation brought by death into the life of the small community
> whose members were slowly pacing after him, he was drawn, *as
> irresistibly as water funnelling downwards*, to dream, to think, to
> work out new forms, to create beauty. He realized, more vividly
> than ever before, that art has two constant, two unending preoc-
> cupations: it is always meditating upon death and it is always
> thereby creating life. He realized that this was true of all great
> and genuine art; it was true of that work of art which is called
> the Revelation of St. John, and of all those works which have
> been completing it throughout the ages.

I have ventured to italicize a phrase in this paragraph, to bring out
how impossible it is, by the time we get to the poems, to take a
reference to flowing water as simply descriptive, meaning no more
than it says.

Moreover, 'nightingale' inevitably carries over to this poem the
significance which accrued to it in 'White Night'. It is Zhivago's
poetic destiny which calls him, at once promising and minatory,
and appropriately in the accents of Pushkin, from the nightingale's
throat. And before the poem is over Zhivago has answered the call
and embraced the destiny. For he answers the question of the seventh
quatrain – 'What paramour . . . ?' – by realizing that the nightingale's
challenge is addressed to him, Zhivago. The evidence is in the next
quatrain, where the nightingale (identified by the allusion to Turgenev)
comes from the bivouac of a wanted man, such as Zhivago then
was, to confront a detachment of the partisans, just as Zhivago did
at just this point in the story.

'Explanation'

Dr Johnson, who believed apparently that poetry is better the more
translatable it is, says in his Life of Denham, of four verses from
'Cooper's Hill':

The lines are in themselves not perfect; for most of the words, thus artfully opposed, are to be understood simply on one side of the comparison, and metaphorically on the other; and if there be any language which does not express intellectual operations by material images, into that language they cannot be translated.

So we may say of this poem that, if there be any language in which the extreme and ecstasy of sexual desire is not expressed by the same word as serves for the extreme and ecstasy of passive suffering, into that language it cannot be translated. Fortunately English is not such a language; and the swing of meaning in English between 'passion' and 'Passion' reproduces almost exactly the ambiguity, crucial to this poem, in the Russian word *strast'*.

It is attractive, and perhaps it is correct, to see 'Explanation' as the one poem by Zhivago in which he does justice to the third woman in his life, the undemanding and shadowy Marina who is his companion in Moscow in the last years of his life. Certainly the first eight lines, with their reference to a specific Moscow building, the Manège, suggest this. On the other hand these recall also Zhivago's bad dream after he has got back to Yuryatin from the partisans (Chapter Thirteen, the 8th section):

> Now he dreamed of a dark winter morning; the lamps were lit and he was in some crowded Moscow street. Judging by the early morning traffic, the trams ringing their bells and the yellow pools of lamplight on the grey snow of the dawn-lit street, it was before the revolution. He dreamed of a big flat with many windows, all on the same side of the house, probably no higher than the third storey, with drawn curtains reaching to the floor.

> Inside, people were lying about asleep in their clothes as in a railway carriage, and the rooms were untidy like a railway carriage, with half-eaten legs and wings of roast chicken and other remnants of picnic foods scattered about on greasy bits of newspaper. The shoes which the many friends, relations, callers and homeless people, all sheltering in the flat, had taken off for the night were standing in pairs on the floor. The hostess, Lara, in a dressing-gown tied hastily round her waist, moved swiftly and silently from room to room, hurrying about her duties, and Yury was following her, step by step, muttering dreary, irrelevant explanations and generally making a nuisance of himself. But she no longer had a moment to give him and took no notice of his mutterings except that she turned to him now and then with a tranquil, puzzled look or burst into her inimitable, candid, silvery laughter. – This was the only form of communication that remained between them. But how distant, cold and compellingly

attractive was this woman to whom he had sacrificed all he had, whom he had preferred to everything, and in comparison with whom nothing had any value!

The time of day, and all the colouring and atmosphere of the scene, are quite different in the poem and in the dream; but the relationship between Lara and Zhivago in the dream is obviously in important respects identical with the relationship between the man and the woman in the poem. The different feel and colour of the scene seem to have been dredged up from farther back – from an incident on Yury's journey from Moscow to Yuryatin with his family. At one point on this journey, the passengers spend three days clearing the snow from the blocked railway-line, beside a village which had been burned down by Strelnikov's independent partisans. This is told in the 15th and 16th sections of Chapter Seven:

> They became almost fond of the ruined station, as of a mountain shelter on a climbing holiday. Its shape, its site, the details of its damage remained in Yury's memory.
>
> Every evening they returned to it when the sun – out of loyalty to old habits – set, just as it had always done, behind the birch outside the telegraphist's window.
>
> A part of the outside wall had fallen in and cluttered up the room, but the window was still there and the corner opposite remained untouched, with its coffee-coloured wallpaper, the tiled stove with a round vent and a copper lid, and the inventory of the office furniture in a black frame. Exactly as before the disaster, the setting sun crept over the tiles and lit a warm brown glow on the paper and hung the shadow of the birch on a hook like a woman's scarf.

This episode seems to come into the narrative for the sole purpose of being recalled by the reader when he gets to this poem, with its grotesque fancy of the sunset nailed to the wall, which corresponds exactly to the shadow of the birch-tree hung on a hook. And for the same reason we are told that the details of the scene 'remained in Yury's memory'. It is the dream's curiously fugitive impression of a railway carriage which seems to have drawn up with it, into the brooding memory of the poet, this scene which he saw from a railway carriage which was temporarily stationary home for 'friends, relations, . . . and homeless people'. These eight lines demonstrate as in a controlled experiment how the poetic imagination modifies the materials which memory presents to it – modifies them in a way that is like, and yet unlike, the ways of dream.

If Lara is in the poem as well as Marina, so is Tonya:

To Yura, his old friend Tonya, until then a part of his life which had always been taken for granted and had never needed explaining, had suddenly become the most inaccessible and complicated being he could imagine. She had become a woman. By a stretch of imagination he could picture himself as an emperor, a hero, a prophet, a conqueror, but not as a woman.

Now that Tonya had taken this supreme and most difficult task on her slender fragile shoulders (she now seemed to him slender and fragile, though she was a perfectly healthy girl), he was filled with that ardent sympathy and shy wonder which are the beginnings of passion.

With this passage, from the 10th section of Chapter Three, Zhivago's wife, first in order of time among the women in his life, is seen to be comprised along with others in the generic figure of Woman which the poem celebrates.

But it is Lara, as might be expected, who is present most insistently. The image from electricity in the 7th quatrain recalls Zhivago speaking to Lara at Varykino (Chapter Fourteen, the 3rd section, italics mine):

When you – a shadow in a schoolgirl's dress – arose out of the shadows of that room, I – a boy, ignorant of you – with all the torment of the strength of my response, at once understood: *this scraggy little girl was charged, as with electrical waves, with all the femininity in the world.* Had I touched you at that moment with so much as the tip of my finger, a spark would have lit up the room and either killed me on the spot or filled me for the rest of my life with a magnetic flow of plaintive longing and sorrow. I was full to the brim with tears, I wept and blazed inwardly. I was mortally sorry for myself, a boy, and still more sorry for you, a girl. The whole of my astonished self asked: if such is the torment of being charged with the energy of love, *what must be the torment of being a woman, of being this energy, of being its source?*

And ten pages later, in the 9th section of this chapter, 'In the rush of some task or other their hands would meet and join and then they set down whatever they were carrying weak and giddy, all thoughts driven from their heads.'

However, if there is more than one woman in the poem, so also there is more than one man. Astonishingly, many of the verses might be spoken not by Lara's lover, Zhivago, but by her despicable seducer, Komarovsky. In particular the penultimate stanza, dwelling on one item after another of a woman's anatomy, is the litany of a sensualist. It recalls nothing so much as Komarovsky's realization, in the 13th section of Chapter Two, that he has committed himself far more deeply than he intended, to the schoolgirl he has seduced:

> What he needed desperately was Lara and there was no possible chance of seeing her that Sunday. He paced up and down the room frantically, like a caged animal.
>
> She had for him the unique charm of the incorporeal. Her hands astonished him like a sublime idea. Her shadow on the wall of the hotel room had seemed to him the outline of innocence. Her vest was stretched over her breast, as firmly and simply as linen on an embroidery frame.
>
> His fingers drummed on the window pane in time to the unhurried thud of horses' hooves on the asphalted carriage-way below. 'Lara,' he whispered, shutting his eyes. He had a vision of her head resting on his arm; her eyes were closed, she was asleep, unconscious that he watched her sleeplessly for hours on end. Her dark hair was scattered and its beauty stung his eyes like smoke and ate into his heart.

But how could Zhivago know what had gone on in Komarovsky's heart and head? It is the same question that we ask about the unintelligent woman who experienced the poem 'In Holy Week', and it must get the same answer: it is part of what the poetic imagination means, thus for the poet to be able to sink his identity in the identity of another. This is what Zhivago says himself at the end of 'The Wedding' and again at the end of 'Daybreak', just as Keats had said it before him. But in any case, where Komarovsky is concerned, we have other evidence of Zhivago's clairvoyance, in the conversation he has with Lara in the 12th section of Chapter Thirteen, where he confesses his jealousy of Komarovsky and justifies it in a way to which Lara has no answer.

It is indeed one of the strengths of Pasternak's treatment of love in *Doctor Zhivago*, as of Zhivago's treatment of it in this poem, that it is unflinchingly erotic.[1] There is no question of distinguishing sharply between a 'pure' love (Zhivago's) and an 'impure' (Komarovsky's). On the contrary one of the things that goes wrong with Lara's marriage to Antipov is that Antipov's love for her is altogether too 'pure' to be sustaining. The image from electricity is not used lightly; what is released in sexual encounter is *energy*, creativity as such – hence the reference to '*spring*'s fever-fit'. And this is as true if the sexual partner is Komarovsky as if it is Zhivago. Even Komarovsky,

---

[1] Accordingly perhaps the oddest of all comments on *Doctor Zhivago* is Renato Poggioli's reference to Zhivago's '*almost fleshless* love for Lara' (my italics). See Renato Poggioli, *The Poets of Russia 1890-1930* (Harvard, 1960), p.333.

at the start of Chapter Four, feels after his fashion 'the passion for the break' – 'in no circumstances must he come near her; on the contrary he must keep away...' And while I agree with F.D. Reeve (*The Kenyon Review* for Winter 1960) that part of what is pointed to in the last quatrain of 'Explanation' is the necessity for the artist of abnegation and self-induced suffering, yet it would narrow the poem further than I like, to suppose that the passion for the break is known in love only by artists.

It is probably unnecessary to point out that, none the less, in the poem woman is not seen and celebrated solely in her erotic capacity. The very touching 3rd and 4th quatrains are there to celebrate woman's doggedness and selfless fidelity, so that the celebration in the poem widens to include, for instance, the wives of the partisans in the *tayga*, and an indomitably resourceful family of spinster sisters in Yuryatin.

When all is said, however, we cannot allow the presence in this poem of women in all their humanness to shut out the sense that the being whom the poet addresses is as much 'Russia' as she is 'Woman'. Renato Poggioli, speaking of statements which could be cited from Pasternak's verse, early and late, remarks:

> all of them sound like apologies which the poet addressed not so much to the régime as to public opinion, or rather, to an élite able to understand equally the reason of poetry and the reason of state. Yet the poet seemed to know, at least in the depth of his heart, that any reconciliation between art and politics was fundamentally impossible. Hence that sense of both pride and shame in all of Pasternak's statements on the subject: the pride of his unconquerable loneliness, and the shame of being unable to pay the Revolution the tribute which all pay, and which may well be justly due to it.[1]

The mixture of shame and sullen pride in the tone taken by the speaker of 'Explanation' answers exactly to Renato Poggioli's description. It is what gives to the poem its memorable and peculiar flavour. And it follows that this is one of the places where Zhivago and his creator are most at one.

'Summer in the City'

In the original this poem, like the others in quatrains, rhymes *abab*.

This poem is a very interesting case indeed; at least I have found it so. For a long time it seemed to me that the point it made was not

---

[1] Renato Poggioli, op. cit. pp.335-6.

sufficiently sharp. I found myself wanting the word 'unfading' in the last line to be 'unflowering'; in this way, I conceived, the reference to lime-trees would make explicit what the earlier stanzas would have implied – the sterility of the relationship between the man and woman, implied also in the growling thunder. But this would have been a stratagem too sophisticated and oblique for the limpid surface of late Pasternak; and on re-reading the prose narrative I realized how impossible it was for the scent of lime-trees, associated as it constantly is with the flowering at Melyuzeyevo of love between Zhivago and Lara, to stand in any way for sterility in human relations. Very late in the day I found what I believe to be the point of the poem, and a very sharp one it is.

Briefly, as I now think, the poem presents a night spent by Zhivago and his wife Tonya, on which breaks in the last stanza, along with the daylight, Zhivago's guilty awareness of how Lara has alienated his affections.

This reading depends upon identifying the thundery night quite specifically as one of which we are told in the 4th section of Chapter Six, a night on which Tonya throws a party to celebrate her husband's return from the Western Front. As the guests are leaving –

It thundered once as if a plough had been dragged right across the sky. Then silence. Then four loud, delayed thuds, like overgrown potatoes being flung out of the soft, newly dug beds in autumn.

The thunder cleared a space in the dusty, smoke-filled room. All at once, like electrical currents, the component elements of life became perceptible: air and water, need for joy, earth, sky.

The side street filled with the voices of the departing guests. They had started an argument of some sort in the house and were still arguing in exactly the same way in the street. Gradually the voices became softer in the distance and at last faded away.

'How late it is,' said Yury. 'Let's go to bed. The only people I love in the world are you and Father.'

We know at this point in the novel that this profession of Yury's, however sincerely he wishes it to be true, in fact is false. We know it because of what, in the prose and the verse alike, is associated with the fragrance of lime-trees. At Melyuzeyevo, the hospital where Zhivago had got to know Lara was 'the former residence of Countess Zhabrinskaya' (the 4th section of Chapter Five). Loitering on his way to an awkward interview with Lara still known to him only as Nurse Antipova, Zhivago had looked out of a window of the rambling house (section 6):

And from the Countess's centuries-old garden, so littered with fallen branches that it was impenetrable, the dusty aromatic smell of old lime-trees coming into blossom drifted in a huge wave as tall as a house.

When, next night, Zhivago gets his interview with Lara, before he shocks them both by stumbling into an implicit avowal of his love for her, Lara is ironing:

The windows were open. In the room the scent of lime blossom mixed, as in an old park, with the caraway-bitter smell of dry twigs; to it were added the charcoal fumes of the two flat-irons which Lara used alternately, putting them each in turn in the flue to keep them hot.

And the lime-scent follows Zhivago to Moscow. In the train which takes him there from Melyuzeyevo he continues to smell it (section 13):

Then, like a message delivered on the way or like greetings from Melyuzeyevo, as though addressed personally to Yury, there drifted in the familiar aromatic smell. It came from somewhere to one side of the window and higher than the level of either garden or wild flowers, and it quietly asserted its excellence over all else. Kept from the windows by the crowd, Yury could not see the trees; but he imagined them growing somewhere very near and spreading over the carriage roofs their tranquil branches covered with dusty leaves as thick as night and sprinkled with constellations of small, glittering wax flowers.

Everywhere along the way there was the noisy crowd, and everywhere the lime-trees were in blossom.

Their scent seemed to be everywhere at once and to overtake the travellers on their journey north, like a rumour flying round each siding, signal-box and half-way halt and waiting for them on arrival, established and confirmed.

Obviously, when the fact of lime-trees is dwelt upon with such wealth of attention, we do wrong if we read them merely as shorthand for the heroine. They are made very fully present in their own right, as products of Russian earth; and indeed the point of associating them with Lara is not to enrich them but to enrich her. By force of this association she comes to typify and embody the Russian earth in her own person.

And thus there is a deeper resonance to the poem. For the loving lie which Zhivago tells Tonya after the party is only the last of many which he has told that evening as, tipsily, he has joined in with the half-baked pro-Revolutionary enthusiasm of his guests. When in the prose 'the component elements of life become perceptible', they challenged and discredited this also; and in the same way the unfading lime-trees of the poem stand for Lara, but also for more than Lara.

'Wind'

In the 16th section of the Conclusion, Lara says to Zhivago's corpse, 'Your going, that's the end of me.' This poem is as it were Zhivago's anticipating this response and answering it.

As in other poems of this sequence, the wind here surely has the symbolic meaning it had for Blok, and for Pasternak in his 'Four Fragments about Blok'.

'Barley-mow'

The original turns on a punning double-meaning of the word 'Khmel', which means in the first place 'hops', and also, more generally, 'intoxication'. A similar ambiguity in the English expression, 'barley-mow', appeared the nearest equivalent. The translation is thus, inevitably, 'free'.

'Indian Summer'

Several images in this poem recall the opening sections of Chapter Twelve, 'Iced Rowanberries', which have to do with how autumn comes to the partisan encampments in the Siberian *tayga*. Certainly 'the white soot of Autumn' in the 5th stanza seems a very interesting and effective conflation of two images in the prose of Chapter Twelve, the 5th section: 'The weather was horrible. A sharp, scudding wind swept torn clouds, as black as flying soot, low over the earth. Snow fell from them in insane white flurries...' The connection is worth making, if only to emphasize how essential this poem is to the sequence, since among so many others of 'nature-worship' here is one which emphasizes rather the mindlessness of nature, and how its processes seem discredited by contrast with the prudent foresight of the human activities of housekeeping. From this point of view, 'derisively' in the 5th line is important; the wood is imagined as scornfully jeering at human precautions against a wintriness which takes nature and the wood unawares. The laugh is turned upon the foolish wood, before the poem is through.

All the same the contrast between human thrift and natural fecklessness is reconciled in the last line of the poem. For it would be banal for Zhivago to mean, by the laughter and commotion from a distance which answer to their likes indoors, only that in other houses the same activities are going on. The sense is, surely, that despite appearances something in the natural order answers to this in the human; the mushrooms, as it were, are asking to be pickled.

For the form the housekeeping takes is of the first importance. As George Katkov observes of the first line, 'The black-currant leaf ... would suggest to a Russian the season of pickling and salting cucumbers and mushrooms. Black-currant leaf was used widely as a herb for making brines.' And thus, more than Zhivago's memories of the *tayga*, what informs the poem are his memories of Varykino – and of his first stay there, with his wife Tonya, rather than his second, with Lara. For, as Katkov says, 'the theme of this poem is the daily round of domestic life seen to proceed in harmony with the changes of the seasons'. To be sure, the harmony is discovered only at the very end, and most of the poem is concerned with establishing, rather, a dissonance. In the diary which Zhivago keeps at Varykino (the first sections of Chapter Nine), he explicitly warns us: 'I am not preaching a Tolstoyan doctrine of simplicity and "back to the land".' Yet the same diary records sentiments which are certainly implicit in the poem; for instance, 'What happiness it is to work from dawn to dusk for your family and yourself, to build a roof over their heads, to till the soil to feed them...' Even more to the point is another entry in the diary, in the 2nd section of Chapter Nine:

> We have been lucky. The autumn was dry and warm. It gave us time to dig up the potatoes before the rains and the cold weather. Not counting those we gave back to Mikulitsin, we had twenty sacks. We put them in the biggest bin in the cellar and covered them with old blankets and hay. We also put down two barrels of salted cucumbers and two of sauerkraut prepared by Tonya. Fresh cabbages hang in pairs from the timbers...

For here, along with the pickling and preserving which lead into 'Indian Summer', is a reference to the cellar where the preserved vegetables are stored. And the cellar, as it is described and dwelt upon a few sentences later, figures with startling effect in the last lines of 'The Bad Days', a poem near the end of the sequence. Accordingly 'The Bad Days', which has as much to do with Christ and the raising of Lazarus as with Zhivago in his cellar, is intended, as I conceive, to recall 'Indian Summer' and to draw tangibility and concreteness from that connection.

As important as Zhivago's memories of Varykino, and far more important than the *tayga*, are what gets into this poem from Zhivago's experiences on his long trek back to Moscow from the Urals. The woods running 'in deep gullies to the river, dropping precipitously'; the unnaturally intense burnt colours of the 2nd stanza ('so ominously rusty brown, the colour of old, dimmed gold') and above all the hazel-tree – these come from the powerfully written 2nd section of Chapter Fifteen, where Zhivago, 'at the end of the summer and the beginning of a warm, dry autumn', moves slowly through a landscape devastated and largely depopulated by the Civil War. And this makes it certain that what is intended in the last lines of the poem is the Rilkean conception of how inanimate nature yearns for the human to perfect it and preserve it. In Rilke the inanimate asks to be preserved in human utterance, in the names man finds for it; though this idea is entertained by Zhivago also (for instance at the end of 'Earth'), in 'Indian Summer' and elsewhere Nature asks rather to be cropped, so that it may renew itself in a new season. In Chapter Fifteen, for instance, it is rye that is 'ominously rusty brown', and Zhivago notes, of 'these flame-coloured fields burning without fire, these fields silently proclaiming their distress', that 'usually when it is cut on time, its colour [the rye's, that is] is much lighter'. The case appears the same with the hazel:

> Usually the nuts are not allowed to ripen, as people, and particularly village children, pick them green, breaking off whole branches. But now the autumn-wooded hills and gullies were thick with rough golden leaves dusted and coarsened by the sun, and festive among them, as if tied with ribbons, were bulging clusters of nuts, three or four together, ripe and ready to fall out of their husks.

But the festive simile reinforces a point explicitly made – that these fruits of the woods differ from fruits of the fields. Zhivago fed on hazel nuts for a week, and no doubt gratefully; but 'he felt as if he saw the fields in the fever of a dangerous illness'.

'The Wedding'

This poem presents the translator with special and probably insurmountable difficulties. It is in the metre of the *chastushka*, a form of popular composition which is mentioned explicitly in the 5th quatrain. Traditionally a peasant dance tune, the *chastushka*, according to George Katkov, is now to be thought of as a 'popular ribald factory song', usually to the accordion. I have no way of being sure about the level and tone of the poem's diction but at some points, as one might expect of language set to this metre, it appears to be racy and colloquially vulgar. See for instance the 8th quatrain, where in place of Hayward's and Harari's (and Kamen's) very stilted reference to Tartarus, I have risked, 'Gone to hell out of it.' This illustrates how, in order to get into current English any vulgar energy and verve, one has to draw upon American rather than British speech – because British youth in fact uses American idiom for such purposes. But even American idiom provides only poor and approximate equivalents.

Apart from the difficulties presented by the language the topography of the poem is hard to understand, as are the social and human relations which it takes for granted. The time-sequence is clear enough, though translation can disastrously obscure it. But what is the relation of the yard to the house where the bride sleeps? And to neighbouring houses? Is the yard a public place, or private, or semi-private? And if it is to some degree private, what is its relation to the public thoroughfare?

Similarly, as regards the man of the house, explicitly mentioned in the 5th line, what is his relation to the bride? Is he the bride's father, and therefore host to the wedding guests? Or is he on the contrary only the resident householder? Or even just a neighbour?

These questions can be settled only by reference to the prose narrative, which thus contributes to this poem in an unusual way – not primarily as a source of images (though it is that too, as we shall see), but as a source of indispensable factual information.

The wedding appears to be that of Lara and Pasha Antipov, recounted in the 3rd section of Chapter Four. (The 4th section, which deals with a second party nine days after the wedding party, is also drawn upon.) Lara has no father. Indeed she lodges alone; and both the wedding party and the farewell party which succeeds it take place at her lodgings. These have been described at the end of the 2nd section of Chapter Four; they consist of a studio-apartment belonging to a painter who is away in Turkestan –

> ...Lara moved to the lodgings Kologrivov had recommended, near the Smolensky Market. The flat was at the top of an elderly-looking two-storey house. There were draymen living in the other part of it, and a warehouse on the ground floor. The cobbled yard was always littered with spilt oats and hay. Pigeons strutted about cooing and fluttered up noisily to the level of Lara's window; sometimes a swarm of rats swarmed down the stone gutter.

Given this information, I find it certain that the felted door behind which we are taken in the 2nd quatrain is that of 'the draymen' who share the house with Lara, who accordingly figure as 'the householder' only in the sense of being senior co-tenants. And the yard, it now seems, is neither wholly private property nor wholly public; the yard of a warehouse abutting on the street whence one may hear quite naturally, as in the 9th quatrain, 'an echo of business deals', as customers come in the morning to argue the price of corn and straw. (As already noted, this is also the yard of the last quatrain of the poem, 'March'.)

If the 2nd quatrain takes the reader into the draymen's quarters, does he ever emerge again? I think in one sense he does not. For they share the first floor with Lara, and it is to their window that in the last quatrain the sound of the wedding floats up (from the yard, not, as Hayward and Harari say, 'from the street'), just as the pigeons fly up and past Lara's window on the same level. A doubt which remains is whether the draymen are the sleepers in the 5th quatrain. I think this may be, but since 'bed' is in the singular, and also because it will be very odd if there is no reference at all to the marriage-bed. I have risked suggesting that the sleepers here are bride and bridegroom tired out after love-making.

And after all we should not be surprised if the poem takes us floating in and out of consciousnesses which are normally distinct. For this experience and the importance of it, is explicitly evoked in the penultimate stanza:

> Life right enough is likewise only an instant
> Only a loosening out
> Of ourselves among all others
> As it might be a thing we gave them.

In the very instant of saying this we float, along with Zhivago, into another consciousness altogether – that of the Jewish boy, Misha Gordon, many years before (the 7th section of Chapter One), on a long train-journey:

> All the movements in the world, taken separately, were sober and deliberate but, taken together, they were all happily drunk with the general flow of life which united and carried them. People worked and struggled, they were driven on by their individual cares and anxieties, but these springs of action would have run down and jammed the mechanism if they had not been kept in check by an over-all feeling of profound unconcern. This feeling came from the comforting awareness of the interwovenness of all human lives, the sense of their flowing into one another, the happy assurance that all that happened in the world took place not only on the earth which buried the dead but also on some other level known to some as the Kingdom of God, to others as history and yet to others by some other name.

It is effective and profound to have this perception proffered to us by those anonymous Russians, the draymen. (Misha, incidentally and significantly, can perceive but not experience this 'profound unconcern' and 'awareness of the interwovenness'; this limitation he sees as part of what it means to be a Jew – at least in Russia.) The value to be put on anonymity – this comes best from those who are anonymous, wholly tangential to the narrative.

This quality of the tangential, and the poignancy of it, are at the heart of the poem. Who is it, for instance, who goes dancing like a peacock? She is a nameless apparition conjured up, like everything else (for this is a poem in which nothing is *seen*), out of the sounds which drift upwards and penetrate the sleeping consciousness of Lara and Pasha perhaps, but more importantly of those complete strangers who sleep next door to them. The peacock-dancer is thus the embodiment of all that is poignantly transitory and fugitive; yet it is worth having Lara hear the sounds also, since this brings home a particularly sharp instance of transience – the way in which on only one day of her life is a woman a bride (and a brilliant peacock), a single day earned by the many more on which she is to be a wife (a domesticated pigeon). The dancer is thus not the particular bride, Lara, but *the idea* of a bride.

As in all the poems, so in this one it is essential to remember that it is the artistic composition of one man, Zhivago. We must suppose that the salient details of the wedding party and the farewell party were supplied to Zhivago by Lara, out of musing recollections. (These would have included, I think, an image from the prose and poetry together – the hobbled horse which strays into the yard during the night.[1]) The fluctuating and merging of consciousness is made plausible to us by the way the sounds penetrate the sleepiness of those who hear them. But in fact the one consciousness which can comprehend all the others, entering into the minds of the draymen and of Lara and even of a Jewish schoolboy, is the consciousness of the poet. And so it is relevant to remember, in relation to the penultimate stanza, Keats's remarks on how the poet lacks 'character':

A Poet is the most unpoetical of any thing in existence; because he has no Identity – he is continually in for – and filling some other Body – The Sun, the Moon, the Sea and Men and Women who are creatures of impulse are poetical and have about them an unchangeable attribute – the poet has none; no identity – he is certainly the most unpoetical of all God's Creatures... It is a

---

[1] Chapter Four, the 4th section – 'A hobbled horse was moving across the yard with short limping jumps. She did not know whose it was or how it had strayed into the yard. The sleeping city seemed dead. It was bathed in the grey-blue coolness of the early hours. Lara closed her eyes, carried to goodness knows what country depths and joys by the noise of the horse's hobbled steps, so unlike any other sound.'

wretched thing to confess; but it is a very fact that not one word I ever utter can be taken for granted as an opinion growing out of my identical nature – how can it, when I have no nature? When I am in a room with People if I ever am free from speculating on creations of my own brain, then not myself goes home to myself; but the identity of every one in the room begins to so press upon me that I am in a very little time an(ni)hilated...[1]

It is in keeping with the sustained drive of *Doctor Zhivago* towards apotheosis of the poet, that what Keats sees as a peculiarity in some ways disabling, Pasternak offers as an ideal norm of feeling.

'Autumn'

If George Katkov is right when he sends us, for the source of this poem, to nothing in *Doctor Zhivago* but rather to 'Chapter from a Novel', a document published in the thirties, 'Autumn' is a poem as to which the pretence that it was written by Yury Zhivago breaks down completely.

This is surely a view to be resisted as long as possible, for if it is accepted it invalidates what I have taken to be the idea and governing principle of the whole sequence. And so it is a relief to find that much of the poem can be traced quite confidently to certain pages of the novel, specifically to passages about how Zhivago returns with Lara to Varykino, where he had earlier been settled with Tonya and his children. In the 3rd section of Chapter Fourteen, when Lara proposes retreating from Yuryatin to Varykino, Zhivago responds: 'But about Varykino. Of course, to go to that wilderness in winter, without food, without strength or hope – it's utter madness. But why not, my love! Let's be mad, if there is nothing except madness left to us.' This is exactly the mood conjured up in the poem. And it is elaborated in the prose, beautifully and to the point:

But after all it's true, isn't it, that we haven't any choice. Put it how you like, but death is really knocking at our door. Our days are really numbered. So at least let us take advantage of them in our own way. Let us use them up saying goodbye to life, let us be alone together for the last time before we are parted. We'll say goodbye to everything we held dear, to the way we looked at things, to the way we dreamed of living and to what our conscience taught us, and to our hopes and to each other. We'll speak to one another once again the secret words we speak at night, great and peaceful like the name of the eastern ocean...

[1] *The Letters of John Keats*, ed. M.B. Forman, 3rd ed., p.228: letter dated 27th October 1818.

When in the 4th section of Chapter Fourteen Yury and Lara, with Katya, make their retreat to Varykino, the effect of hysteria in the whole venture is sustained in Zhivago's deliberately madcap driving of the sleigh. It is significant however that the move, as well as the debate about it, happens in midwinter; and the autumnal imagery must therefore be drawn from another chapter of Zhivago's life, perhaps from the autumn which he experienced with the partisans in the *tayga*.

An attractive but ultimately unacceptable reading of the poem is offered by F.D. Reeve, writing in *The Kenyon Review* for Winter 1960. Reeve writes, of the last stanza:

> Zhivago cannot endure the continued immediacy of so much life, the pressure of so much undefined insistence. The world being what it is, and not Lara's world, he can preserve her vitality only by fraud and by art. He can keep her only by sending her away and by transforming into the ordered language of poetry, as a definition, his sense of the electricity that passed between them.

It is good to find a reader for whom it matters that Zhivago is a poet. And undoubtedly the paradoxes of aestheticism are not foreign to Zhivago's experience, any more than to Pasternak's. Moreover this comment makes as good a guess as any at two very riddling passages – one in the verse (the last stanza of 'Explanation'), and one in the prose, Zhivago's tricking of Lara into going with Komarovsky to the Pacific sea-board,[1] a perverse step which it is possible, but not very plausible or interesting, to attribute to straight-forward altruism. On the other hand, as a gloss on this poem in itself, Reeve's comment is surely top-heavy: it depends on taking 'beauty' ('krasota'), in the penultimate line, as strictly the beauty of art; and the context gives no warrant for reading this common and powerful word so narrowly.

'Fairy Story'

In the 9th section of Chapter Fourteen Zhivago feels that the wolves round Varykino represent the hostility which will drive him and Lara from that retreat – an intangible hostility which 'loomed like a prehistoric beast or dragon... who thirsted for Yury's blood and lusted after Lara'. And there are other hints in this section of the prose narrative by which Pasternak seems to invite us explicitly to explore the background to this poem by considering the place in the

---

[1] Accordingly there may be significance in the punning play, in the passage last quoted from the novel, on the word 'pacific'.

Russian tradition of the legend of St George and the Dragon. Edmund Wilson followed this signpost in his valuable essay, 'Legend and Symbol in *Dr Zhivago*',[1] and so did George Katkov in his notes to translations by Henry Kamen.[2] Mr Katkov's observations are particularly welcome, since they have to do, not just with the substance of the poem, but with its style:

> The story of St George, as it spread through the oral tradition of the 'Religious poems' (*dukhovnye stikhi*), sung by the Russian equivalent of minstrels, is a fusion of the Byzantine story of the martyrdom of St George and the western version of the liberation of the 'maiden' from the dragon. This explains the mixed style of imagery, in which the Russian landscape combines with a somewhat westernized medieval style.

In my version I have tried to reproduce this 'mixed' and 'westernized' style, by drawing on the diction of Spenser's *Faerie Queene* which itself is modelled in part on that of the English mediaeval romances.

A supplementary 'source' for the poem may be found in Chapter Seven, 'The Journey' (the 24th section):

> The white northern night was ending. Everything was clearly visible, the mountain, the thicket and the ravine, but as if they did not quite believe in themselves and existed only in a fairy-tale . . .
>
> The waterfall, though not far away, could be seen only from the edge of the ravine beyond the thicket. Vassya Brykin, the escaped conscript, had tired himself out with joy and terror looking at it.
>
> There was nothing comparable to the waterfall anywhere in the neighbourhood. It was unique and this made it terrible, transformed it into a being endowed with life and consciousness, perhaps that of the dragon or winged serpent of these parts, who levied tribute and preyed upon the countryside . . .

The references here to fairytale and dragon lead into the poem as directly as those which come along with St George. A few sentences later we learn that Vassya Brykin has been hiding by the waterfall for two days, after his escape from the troop-train bound for the Eastern Front. ('He sped to the fray'), and that he is accompanied by the woman Tyagunova, a virago whom we have met as the mistress of an older conscript. (For Vassya is no more than a boy.) What Vassya says to her reveals, or hints, that at the time of the escape Tyagunova had tried to murder her rival Ogryskova.

[1]   *Encounter*, 69 (June 1959).
[2]   Pasternak. *In the Interlude – Poems 1945-1960*, tr. by Henry Kamen (1962), pp.123-4.

This gives point to stanza 13, in which the physical confusion between woman and serpent seems conveyed with grotesque insistence in the Russian. (It is incidentally all-important, surely, to preserve meticulously Zhivago's switching from 'dragon' to 'serpent' and back again.) At this point in the poem the woman in the serpent's toils cannot help but recall the figure of Eve the temptress. And indeed the Freudian imagery seems to be consistently sustained, so that the whole can be read as an allegory of sexual encounter.

But what is more important is to realize that the woman in the poem, if she is Tyagunova, is also Lara, when seduced for instance by her mother's protector Komarovsky (hence 'ransom' and 'scapegoat'), just as she is also the Mary Magdalene of later poems in the series. In fact this poem should prevent us from sentimentalizing Lara, the heroine. Seen through Zhivago's eyes she is profoundly ambiguous, a force as much destructive as creative. And of course in the plot Lara does in many important ways destroy Zhivago her lover, just as she destroyed her husband, Pasha Antipov, by transforming him into the Gerald-Crich-like figure of the avenging man of will, Strelnikov. (I refer to D.H. Lawrence's *Women in Love*.) Moreover Lara is identified with a waterfall when Zhivago dreams, in the 8th section of Chapter Thirteen, of maltreating his son by Tonya, the child Sasha whom he has abandoned for Lara's sake.

It is important to realize that 'Fairy Story' is presented, like the rest, as Zhivago's poem, not Pasternak's. At first it may seem that this cannot be, because Zhivago, in the train from which Brykin has escaped, has no way of knowing what has happened to Brykin. But I think we should take the poem, and also the corresponding section of the prose, not as the omniscient narrator's account of what happened to Brykin, but as Zhivago's imagining of what might have happened, or (better) what, according to the logic of the poetic imagination, *should* have happened.

Indeed, it is only on this understanding that, for instance, the 17th section of Chapter Seven can be seen to provide anything more than anecdotal local colour; for in this section nothing happens except that Zhivago and his wife overhear Ogryskova and Tyagunova quarrelling about who shall have Brykin. It was essential that Zhivago should have this information in order that the image of predatory temptress woman should come together with the waterfall he hears later in the journey (in the 21st section), so as to make his poem for him. There could not be a better example of how the novel cannot be appreciated – the necessity of its component parts cannot be recognized – until prose narrative and poems are considered as making up one thing. To put it another way, the escaped conscript is connected with the waterfall, not because the waterfall was near where he escaped (it is not certain that it was), but because we are told about the waterfall, that 'Its freshness *and freedom* widened the expanse of the night and it was this that had filled Yury with happiness in his sleep' (the 21st section of Chapter Seven – my italics).

In Chapter Fourteen (the 9th section), we are given Zhivago's experience when writing this poem:

> He started with a broad, spacious pentameter, but its harmony, derived from the metre itself and independent of the sense, annoyed him by its slick, humdrum sing-song. He gave up the pompous rhythm and the caesura and cut down the lines to four beats, as you cut out useless words in prose. The task was now more difficult but more attractive. The writing was livelier but still too verbose. He forced himself to still shorter lines. Now the words were crammed in their tetrameters [*sic*] and Yury felt wide awake, roused, excited; the right words to fill the lines came, prompted by the measure. Things hardly named assumed form by suggestion. He heard the horse's hooves riding on the surface of the poem as you hear the trotting of a horse in one of Chopin's Ballades. St George was galloping over the boundless spaces of the steppe. He could watch him growing smaller in the distance. He wrote in a feverish hurry, scarcely able to keep up with the words as they poured out, always to the point and of themselves tumbling into place.

There is something wrong here, since, if the lines were shortened 'to four beats', *and then shortened again*, it can hardly be tetrameters that the words were 'crammed in'. And in fact this is a mistranslation: the word is 'trimeter'. Sure enough, no line in the poem is longer than a trimeter, and most are shorter still.

We should note that there is a real distinction between 'harmony derived from the metre itself and independent of the sense', and 'the right words... came, prompted by the measure'. For prompting is not dictation. And in another excerpt from the diary (6th section of Chapter Nine), Zhivago exclaims, thinking of Pushkin: 'What a lot depends on the choice of metre!'

'August'

Henry Gifford has helped me generously by answering my queries about this poem. From him I learn, for instance, as regards the puzzling second line of the third stanza from the end, that the Orthodox Church observes in early August three days called respectively the First, the Second, and the Third Saviour; August 6th (O.S.) is the second of these.

The stately resonance of these lines, dignified by Church Slavonic, should not lead us to read into the poem more levels of meaning than one. The 'gold' of this day, for instance, has been established insistently through 'saffron' and 'ochre' and 'red-as-ginger'; the colouring is literal, not (except very marginally indeed) ritualistic or symbolic. And in the same way 'the azure of Transfiguration' boldly registers the other component in the landscape as physically observed – the blue of the skies which, in the seventh stanza, are neighbours to the tree-tops.

Double-meaning appears only in the last stanza, and in fact in the last line; where there is a sort of pun in the words translated as 'authorship' and 'working wonders'. The wonders can be miracles. And the authorship can be, as it is in English hymns of the eighteenth century, the originating activity of God the Creator. The poem thus leads up to an apotheosis of the artist, who in his art both transfigures the world and can be transfigured himself. And of course the poet is resurrected posthumously in his poems.

'Winter Night'

At the end of stanza 4, Obolensky's 'crossed destinies' (*Penguin Book of Russian Verse*) is very beguiling. But it invokes a little too loudly the 'star-crossed lovers', Romeo and Juliet. And this invokes for Zhivago and Lara a stock response from the reader which makes the rest of the poem superfluous.

In the penultimate stanza to write 'wings', as Obolensky does, seems foolish. For the Russian word can mean 'arms' as well as 'wings'; and an angel has arms as well as wings, but a cross has only arms. Moreover the gesture is surely one of benediction. In the 3rd section of Chapter Fourteen Zhivago says to Lara, 'It's not for nothing that you stand at the end of my life, my secret, forbidden angel, under the skies of war and turmoil, you who arose at its beginning under the peaceful skies of childhood.'

What the poem recalls very insistently is Lara, in Chapter Fourteen (the 8th section), waking and sleepily whispering to Zhivago, 'Still at work, my love? . . . Burning and shining like a candle in the night.' And most readers, surely, will associate the poem with Lara's and Zhivago's tormented idyll at Varykino (Chapter Fourteen), though they will read erotic meanings into the image of discarded clothing, and so will want the candle to stand for Zhivago's love-making as well as for his working through the night at his poems. Indeed no one will deny that the subject here *is* erotic. And as Obolensky points out, the rendering of it with such chasteness is what we are prepared for in the 14th section of Chapter Fourteen, where we learn how hard Zhivago works at his poems:

The reason for this correcting and rewriting was his search for strength and exactness of expression, but it also corresponded to the promptings of an inward reticence which forbade him to expose his personal experiences and the real events in his past with too much freedom, lest he should offend or wound those who had directly taken part in them.

And yet in the 8th section of Chapter Fourteen we have been told that this poem, together with 'Christmas Star', had been composed before the return to Varykino though only there was it committed to paper. It appears therefore that it cannot treat of Zhivago's life there with Lara. And in fact there are strong indications that the episode it is meant to recall chiefly is from much earlier in Zhivago's and Lara's story, Lara's conversation with Pasha Antipov in the 9th section of Chapter Three, 'Christmas Party at the Sventitskys''. This took place in the same room in which, at the end, Zhivago lies in his coffin. And Lara grieving over the corpse, makes the connection:

She strained her memory to reconstruct that Christmas conversation with Pasha, but she could remember nothing except the candle burning on the windowsill and melting a round patch in the icy crust on the glass.

How could she know that Yury, whose dead body was lying on the table, had seen the candle as he was driving past, and noticed it, and that from the moment of his seeing its light ('The candle burned on the table, the candle burned'), all that was pre-ordained for him had seized control of his life?

What is quoted in parenthesis here is the refrain to Zhivago's poem, which I have rendered, 'And the candle burning on the table, The candle burning'. When Lara at Varykino alludes to the same lines, we may suppose that she is quoting back to the author his own poem, which he has recited to her at some earlier stage. And thus the poem may refer to the Varykino idyll after all. Indeed, it's essential that it should. For Lara's quoting of his own poem back at Zhivago is only one of many indications that by this stage in their story both Zhivago and Lara see each thing that happens to them as prefigured and pre-ordained; that they see themselves, in fact, as already characters in a story or at least in a developing drama. 'Hamlet', the first poem in the sequence, struck this note from the beginning and should have prepared us to listen for it later, as here.

As for the word 'candle', whenever it occurs in the narrative at any point after this episode, it has a symbolic resonance. However, this is symbolism at its most irreducible, at its furthest from allegory;

for it is the very wealth of association that accrues to the word which prevents it from ever bearing a single formulable meaning. By the 16th section of Chapter Fourteen, for instance, the most common-place exchange about having enough candles, and whether they are of wax or tallow, bristles with symbolic overtones just because the speakers are Lara's lovers Zhivago and Antipov / Strelnikov.

Note. G. Katkov (*In the Interlude*, tr. by H. Kamen, p.234) finds the reference to February in the last stanza an odd one, since in the prose the reference to a *Christmas* party is so emphatic. He speculates that 'by letting Zhivago postpone the completion of the poem to a much later date Pasternak wanted . . . to give him an opportunity to relate the seemingly trivial episodes of his life to the great historical events that served as a background to it. The February in the poem might well be the February of 1917; . . .' I find this far-fetched.

'The Breach'

This poem, and 'Rendezvous' which follows it immediately, are obviously companion-pieces, products of the same experience, two beams of light falling at different angles on the one disturbance. One passage of the prose, in the 13th and 14th sections of Chapter Fourteen, tells of the composition of both poems. But 'The Breach' presents the experience nakedly and harshly, with all the jangle of jarred nerves; in 'Rendezvous' the trouble is distanced and more under control, though not for that reason less harrowing. Hence much of 'The Breach' can be glossed from the prose almost word for word, as 'Rendezvous' cannot:

> He came in, locked the door behind him and took off his coat. When he came into the bedroom which Lara had tidied up so well and so carefully that morning, and which her hurried packing had again turned inside out, when he saw the untidy bed and the things thrown about in disorder on the chairs and the floor, he knelt down like a child, leaned his breast against the hard edge of the bedstead, buried his head in the bedclothes and wept freely and bitterly as children do. But not for long. Soon he got up, hastily dried his face, looked round him with tired, absent-minded surprise, got out the bottle of vodka Komarovsky had left, drew the cork, poured half a glassful, added water and snow, and with a relish almost equal in strength to the hopelessness of the tears he had shed, drank long, greedy gulps.

It is worth reading through to the end of the paragraph. When the narrative switches to the vodka-bottle, this is not to cover up with a gruff masculinity the supposed mawkishness of weeping. The clues are plain enough in 'absent-minded surprise'. Such abrupt veerings of attention are typical of a mind mastered by experience it cannot come to terms with. And this is the state of mind in the poem also: it merely breaks off, it does not reach a conclusion – if it ends with a burst of tears, they are not the sort of which one says, 'If only he could weep, he would feel better.' He has wept before, as the second stanza tells us; and no doubt he will weep again. (It goes without saying that we should not imagine Zhivago writing the poem at this stage; doubtless he recollects and re-enacts it much later – the poem is a controlled dramatizing of an out-of-control condition.)

It is because the state of agitated bewilderment has been established, that the questions in the third stanza are seen to be real ones. (In fact, rhetorical questions are quite foreign to Zhivago's way of writing.) The stanzas which follow, each an attempt to answer his own question why he should think of the sea – these are the meat of the poem. And if referring back to the prose should lead us to locate the poem in the first three stanzas and the last four, considering the sea-images that come between as just a decorative amplification of this discursive material, it would be better not to turn to the prose at all.

Some of the marine analogies are twisted, they cut more ways than one; this is why they can express mental agitation more faithfully than discursive statement could. No one of them reproduces the relatively straightforward analogy established in the prose (the 13th section of Chapter Fourteen), as Zhivago silently addresses the vanished Lara:

> This is how I'll trace your image. I'll trace it on paper as the sea, after a fearful storm has churned it up to its foundations, leaves the traces of the strongest, furthest-reaching wave on the shore. Seaweed, shells, pumice, all the lightest debris, all those things of least weight which it could lift from its bed are cast up in a broken line on the sand. This line endlessly stretching into the distance is the tide's high-water mark. This is how you were cast up in my life, my love, my pride, this is how I'll write of you.

What comes nearest to this is the 6th stanza:

> As the inundation of reed-banks
> By chopped seas after a storm,
> Ebbed over the floor of his soul
> Her features and her form.

(The sea here appears to be an inland sea, like the Caspian.) The relationships in this simile between man and woman, memory and separation on the one hand, reed-banks, chopped seas, sea-floor and storm on the other, are manifold and complicated, even mutually contradictory, beyond any teasing out in explication. What seems certain is that they give no warrant for the comfortable assurance like Henry Kamen's:

> So all her features drown in him:
> Their hidden image he will keep.

On the contrary, this is one place where this poem and 'Rendezvous' seem especially closely connected. The latter poem claims to hold an image of Lara which is indeed secure and inviolable. But this became possible only after the generalizing and universalizing which supervened, as we learn in the 14th section of Chapter Fourteen, on Zhivago's writing about the lost Lara. An image which ebbs on the sea-floor, that floor being reed-banks which stand clear of the water except in certain special conditions – this image is a very different matter, altogether more fluctuating and uncertainly agitated.

There is another sense in which the marine comparisons are at the heart of this poem. This sense is secondary because it has to do with 'The Breach' less as a poem than as a cryptogram or message in code. Just for this reason it is likely to excite commentators much more, if only because it can be illustrated at great length. To be brief, however, 'The Breach' seems to be the poem which gathers together more insistently than any other the punning significance of Lara's name, first pointed out by Edmund Wilson. 'Lara' is short for 'Larissa', which in the Orthodox calendar means 'sea-gull'; a pre-Christian mythological Larissa was wife to the sea-god Poseidon.[1]

One may be forgiven for suspecting at the start that this is a discovery of ingenious commentators, rather than anything truly in the written work. But the pointers are too many, and underlined too heavily; there can be no doubt that Pasternak intended the pun. Of many passages that might be cited, one is particularly striking. It comes from Chapter Five, which otherwise is seldom drawn upon for the poems. At Melyuzeyevo, to which Zhivago is moved with his military hospital as the Western Front breaks up around him, Lara is serving as a nurse. Soon after she leaves to find her way home, on a night of storm a knocking at the door suggests to Zhivago and the oddly marooned little Frenchwoman, Mademoiselle Fleury, that Lara, balked of her intention, has returned and is seeking refuge.

> Mademoiselle came back. 'Well?' said Yury. 'You were right. There's no one.' She had been all round the house; a branch knocking on the pantry window had broken one of the panes and there

[1]   Edmund Wilson is prepared to see also a more specific reference to the Trotskyite heroine Larisa Reisner (1895-1926), to whom Pasternak in 1926 devoted a poem 'In Memoriam Reisner'.

were huge puddles on the floor, and the same thing in what used to be Lara's room – there was a sea, positively a sea, an ocean...

They had been sure that, when they opened the door, Lara would come in, chilled through and soaked to the skin, ... and would tell them her adventures, pushing back her hair and laughing.

They had been so sure of it that when they locked the door the imprint of their certainty remained in the street, round the corner, like the watery wraith of this woman, or of her image which continued to haunt them.

It is the cumulative effect of passages such as this, interspersed with others where the marine reference is more cursory and natural, which makes it indisputable that either a running comparison of Lara with the sea was intended throughout, or else (what Edmund Wilson does not allow for) that an experience such as this at Melyuzeyevo naturally though quite illogically makes the connection habitual with Zhivago.

George Katkov reports: 'Pasternak told his friends that the poem was a description of his own feelings when he learned of the first arrest of Ivinskaya in 1948.' This is very interesting, and no doubt true. But we can see that there is quite enough in the recorded experience of Yury Zhivago, to sustain the fiction that 'The Breach' is his poem rather than Boris Pasternak's.

'Rendezvous'

This poem was published, with others of the sequence, in *Znamya* (Moscow) in April 1954. This first version, published in advance of the novel, lacked what is now the last stanza. George Katkov, who points this out, finds the last quatrain 'mysterious', and explains it by saying, 'Like other poems in the cycle, Meeting [i.e. Rendezvous] has a closer relation to Pasternak's own real life than to the events of the novel.' But is this really so? Is the last stanza so mysterious if we regard it as the work of Zhivago rather than Pasternak? Undoubtedly Katkov is right to say, 'The meeting is an imaginary one; the poet is meeting an image which is engraved... in his heart.' But this was an experience of the poet Zhivago, no less than (doubtless) of the poet Pasternak. Chapter Fourteen says as much. In its 13th section, after Zhivago has tricked Lara into leaving him, he soliloquizes:

I'll stay with you a little, my unforgettable delight, for as long as my arms and my hands and my lips remember you. I'll weep for you so that my lament will be lasting and worthy of you.

I'll write your memory into an image of infinite pain and grief.
I'll stay here till this is done, then I too will go....

In so far as this 'lament' can be located in any one poem, rather than
in the sequence as a whole, it may surely be located here. If so, we
should look in this poem for 'an image of infinite pain and grief'.
And it is at this point that the distinction between Pasternak and
Zhivago turns out to be, as usual, something more than a quibble.
For Katkov, treating the poem as immediately Pasternak's, reads
the last stanza so as to make the poem end, as it were, on an up-beat.
For him, the revelation that the meeting was imaginary means that
the union of the lovers is inviolable: 'It is this humble vision which
makes the union of the lovers possible in spite of the "mercilessness
of the world" which has separated them, and this accounts for the
mysterious last strophe...' But surely F.D. Reeve does better (in
The Kenyon Review for Winter 1960), when he sees the question
posed in the last quatrain as not rhetorical but real, something not
to be answered until the poems about the Magdalen at the end of
the sequence. For him the stanza 'asks what man is for: how does
he make an adequate definition of himself?' Whereas for Katkov
the question in the last stanza sends us back to the arrogant affirma-
tion of the 8th, for Reeve it opens up a whole dimension beyond
that. And this seems to me preferable for several reasons: in the first
place, so far as I understand Pasternak's view of poetry as essentially
musical, this tends to produce poems which move always forward
and end a long way from where they began, poems which are open-
ended rather than neatly turned back upon themselves; in the second
place, as I have hinted already, Reeve's reading makes the poem
indeed a lament, full of pain and grief; and thirdly one should surely
be chary of taking from Pasternak what seems to be a peculiarly
Russian virtue, the capacity for asking massively direct Tolstoyan
questions like, 'What is life for?'

Moreover, to take this poem on Katkov's terms leaves Pasternak
wide open to an objection which is made to *Doctor Zhivago* by readers
who are otherwise sympathetic:[1] that Pasternak too readily and too
sweepingly writes off as incurably corrupt the whole world of political action and social organization. Only a mealy-mouthed humani-
tarian would object to 'No matter the world's unpitying heart' at
the point where this comes in the poem; it is a lyrical cry of defiance
from the personal fastness to which the world's ferocity has driven
the speaker. But if this were to be the statement made by the poem
as a whole (which is what Katkov's reading amounts to), one might

---

[1] See, for instance, John Strachey, *The Strangled Cry*.

legitimately object that it was inadequate and inhuman in the poet to regard the woes of the world as solved merely because he can retreat from them into an inviolable privacy. To regard the stanzas which follow as opening up dimensions beyond that act of private defiance – this is to see the writer acknowledging the inadequacy of that attitude, or at least recognizing the price that has to be paid for it.

A poem is necessarily a public document, as soon as it is published. And so, however closely this poem may correspond to passages in Pasternak's private life, it must be flawed as a poem unless it corresponds also to realities which are public and available. Those realities are experiences common to all mankind, ultimately; but in this sequence of poems there stands, between the private life of the poet and the life common to his readers, the life of the exemplary and representative man, Zhivago. And his imaginary interview with the lost Lara seems to be what we are told of, in an important passage of Chapter Fourteen. This is in the 14th section of that chapter:

> He drank vodka and he wrote about Lara, but the more he crossed out and rewrote what he had written, the more did the Lara of his poems and notebooks grow away from her living prototype, from the Lara who was Katya's mother, the Lara who was away on a journey with her daughter.
>
> The reason for this correcting and rewriting was his search for strength and exactness of expression, but it also corresponded to the promptings of an inward reticence which forbade him to expose his personal experiences and the real events in his past with too much freedom, lest he should offend or wound those who had directly taken part in them. As a result, the steaming heat of reality was driven out of his poems and so far from their becoming morbid and devitalized, there appeared in them a broad piece of reconciliation which lifted the particular to the level of the universal and accessible to all. This was not a goal which he was consciously striving for; it came of its own accord as a con-solation, like a message sent to him by Lara from her travels, like a distant greeting from her, *like her image in a dream* or the touch of her hand on his forehead, and he rejoiced at this ennobling of his verse.

I have italicized the phrase in the prose which seems to bring it closest to the experience of the poetry. But there is much here that is of more importance. In particular, 'No matter the world's unpity-ing heart' looks quite different from this vantage-point: the poet is able to say this, not only because the image of the loved woman is engraved on his heart indelibly, but because that image has become universalized so as to take up into itself all the woes of others. And thus the poet need no longer take account of the world's ruthlessness, only because he takes account continually of the world's victims, as typified and embodied in the one he loves. There is no question, after all, of withdrawal into the privately inviolate.

And indeed, if we are only attentive enough, the poem says this on its own account, without help from the prose gloss. For the point of the metaphor of the engraving on the heart (in itself a faded conceit out of common stock) is not so much the indelibility of the image as what the next quatrain goes on to say – how the image personifies 'humility', all the long-suffering meekness in existence.

One last observation. If Zhivago were a poet of flesh and blood, instead of a created fiction, one could say with some confidence what, as it is, one may only surmise – that the particular circumstances which attend the dream-image are drawn, probably at a subconscious level, from the adventitious juxtaposition in the poet's buried experience, of Lara's face with faces of stone. Chapter Thirteen is entitled 'Opposite the House of Caryatids', as if to emphasize how Lara's rooms in Yuryatin look across the street to the house with curiously carved human figures which have been described earlier. But it is in the 16th section of Chapter Nine that Zhivago remembers how Lara had responded to his attempt to break off his association with her, so as to return to his wife:

> Lara had realized how unhappy he felt and had no wish to upset him further by a painful scene. She tried to listen to him as calmly as she could. They were talking in one of the empty front rooms, tears were running down her cheeks, but she was no more conscious of them than the stone statues on the house across the road felt the rain running down their faces. She kept saying softly: 'Do as you think best, don't worry about me. I'll get over it.' She was saying it sincerely, without any false generosity, and as she did not know that she was crying, she did not wipe away her tears.

If the dream-image of Lara in the poem is running with water and condensations and melted snow, rather than relate this to any etymological pun on her name (Lara = Larissa = the sea), I would connect it with this image of an earlier attempted separation of the lovers, and with the humility of Lara's demeanour on that occasion. To make the face of flesh approximate to a face of stone acts on our imaginations so as to idealize and universalize the particular, in the way which Pasternak says that Zhivago attempted and attained.

'Christmas Star'

D.D. Obolensky has pointed out that this poem must be related to
a passage from the early autobiography *Safe Conduct*, in which Pasternak, remembering a visit to Venice, is led on from that, by no
very natural connection, to reflect on the various versions of Christmas which co-exist in his imagination:

> There is a special Christmas Tree East, the East of the pre-
> Raphaelites. There is the presentation of the starry night according
> to the legend of the worship of the Magi. There is the age-old
> Christmas relief: the top of a gilded walnut sprinkled with blue
> paraffin.

The last sentence I take to be a mannered allusion to the Christmas
of the children's party, with its traditional toys and curios. If so, the
part of the poem most directly anticipated here is the curiously affecting quatrain which begins, 'All the quiver of candle-light, all festoons'. In these four lines, as in the six which precede them, about
'a strange glamour', Pasternak is an impenitent modernist: the
strangeness of the vision is in its cubist perspective which juxtaposes
three or four incompatible series of images and landscapes. Museums
and art-collections provide one series of Christmas images, fairies
and wizards another, aspirations after peace on earth another, children and Christmas trees yet another; by locking each series in with
all the others, the poem presents a composite Christmas, a factually
impossible scene compounded of all the different Christmases available to the imagination.

This is worth insisting upon because Pasternak's revulsion from
his earlier writings at the time of *Doctor Zhivago* has been eagerly
interpreted, by those with an anti-modernist axe to grind, as a condemnation of the modern movement in European poetry by one
who has been a leading light of that movement. But 'Christmas
Star' shows that, however thoroughly by this time Pasternak was
out of love with a poetic sophistication parading itself, he was not
ready to abandon poetic structures which post-symbolist practice
had made possible. And those who interpret Pasternak's change of
heart more narrowly still, as a return to regular metres and regular
rhyme-schemes, may be assured that this version reproduces faithfully the waywardness of the original in these respects. Moreover,
in this poem as in others, the use I make of approximate and consciously imperfect rhymes goes very little further than Pasternak's
practice.

In this poem, however, the poet seems to emphasize these features
in order to achieve a deliberately rough-hewn effect. For if in certain

lines the Christmas of the children's party is evoked, and other Christmases also, the framework of the poem as a whole is what *Safe Conduct* calls 'the East of the pre-Raphaelites'. By 'pre-Raphaelites' Pasternak means, of course, not any English painters of the nineteenth century, but Italians of the fifteenth. And in the poem the placing of the Nativity in a rocky cave recalls the identical odd convention used by so-called primitives of the quattrocento, such as Ghirlandaio. This deliberately 'primitive' image calls for off-rhymes, changes of metrical pattern, and uneven blocks of lines so that the poem shall be in keeping, equally 'primitive' all through.

This is corroborated by a passage in Chapter Three of *Doctor Zhivago* which others have remarked as bearing very directly on this poem. In the 10th section of this chapter the young Zhivago, who has promised one of his friends an article on Blok for a student paper, is driving a sleigh with his future wife Tonya through the frost-bound Moscow streets. Their destination is that Christmas party at the Sventitskys' which gives a title to Chapter Three as a whole:

> It occurred to him that Blok was a manifestation of Christmas in the life and art of modern Russia – Christmas in the life of this northern city, Christmas underneath the starry skies of its modern streets and round the lighted trees in its twentieth-century drawing rooms. There was no need to write an article on Blok, he thought, all you needed do was to paint a Russian version of a Dutch Adoration of the Magi with snow in it, and wolves and a dark fir forest.

Italian or Dutch, hardly matters; what matters is the precious naïveté of a primitive artist who, undeterred by considerations of historical and geographical accuracy, makes over the landscape, the personages, and the actions of the Nativity story into terms immediately familiar to himself and his fellows. This naïveté, the vividness of apprehension not joined to any sense of needful subordination of detail, gets into the poem in, for instance, the observation that some of the Wise Men's donkeys were smaller than others. And there is a corresponding, equally poignant naïveté, but in literary not painterly terms, when angels and shepherds announce themselves with one voice to Mary; we are relied upon not to ask superfluous questions about who was the spokesman, or when and how the shepherds came to terms with their immaterial companions.

With this passage from Chapter Three we necessarily turn from considering 'Christmas Star' as a poem by Pasternak, to thinking of it as a poem by Zhivago. Does this make any difference? It does, undoubtedly; for it compels us to take seriously the possibility that this is indeed the poem which the young Zhivago imagined he might write – a poem, that is, which stands in place of an essay about Alexander Blok, in other words a poem about Blok.

One should notice first a crucial detail which establishes the poem as Zhivago's, not Pasternak's:

> Across the sheeted snow-field, mica-bright,
> Led round a hut the prints of naked feet.
> About these prints, as to flame of a candle-end
> Padded and shifted sheep-dogs in the starlight.

Are flames at candle-ends more disturbing to sheep-dogs than other kinds of flames? If not, then the simile which alludes to them seems quite gratuitous. And yet it is nothing less than Zhivago's signature to his poem. This we realize only if we have noticed how, through the sixteen chapters of prose narrative, candles have come to have for Zhivago an occult and momentous significance such as they have for no one else but Lara. Nowhere in the narrative are the clues to this sown so thickly as in the pages just before and after Zhivago's reflections about Blok and Christmas. Throughout 'Christmas party at the Sventitskys' the point about lighted candles is hammered home with an insistence almost heavy-handed. The passage about 'a Dutch Adoration of the Magi' goes on:

> As they drove through Kamerger Street Yury noticed that a candle had melted a patch in the icy crust on one of the windows. *Its light seemed to fall into the street as deliberately as a glance, as if the flame were keeping a watch on the passing carriages and waiting for someone.*
>
> 'A candle burned on the table, a candle burned...' he whispered to himself – the confused, formless beginning of a poem; he hoped that it would take shape of itself, but nothing more came to him.

As we know from a few pages before, this candle which Zhivago sees was burning in the room where Lara had just given a crucial interview to her future husband, and at the end of the novel Zhivago's dead body lies in the same room. Pasternak is so little concerned with verisimilitude in the normal tradition of the realistic novel, that on the contrary he contrives such webs of unlikely coincidence specifically so as to advise the reader not to look for the significances of realism, but for meanings of another kind. And the meaning of 'candle' is surely spelt out for us in the sentence I have ventured to italicize. That meaning is, or is to become, extremely important – as appears from the way in which, not just 'Christmas Star', but another poem also, 'Winter Night' (its refrain here anticipated), leans heavily and explicitly on these sentences of the prose.

And yet the significance of 'flame of a candle-end' *is* realistic, in this important sense: that without something of the sort there could not be a faithful and complete account of what poetic composition is, and how it works. One of Pasternak's aims in *Doctor Zhivago* is to give such an account. And he gives it in the only way possible for exact fidelity and comprehensiveness – that is, by a working model; by making Zhivago a poet and showing how his poems come to him. Zhivago, like other poets, is influenced by some images of a private, even obsessive kind; and 'candle' is the example which Pasternak endows him with, of images of this kind. By a brilliant finesse Pasternak is able to show his poet drawing on associations of a wholly private kind, and at the same time to avoid the impenetrable obscurity which normally is inescapable in such writing.

The point to be made in calling the candle-end Zhivago's signature is that this reference establishes 'Christmas Star' as the work of a certain man who envisaged an account of Blok in the shape of a primitive Nativity-painting. And this means that the presence of Alexander Blok, in this poem where he is never named, is something to be looked for.

To establish his presence beyond cavil would require an exhaustive essay on Blok, his life, and his writings. One may think first of Blok's iconoclastic and glancing treatment of a Scriptural theme in his most famous poem, 'The Twelve', where the twelve apostles figure as a patrol of Bolshevik riflemen roaming the streets during the Revolution. But Zhivago could have known of this poem neither at the time of the Sventitskys' party, nor when he wrote 'Christmas Star'. In Chapter Fourteen we learn that 'Christmas Star' had been composed before Zhivago's return to Varykino, though it was there first committed to paper (and modified in the process). On the other hand Blok's *Italian Verses* (1909) include both an Annunciation and an Assumption; and it may have been these that Zhivago had in mind when he wrote his Nativity for Blok's sake. In the second place 'the wind over the steppe' should be compared with 'The Wind. Four Fragments about Blok', among Pasternak's poems published after *Doctor Zhivago*. What these four splendid lyrics appear to say is that Blok was no 'civic' or 'moral' poet, to be taken up into a national tradition, but amoral as the wind, as ambiguous as that natural force, and incidentally as destructive.

For this, it seems to me, is the most important aspect of Blok to be remembered in this connection: the extent to which his achievement, in other poems besides 'The Twelve', lay in his grasp, from the start and from before the start, of the essential ambiguity in the Revolution – a convulsion as of physical nature, at once a liberating renascence and a fury of cruel destruction. Though translators have unaccountably obscured the fact by suppressing for instance the reference to arson in one of Zhivago's quatrains about the blazing of the new star, a great deal of the power in his treatment comes of his seeing the even greater historical convulsion of the Nativity just as Blok saw the Revolution, as ambiguous, at once tender and appalling. These quatrains seem to approach the point made by W.B. Yeats in 'The Second Coming' – that when the superhuman invades the human realm, all the human can say of it is that it is non-human; in consequence, from the human standpoint the superhuman will always be confused with the subhuman, the bestial with the divine.

These connections with Blok may seem tenuous. But in the first poem of the sequence, as in virtually all which follow 'Christmas Star', the office of the poet is likened to, or even identified with, the role of Christ. Seeming to see allusions to Blok in 'Christmas Star' one is only detecting the same train of feeling; with the difference that the poetic office is here filled not by Zhivago but by the greatest Russian poet of the generation before his. Moreover, what is the alternative? Is 'Christmas Star' no more than a touching and accomplished pastiche? What happens, on any other reading, to those insistences in the prose–clue about 'the life and art of *modern* Russia', 'its *modern* streets', 'its *twentieth-century* drawing rooms'? Zhivago, with of course Pasternak behind him, regards Blok as the poet who baptized Russian poetry into the present century. For Russians this was a baptism of fire as for no others. Would there be impiety, or disproportion even, in a Russian's comparing the convulsion of the Revolution with the convulsion which began at Bethlehem and ended at Calvary? Or with his seeing, in the one great Russian poet who in his maturity lived through the Revolution and came to terms with it in his art, an analogue of the Redeemer?

'Daybreak'

This is hard to translate. The baldly assertive style seems to lay claim to sublime perceptions which it does not bother to earn; more than in most of Zhivago's poems, the poetry is in the spaces between the quatrains, more than in the verses themselves.

According to George Katkov, there is Pasternak's authority for saying that the 'you' addressed in the first stanzas is Christ. Accordingly Katkov believes that the poem deals directly with what Pasternak described as his own condition following 'an illumination which came over the poet in the first months of World War II'; thereafter he described himself as 'an atheist who has lost his faith'.

Realizing the need to relate the poem not only to Pasternak's life but more immediately to Zhivago's, Katkov decides (*In the Interlude*,

tr. Kamen, p.236): 'The poem relates to the last part of Zhivago's life
... when he shared his room with the peasant painter Vasya.' This is
the period when Zhivago publishes 'his views on medicine, his defini-
tions of health and sickness, reflections on evolution and the mutation
of species, his theory of personality as the biological basis of the
organism, and thoughts about religion and history (his views had
much in common with those of his uncle and Sima)...' And bearing
heavily on this last clue, Katkov would have it that a main source for
the poem is the same as that for the Magdalen poems which are to
follow – that is to say, in the 17th section of Chapter Thirteen, the
homily which, overheard by Zhivago, Sima Tuntseva delivers to Lara.

The trouble is that no one would arrive at this reading from a
study of the poem itself or in its place in the sequence. Undoubtedly
Pasternak's statement of his intentions is illuminating; but it leaves
open to question how far the intentions have been fulfilled. For
instance, 'All night I have read your will' is inexplicable, until Pasternak's testimony reveals that what is meant is reading the Gospels;
but what reader would arrive at that solution, with nothing to go
on but what the poem itself provides?

We owe it to Pasternak, if not to Zhivago, to think that over and
above this secret meaning he provided another, more superficial,
which still hangs together and holds the attention. The first line in
itself promises a love-poem. And though it's true that the next few
lines cannot be made to fit Zhivago's relations with any of the women
in his life, the piece can still be read as a love-poem all through.
Moreover I believe that this was intended by the author. For in his
autobiography *Safe Conduct* Pasternak invokes many of the distinctive images of this poem, when speaking of the effects of a youthful
love-affair in Marburg:

> I was surrounded by transformed objects. Something never
> before experienced crept into the substance of reality. Morning
> recognized my face and seemed to have come to be with me and
> never to leave me... Gradually the town began to move. Carts,
> bicycles, vans and trains began slithering in all directions. Above
> them like invisible plumes serpentined human plans and designs.
> They wreathed and moved with the compression of very close
> allegories which are understood without explanations. Birds,
> houses and dogs, trees and horses, tulips and people became shor-
> ter and more disconnected than when childhood had known
> them. The laconic freshness of life was revealed to me, it crossed
> the street, took me by the hand and led me along the pavement.[1]

[1] *Safe Conduct*, tr. by Beatrice Scott. *Boris Pasternak. The Collected Prose Works*, ed.
by S. Schimanski (London, 1945), pp.76-7.

Love for a woman, love for God...It would be foolish to think that if the poem is about the one, it cannot be about the other. On the contrary there is a massive tradition of regarding the one as a paradigm of the other, especially when it leads, as it does in the poem, into the widest possible dispersal of sympathy among all modes of being. And thus there is no need to exclude George Katkov's observation that 'In "Daybreak" the import of the New Testament as a whole for modern metropolitan urban conditions is revealed.'

'The Miracle'

It is disconcerting that when Zhivago gives this account of a specific instance of that 'wonder-working' which he referred to in the poem 'August', the miracle he chooses to write of is not a blessing but a curse, where the wonder-working power expresses itself not in creation but in annihilation. To be sure the poem makes provision for the instructive moral which commentators draw from the corresponding passages in Scripture: a sterile self-sufficiency is always evil, we must fructify in help and sympathy for others. But important as this precept is in Zhivago's scheme of things, it would be wrong, I believe, to think this is the point of the whole poem: for these are religious or metaphysical poems, only incidentally ethical. And in the sequence as a whole, considered as a sustained religious meditation, one reason for 'The Miracle' is not hard to find: for the disconcerting shock it gives should prepare us for the note of sombre exultation at the end of 'Gethsemane', and thus of the whole sequence, where Christ, the doomed god, glories in his unimpaired omnipotence. In other words, the God whom Zhivago gives us is at least as much the God of the Old Testament as of the New: the emphasis at the end is far more on a God of Power than a God of Love. And this is one way to explain why he chose, from among the miracles in the New Testament, this incident of the barren fig-tree, where Christ's action has a sort of primitive ferocity.

However, the poem departs in interesting ways from the account given, for instance, by St Mark. In the first place, where Mark puts Christ in the company of his disciples, Zhivago insists that on the contrary Christ is utterly alone. And secondly, whereas in the Gospel Christ is angered by the fig-tree because he is hungry, in Zhivago's account Christ's motive is harder to define: the hunger which the fig-tree cannot allay is metaphysical.

On a casual reading it may seem that the fig-tree calls down the divine wrath because it embodies all that is desolate and sterile in the wastelands about it, and because this reflects with intolerable

exactness the desolation and sterility in the traveller's soul. It is true
that images of sterility and stagnation are powerfully accumulated
in the first lines of the poem. But on the other hand the air is balmy
over the wilderness, and it is not so much a wilderness as not to
harbour lizards and (perhaps the clinching point) it has in it the
sounds of gushing springs and running streams. It is not for nothing
that these images of refreshment are suddenly introduced before the
curse is uttered. They make it clear that the sterility which is exter-
minated is only partly outside the observer's mind, he brings most
of it with him and projects it upon his surroundings; a landscape of
the mind is imposed upon, and supplants, the landscape of actuality.
And this makes the story more barbaric than ever, the 'moral' even
less acceptable. The unfortunate fig-tree is blasted much less for any
sterility it has in itself than for a sterility in the squinting eye of the
beholder. The tree is punished out of the same childish petulance
with which, when we are out of sorts, we slash at dandelion-heads
with a walking-stick. And what are we to make of this?

   We begin to make something of it only if we attend to the untranslatable ambiguity in the word *chudo* which gives this poem its title.
The word means 'miracle'; but also, more generally, 'wonder',
'marvel'. Elsewhere in the sequence, though pre-eminently here,
Zhivago exploits this play of meaning in the word so as to talk, at
one and the same time, of the miraculous capacities of God and of
the prodigy of the poet's gift of utterance which is, so we are made
to infer, no less miraculous. This ambiguity in the 'wonder-working'
of an earlier poem should have prepared us to see, in the solitary
traveller here, a human poet no less than an incarnate God. This
poet looks to the landscapes about him (which might well be the
landscapes of politics as well as physical scenery) to take him out of
himself and cure his sterility by making the act of poetic utterance
possible. The landscape fails him: the lizards do not move him for
instance to 'bless them unawares'; of them, and the springs and
streams about them, he might say, with Coleridge in another place,
'I see, not feel, how beautiful they are'. Focusing upon the fig-tree
all his anger at this unhelpfulness, he after all does better than slash
at a dandelion-head. For his anger finds utterance; and it does not
matter that the utterance is a curse, not a blessing. For 'a miracle is
a miracle, a miracle is God'. Poetry can be made from invective.

   Coleridge, dejected because the springs of poetry had run dry in
him, uttered his state in the great poetry of 'Dejection, an Ode',
from which I have just quoted. I find it more helpful to remember
this, when considering the important penultimate line, than to follow George Katkov when he says: 'Pasternak seems to think that
belief in the miracles of the New Testament differs from belief in

magic, because the miracle in Christian interpretation is a revelation of God's providence which occurs, not at the moments of our strength, but at times when we are dismayed and go astray.' It is surely the miracle-worker himself who is startled by the miracle when he is 'all at odds', not those he does the miracle for.

Katkov, who agrees about the ambiguity of 'miracle', goes on to say, 'There can be no doubt that Pasternak believed his own poetry to be "miraculous" in that sense.' This is surely true. But it is important to get the emphasis right. For Pasternak has been accused of 'surrendering to the irrational'; and it is important not to seem to credit him with belief in Gothic fancies such as sometimes trapped his contemporary Yeats into a sort of half-belief. Of course, to those whose idea of rationality is bounded by the anti-religious and anti-poetic rationalism of the Enlightenment, Pasternak does indeed embrace the irrational. But, I take it, he does not believe that, because he is a poet, he can blast fig-trees or raise the dead or make the blind see – except metaphorically. Metaphorically he can do all these things; for within the created world of a poem the creator's fiat is absolute. In the poem he is indeed free of natural law, free to bless and to curse at his will. He can for instance write a book, partly in prose, partly in verse, in which he takes it for granted that the Russian Revolution did more harm than good. If that book creates a world which hangs together, is recognizably close to the world we live in, and strongly moves our sympathies, there is no appeal against the creator's verdict on the Revolution. So long as the reader inhabits the world of that book, the Russian Revolution is for him precisely what the creator of that book decreed that it should be. And the anger and dismay which *Doctor Zhivago* caused to the heirs of that Revolution show how impossible it is to overlook or to take lightly the sense in which indeed the poet is a miracle-worker, the act of poetic utterance miraculous. 'A miracle is a miracle, a miracle is God.' Believing along these lines, Pasternak is echoing a Renaissance thinker like Philip Sidney, for whom poetry is the noblest human activity because it is that activity in which man, as 'maker', most nearly approaches the creativeness of God.

What is meant by the poet's being in his poem freed from the laws of nature is made clear by a curious and arresting passage in the 7th section of Chapter Twelve, 'Iced Rowanberries'. Zhivago at this point, still in the *tayga* with the partisans, is listening to a long rambling monologue by the woman Kubarikha, addressing the bystanders after she has claimed to charm infection out of a sick cow. Zhivago realizes that some of Kubarikha's gibberish, about a woman's shoulder being cut open by a sword to reveal 'a measure of corn or a squirrel or a honeycomb', is 'the opening passage of an ancient chronicle, either of Novgorod or Ipatyevo, but so distorted by the errors of copyists and the repetitions of sorcerers and bards that its original meaning had been lost'. Before long he is launched upon a grotesque day-dream about Lara's left shoulder being thus opened. But first he reflects:

> No deep and strong feeling, such as we may come across here and there in the world, is unmixed with compassion. The more we love, the more the object of our love seems to us to be a victim. Occasionally, a man's compassion for a woman exceeds all measure, and his imagination removes her from the realm of possible happenings and places her in situations which are never encountered in life. He sees her at the mercy of the surrounding air, of the laws of nature and of the centuries which preceded her.

If the man in question is a poet, he saves the loved woman from the rule of the laws of nature by placing her in a poem 'in situations which are never encountered in life'. A clear example of this in the poems of Zhivago is 'Rendezvous', where the dream-image of Lara comes to us first as very precisely 'at the mercy of the surrounding air' (with snow in her hair, all over her clothes, and even in her mouth), and is gradually rescued from natural law by the supernatural power of the poetic utterance about her. Once again, there is nothing of magical mumbo-jumbo about this contention: almost any European poem since Rimbaud shows the poet breaking free of natural law, and, by juxtaposition of images, creating perhaps a time in which Nineveh and New York are contemporaneous. The miraculous power of poetry is thus not an article of faith, but a plain statement of observable fact.

If the last stanza of 'The Miracle' may thus rely to some extent on Zhivago's recollections of the cow-healer Kubarikha, much more of the poem, I suggest, draws its images from a later episode of Zhivago's life, which provided material also for the poem 'Indian Summer'. This is in the 2nd section of Chapter Fifteen, where Zhivago is toiling slowly back to Moscow through countryside ravaged and depopulated by Civil War. To be sure, that country is by no means sterile; on the contrary it is strangled by its own fertility, now that no people are left to crop it – and, as I have argued, this is the central matter of 'Indian Summer'. On the other hand the image of the sun scorching the herbage is common to both poems and to the passage of prose; and there is what I am prepared to think a deliberate echo, in 'a few clouds raggedly followed':

> Everything was in ceaseless, slow, measured movement: the flowing river, the road running to meet it and Yury walking along

the road in the same direction as the clouds. Nor were the rye fields motionless. Something stirred in them, something which filled them from end to end with a small incessant rummaging and which nauseated Yury.

Never had there been such a plague of mice. They had bred in unbelievable multitudes such as had never been seen before. They scurried over Yury's face and hands and inside his sleeves and trousers at night when he was caught by darkness and forced to spend the night in the open; they raced across the road by day, gorged and teeming, and turned into squeaking, pulsing slush when they were trodden underfoot.

The nausea that Zhivago feels for the mice, nature-poet as he is, is the nearest he comes to uttering a curse on the natural order. Moreover he is alone, travelling to the town, Moscow, where he will foregather with those who figure as his by no means staunch disciples, Gordon and Dudorov. (The passage immediately precedes Zhivago's meeting with a disciple who for a time is more loyal, Vassya Brykin.) One other reason why 'The Miracle' deserves its place is that it reveals Zhivago as a nature-poet certainly, with love and veneration for the natural creation; but, unlike a nature-poet such as Wordsworth, he realizes that his art of utterance ultimately transcends the natural and must, if necessary, do it violence.

'Earth'

The best note to this poem is a comment by Henry Gifford (*Poetry*, May 1962, p.125): 'Pasternak and his contemporaries may have been restless as were poets everywhere half a century back. They tried new metres; they revolutionized rhyme; they extended the language. However, their situation wasn't that of American and English poets: they had not to face the full urban paralysis of feeling and language. The Russian city, even today, keeps touch with nature.' This is not just what Zhivago's poem takes for granted; it is also, in part, what his poem says.

But another thing it seems to say is that in a society vowed to thorough-going renovation, to optimistic spring-cleaning, the poet's task is to recollect how there is a tragic, irremediable dimension to life – a dimension which the non-human Creation reminds him about. For the images appear to come to Zhivago out of the period of his short-lived enthusiasm for the Revolution, when he was at Melyuzeyevo. It was there (Chapter Five, section six) that 'the houses and fences huddled closer together in the dusk'. And it is there (section eight) that Zhivago expatiates to the Lara he as yet hardly knows:

Last night I was watching the meeting in the square. It was an astonishing sight. Mother Russia is on the move, she can't stand still, she's restless and she can't find rest, she's talking and she can't stop. And it isn't as if only people were talking. Stars and trees meet and converse, flowers talk philosophy at night, stone houses hold meetings. It's like something out of the Gospels, don't you think? Like in the days of the apostles...

Lara responds, 'I know what you mean about stars and trees holding meetings. I understand that. It's happened to me too.' But Lara (and this is surely central to the irreplaceable value she comes to have for Zhivago) has lived in the tragic dimension since long before. For Zhivago expostulates: 'And then, in the midst of all this general rejoicing, I come up against your puzzlingly sad, absent look...' (At this point in the novel Lara and 'Mother Russia' are almost the one same thing.)

Thus the friends with whom Zhivago foregathers at the end of this poem are not I think his friends of Melyuzeyevo days, but rather (to take Henry Gifford's hint) his fellow-poets of a later period in Moscow. And their task, so the poem seems to say, is to insist, continually and unseasonably, on the irremediable because tragic aspect of human life.

'The Bad Days'

This is a poem about Jesus; to take its place in the sequence it ought to be about Zhivago too. But at first it's not clear how Zhivago comes into it.

To be sure, there is a plain general resemblance between the atmosphere evoked by the poem and that established in the later sections of Chapter Thirteen, when Zhivago and Lara, re-united after Zhivago's escape from Siberia, are forced to move from Yuryatin to Varykino by the thickening air of suspicion, investigation and terror in the Urals town. Thus, what corresponds to the first four stanzas of the poem is Zhivago saying to Lara, in the 16th section of Chapter Thirteen:

> You know it looks as if I'll be forced to resign from my job. It's always the same thing – it happens time and again. At first everything is splendid. – 'Come along. We welcome good, honest work, we welcome ideas, especially new ideas. What could please us better? Do your work, your research, struggle, carry on.'
>
> Then you find in practice that what they mean by ideas is nothing but words – claptrap in praise of the revolution and the regime. I'm sick and tired of it. And it's not the kind of thing I'm good at.

Certainly we should think that it is from his memory of this experience that Zhivago wrote the first four stanzas of his poem. Less
certainly the sixth stanza may well derive from Lara's note, a few
sentences later, about the second of the 'certain regular stages' which
the regime goes through:

> Then comes the second stage. The accent is all on the dark forces,
> the false sympathizers, the hangers-on. There is more and more
> suspicion – informers, intrigues, hatreds. You are perfectly right
> that we are entering on the second stage.

And undoubtedly relevant is Komarovsky of all people, in the 1st
section of Chapter Fourteen, telling Zhivago: 'You are a mockery
of that whole world, an insult to it.'

But, while we must stop short of looking for the one-to-one
correspondences of allegory, I think we have the right to look for
more than this general analogy. We have the right to ask, for instance:
What was Zhivago's temptation in the desert? And part of the answer
might be in the 3rd section of Chapter Thirteen, where Zhivago is
reading the proclamations posted on the House of Caryatids in
Yuryatin. He reflects:

> Only once in his life had this uncompromising language and
> single-mindedness filled him with enthusiasm. Was it possible
> that he must pay for that one moment of rash enthusiasm all his
> life by never hearing, year after year, anything but these unchang-
> ing, shrill, crazy exclamations and demands, ever more lifeless,
> meaningless, and unfulfillable as time went by? Was it possible
> that in one short moment of over-sensitive generosity he had
> allowed himself to be enslaved for ever?

Of course it was not possible, as the narrative and poems alike show.
And in fact Zhivago's initial sympathy with the Revolution is so
short-lived, and sketched in so lightly, that while it may present
itself to him as a surrender, to the reader it figures only as a sway
towards a temptation which is then vigorously resisted.

In any case, as J.M. Cohen rightly says,[1] 'Pharisaism, not the
Revolution, was the enemy, because it was remorselessly destructive
of creative energy.' And the passage just quoted is only one of many
in which Pharisaism is seen as above all, whether in its Revolutionary
guise or some other, a vice of language, of language that is lifeless,
meaningless, shrill. Unless we recognize with Pasternak that the
shrillness of language pulled loose of meaning is a vice which infects
every department of corporate life, we shall see his and Zhivago's

[1] J.M. Cohen, 'Servant to the Ages'. *The Spectator*, 6 April 1962.

apotheosis of the poet, the artist in language, as merely megalo-
mania, or else as the symptom of a historical phase of thinking on
these matters which went out for us with Oscar Wilde. And this
would be to evade the challenge of *Doctor Zhivago* altogether.

But finally, what in Zhivago's experience corresponds to the miracle alluded to in the last stanza? Both Eugene Kayden and Henry
Kamen, in their versions of this poem, name Lazarus in the last line;
where Zhivago's poem does not name him at all. To name him is
to make the poem wholly about Jesus, not about Zhivago at all.
And it is to shut out all memory, for instance, of a passage from the
2nd section of Chapter Nine:

> I love the warm, dry winter breath of the cellar, the smell of
> earth, roots and snow that hits you the moment you raise the
> trap, as you go down in the early hours before the winter dawn,
> a weak, flickering light in your hand.

It is true that the word for 'cellar' is not the same – in the prose
it is 'pogreb', in the verse 'podval';[1] but on the other hand there is
an echo in the word for a candle going out – in the prose 'oogasnoot',
in the verse 'gasla'. And the point of recollecting the prose is that
there the cellar which Zhivago descends to is used for the storing
of vegetables through the winter, of twenty sacks of potatoes, of
'two barrels of salted cucumbers and two of sauerkraut prepared by
Tonya', of 'carrots buried in dry sand, and radishes and beet and
turnips'.

For 'resurrection' or, as I translate it here, 'the risen', is not used
by Zhivago solely to refer to human life. On the contrary it is as
often as not vegetable life that he has first in mind. We have already
encountered in the sequence one poem, 'Indian Summer', which
turns wholly on the business of bottling and pickling and preserving;
and when, in the last section of Chapter Six, the elusive and omni-
potent Yevgraf advises Tonya to retreat to the Urals, he speaks
particularly of the vegetables she will grow there, and of the valuable
earthiness of that environment.

How crucial this is comes out when J.M. Cohen can assert (*The
Spectator*, loc. cit.) that Pasternak sees Christ 'not in His office of
Redeemer – for with this aspect of Christ's mission Pasternak, being

---

[1] 'Podval', however, occurs elsewhere in the prose, and in a context not without
significance. This is in the third section of Chapter Seven, where Zhivago and his
father-in-law are allowed for the first and last time into one of the state stores reserved
for the privileged. This is in a cellar: 'They came out of the vault intoxicated, not by
the mere thought of food, but by the consciousness that they too were of use in the
world and did not live in vain, and had deserved the praise and thanks which Tonya
would shower on them at home.' This too is the experience of a sort of 'resurrection'.

by birth a Jew, did not identify himself – but in that of the Suffering Servant, prefigured in Isaiah'. Pasternak's Christ is certainly the Redeemer to the extent that he is repeatedly associated, or even identified, with earth and growth from the earth, for instance in 'In Holy Week' and at the end of 'Magdalene II' as well as here. The act of preserving vegetable life, through from autumn to spring, is an exact, homely image for the Redeemer's promise of resurrection from the grave. The autobiography, *Safe Conduct*, published in 1931, shows how constant for Pasternak was the association of Resurrection with vegetable life stored in cellars. The subject of this ornate prose by the younger Pasternak is the cellar of a florist and the scent of the flowers stored there:

> Their sweet never-coughed-through breath filled the wide rim of the trapdoor from the cellar's depths. They covered one's chest with a kind of wooded pleurisy. This scent reminded one of something and then slipped away, duping one's consciousness. It seemed that a conception about the earth which the spring months composed on the theme of this scent, encouraged them to return year by year, and that the sources of the Greek belief in Demeter were somewhere very near at hand.[1]

'Magdalene I'

I have been compelled in my translation to take more liberties than I like, notably with the order of images inside each stanza.

The most obvious source for this poem in Zhivago's experience is the conversation he overhears, in the 17th section of Chapter Thirteen, between Sima Tuntseva and Lara. This is less a conversation than a monologue or informal homily by the eccentric Sima, on the liturgical texts for Easter in the Orthodox Church. Two passages are particularly relevant. The first is where Sima says:

> It has always interested me that Mary Magdalene is mentioned on the very eve of Easter, on the threshold of the death and resurrection of Christ. I don't know the reason for it, but this reminder seems to me so timely at the moment of his taking leave of life and before he takes it up again. Now look at the way the reminder is made – what genuine passion there is in it and what a ruthless directness.

Passion and ruthless directness are what the translator finds in the poem, and must do his best to reproduce in English. However,

---

[1]   *Safe Conduct*, tr. Beatrice Scott. *Boris Pasternak. The Collected Prose Works*, ed. Stefan Schimanski (London, 1945), p.59.

Zhivago's poem takes for its point of departure a more specific observation by Sima, on a particular passage from the liturgy, in which the Magdalen must be imagined as speaking:

> Again she grieves in a terribly tangible way over her past and over the corruption which it rooted in her, so that every night, it comes to life in her once more. 'The flaring up of lust is to me like night, the dark, moonless zeal of sin.'

The terrible tangibility is certainly taken over and pushed even further by this poem which moves from one image of squalid prostitution to another. In the shocking and extremely powerful image of Eternity as the harlot's client (the word is 'vechnost', which has ominous overtones of 'oblivion', to qualify the more consolatory ring of English 'eternity'), this word 'eternity' should not be narrowed down to merely a name for Christ; yet since Christ to any sort of Christian embodies eternity, undoubtedly at one level of apprehension the harlot's customer is Christ himself, perhaps in a quite literal and physical sense. And thus in the last stanza, though the expressions 'between my knees' and 'strain into my body' doubtless build up in the first place a traditional statuesque image, of the Marys cradling and comforting the body of Christ as it is brought down from the cross, they cannot help but carry also a defiantly erotic meaning; and this means that there may even be deliberate phallic overtones to the reference to the shaft of the cross. This sustained ambiguity rather plainly has something to do with a digression which Sima makes in her homily, on the ambiguity of the Russian word 'strast', an ambiguity to which fortunately there is an exact analogy in English, between the theological and the erotic sense of the word 'passion'. Sima at this point is confessing her lack of sympathy for the ascetic and self-mortifying side of Christian doctrine and practice.

All the same, this element in the poem should be acknowledged only in passing. It is present but very much subordinate. As regards erotic 'passion', for instance, Sima's objection to the ascetic's fascination with it is on the score of vulgarity. And no reader of the poem can afford to ignore Lara's impatience with it when in Chapter Fifteen, bowed over Zhivago's corpse, she reflects upon their mutual love:

> It was not out of necessity that they loved each other, 'enslaved by passion', as lovers are described. They loved each other because everything around them willed it, the trees and the clouds and the sky over their heads and the earth under their feet. Perhaps their surrounding world, the strangers they met in the street, the

landscapes drawn up for them to see on their walks, the rooms in which they lived or met, were even more pleased with their love than they were themselves.

What saves Pasternak's narrative from the trite tastelessness of the *'grande passion'* is this insistence that the pleasure his lovers took in each other spilled over on to (the progression is significant) first, other people, then landscapes and the natural, and last, utilitarian artefacts like 'rooms'.

It is more important to realize that this is the point in the sequence of poems at which the identification of Zhivago with Christ is made inescapable.[1] To put it more exactly, since the poem is Zhivago's rather than Pasternak's, this is the point where Zhivago brings himself to face the possibility of this identification, and to take on the responsibility of it. In the immediately preceding poems, 'The Miracle', 'The Earth', and 'The Bad Days', the reader has seen Zhivago's experience and Christ's experience steadily converging; and I think we should believe that the fact of this convergence dawns on Zhivago himself only as it dawns on his reader. It is something which he finds harder and harder not to recognize; and in the Magdalen poems he recognizes the fact and all its implications. He recognizes and accepts his own identity with Christ by recognizing how inevitable, from Lara's point of view, is her own identity with Mary Magdalene. This has been abundantly prepared for in the prose narrative, perhaps nowhere more explicitly than in the third section of Chapter Fourteen, where Lara says, 'Yury, darling, you are my strength and my refuge, God forgive me the blasphemy.' Undoubtedly we should take it that this experience, of being addressed in words which had been addressed to Christ, is one of the things which enable Zhivago to write this poem. What need he had of all the help he could get, will emerge if we consider that the poem is a prophetic vision by Zhivago of what Lara will feel when she bows above his own dead body. For this is indeed the case: the poem describes much the same arc of feeling as Lara has experienced in the 15th and 16th sections of Chapter Fifteen. For instance, the only adequate gloss on the last stanza is surely this, from the account of Lara's feelings when she was alone with Zhivago's corpse:

This it was that had brought them happiness and liberation in those days. Knowledge, not from the head, but warm knowledge

---

[1]   In *Literaturnaya Gazeta*, 25 October 1958, five Russian critics pointed out that 'Zhivago's entire path through life is consistently likened to "the Lord's passion" in the Gospels'. I cannot agree with D.D. Obolensky (in *Slavonic and East European Review*, December 1961) that there is 'some exaggeration' in this claim.

imparted to each other, instinctive, immediate.

Such knowledge filled her now, a dark, indistinct knowledge of death, a preparedness for death which removed all helplessness in its presence. It was as if she had lived twenty lives, and had lost Yury countless times, and had accumulated such experience of the heart in this domain that everything she felt and did beside this coffin was exactly right and to the point.

Once Mary Magdalene is identified with Lara, a whole new series of references from the prose are taken up into Zhivago's poem. For instance, the guilt and shame which Lara feels when alone with the dead Zhivago is not at all for sexual promiscuity and abandonment in her past, but (as we learn later) for having deserted the child she had by Zhivago. (At the risk of being schematically allegorical in my reading, I am prepared to think that this lost child may 'stand for' the earlier poems by Pasternak which we know he repudiated with contumely by the time he wrote *Doctor Zhivago*.) On the other hand the narrative has by no means shirked from indicating that Lara is lustful. The power and conviction of Lara's portrayal as early as Chapter Two comes from the acknowledgement that when she was seduced in adolescence this was no accident, that something in her responded to the voluptuary in her seducer: 'A tired smile puckered her eyes and loosened her lips, but in answer to his amused glance she gave him a sly wink of complicity.' And in the 5th section of the next chapter we are told explicitly how she could lose herself in 'the nightmare of sensuality which terrified her whenever she awoke from it'. It is these touches which make of Lara's seduction something more interesting and credible, and thus more affecting, than the stereotype of the pure and passive virgin cruelly violated. One might agree with Stuart Hampshire (in *Encounter*, November 1958) that 'The villain is an abstract sketch of bourgeois corruption', but certainly not when he adds, 'and the story of his relation with the heroine is mere melodrama'.

In Chapter Thirteen the point is made all over again that there is something in Lara which responds to Komarovsky, her original seducer. In the 12th section of this chapter Zhivago gets Lara to acknowledge that this is so:

He is the man of whom I shall always be incurably, insanely jealous.

How can you say such a thing? Don't you see, it isn't just that I don't love him, I despise him.

Can you know yourself as well as that? Human nature is so mysterious and so full of contradictions. Perhaps there is something in your very loathing of him that keeps you bound to him more surely than to any man whom you love of your own free will, without compulsion.

What a terrible thing to say! And as usual, the way you put it makes me feel that this thing, monstrous and unnatural as it is, is perhaps true...

We must surely think that if Zhivago had not wrung this admission out of Lara he would not have started a poem which is put as much into her mouth as into Mary Magdalene's, by making her confess to 'the flaring up of lust... the dark, moonless zeal of sin'.

In the sequence of these poems, Zhivago's identifying of himself with Christ depends upon, and is validated by, the identification of Lara with the Magdalen. And this means that there is at least one other beam of light which must be allowed to fall from the prose narrative on this poem. For what is it in Zhivago's death which Lara, as the Magdalen figure, recognizes as divine? In the 16th section of Chapter Fifteen Lara speaks to the dead Zhivago:

Think of it! Again something just our kind, just up our street. Your going, that's the end of me. Again something big, inescapable. The riddle of life, the riddle of death, the beauty of genius, the beauty of loving...

The unexpected item in this catalogue is 'the beauty of genius'. It seems that for Lara – and so by implication for us, and for Zhivago himself – what makes Zhivago identical with Christ is above all his capacity as an artist.

'Magdalene II'

Like the first poem about the Magdalen, this too leans very heavily on the 17th section of Chapter Thirteen, where the mildly dotty Sima Tuntseva speaks to Lara about the significance of Easter in the liturgy of the Orthodox Church, with particular reference (so George Katkov says[1]) to 'a Slavonic translation of a Byzantine spiritual poet, the nun Kassia of the ninth century'. (In Chapter Fifteen we learn of Zhivago's own 'philosophy of life', adumbrated in booklets published after his return to Moscow, that 'his views had much in common with those of his uncle and Sima'.) At the same time of course the identifications of Zhivago with Christ and of Lara with Mary Magdalene are by this time so firmly established that it's impossible not to think of the point, much later in the novel,

[1]   G. Katkov, in *Pasternak. In the Interlude*, tr. by H. Kamen (paperback edn., p.133).

where Lara, alone with Zhivago's corpse, communes with him, and speaks to him.

The most relevant passage from Sima's commentary appears to be her gloss on a passage from the liturgy for either Tuesday or Wednesday of Passion Week:

> She begs Christ to accept her tears of repentance and be moved by the sincerity of her signs, so that she may dry His most pure feet with her hair – reminding Him that in the rushing waves of her hair Eve took refuge when she was overcome with fear and shame in paradise. 'Let me kiss Thy most pure feet and water them with my tears and dry them with the hair of my head, which covered Eve and sheltered her when, her ears filled with sound, she was afraid in the cool of the day in paradise.' And immediately after all this about her hair, she exclaims: 'Who can fathom the multitude of my sins and the depth of Thy judgment?' What familiarity, what equal terms between God and life, God and the individual, God and a woman!

Nothing matters here more than that last exclamation, 'What familiarity...!' For there are indications also in the vocabulary of the poem that what is aimed at is a shocking, almost brutal directness of address; and plainly the translator must try to bring this over.

Thus the woman who speaks the poem, if she is Mary Magdalene, is also Eve, and certainly she is Lara. Nor should we exclude J.M. Cohen's perception[1] that 'the repentant Magdalene seems to represent the poet's unredeemed nature: what he would in fact have been but for the consciousness of his prophetic destiny'. For, as Cohen realizes, this gives added point to the fine poignancy by which the woman's inadequacy is revealed, the stroke of genius which makes her think, when the ground trembles at the rending of the veil of the temple, that it does so out of sympathy for *her*.

But there is another passage in the novel the relevance of which has been overlooked, though it is relevant at a more profound level and therefore more crucially. This is the 15th section of Chapter Six, which deals with Zhivago's attack of typhus in Moscow, after his return from the front but before he retreats with his family to the Urals. In delirium Zhivago dreams that he is writing a poem:

> The subject of his poem was neither the entombment nor the resurrection but the days between; the title was 'Turmoil'.
>
> He had always wanted to describe how for three days the black, raging, worm-filled earth had assailed the deathless incarnation

---

[1]   J.M. Cohen, 'Servant to the Ages'. *The Spectator*, 6 April 1962.

of love, storming it with rocks and rubble – as waves fly and leap at a sea coast, cover and submerge it – how for three days the black hurricane of earth rages, advancing and retreating.

This astonishing feat of bizarre imagination gets into the last stanza of the poem in the no less astonishing word which I have translated 'ram' – the word 'stolknoot', for which the dictionary gives 'collide (with)'.

What is more important, however, about this passage from Chapter Six is that in Zhivago's delirium the writing of his poem ('He was writing what he should have written long ago and had always wished to write, but never could') is tied up very closely with the figure of his half-brother Yevgraf. And indeed, as Edmund Wilson has realized, no other passage gives clearer clues to the significance of this mysterious figure:

He knew for certain that this boy was the spirit of his death or, to put it quite plainly, that he was his death. Yet how could he be his death if he was helping him to write a poem? How could death be useful, how was it possible for death to be a help?

This of course is the very question which the Crucifixion poses for Mary Magdalene near the end of this poem. And the answer she finds in the last stanza is the answer which Zhivago finds in Chapter Six when, after talking of 'the black hurricane of earth', he passes the crisis in his illness:

Two lines kept coming into his head: *'We are glad to be near you'* and *'Time to wake up'*.

Near him, touching him, were hell, corruption, dissolution, death; yet equally near him were the spring and Mary Magdalene and life. – And it was time to awake. Time to awake and to get up. Time to arise, time for the resurrection.

The sudden introduction of the name of the Magdalen, at this stage in the novel where Lara's identification with her has not yet been established, seems to point very deliberately to this poem, and to the placing of 'resurrection' in its last line as in the last word of this section of the prose. And thus the reader who wants to reduce the poem, to internalize its drama by changing its metaphysical terms into psychological ones, can do so; he can read the Magdalen's prophetic complaint to Christ on the cross as the complaint of one of a man's selves to his other self, as he foresees, and undergoes in imagination, the ordeal of an all but mortal illness.

To the question, 'How can death be useful?' the answer which the Magdalen finds at the foot of the cross, and Zhivago in his struggle with typhus, is the enigmatic paradox, 'Life-in-Death'. What brings the unrefreshing paradox home to us, as a refreshing lived experience, is chiefly the imagery which the poet finds for it: 'So much of colony, of river-run and spinney...' But in the poem the paradox is brought home in another way, by a deliberate double-meaning:

> Who is it for in the world, so much bounty?
> So much hurt, such a capacity?
> Is there so much of being and life in the world?
> So much of colony, of river-run and spinney?

The third line may be taken to mean: 'Is there enough human life in the world to deserve that Christ be sacrificed for it?' And this is apparently how previous translators have taken the line. But along with this reading which expects the answer No, there is surely another which expects the answer Yes. For we may take the line to mean: 'Is there (qualitatively) so much of life in the world as Christ, hanging on the cross, embodies and gathers up into Himself?' Unless this second meaning is present along with the first, there is no point to 'river-run and spinney' along with 'colony'. And in fact Pasternak repeatedly shows that the resurrection which Christ brings about, as does any prophetic poet when he writes a poem, is a resurrection not just of human life but of life more generally – of a life which he images most often in vegetable life, as here with 'spinney'.

In the prose this dimension of meaning is hinted at only weakly by 'the spring' – 'yet equally near him were the spring and Mary Magdalene and life'. It is given more substance in the section which follows, and closes Chapter Six, where we learn that during Zhivago's illness his half-brother has been constantly at his bedside and has talked to Tonya, urging her to retreat to the Urals:

> I asked him what he thought, and he said it was a very good idea. We could grow vegetables and there's the forest all round. There isn't any point in dying without a struggle, like sheep.

But this has more to do with the poem called 'The Bad Days' than with either of the Magdalen poems. What is more to the point here is a reflection in the 13th section of Chapter Fifteen, on the behaviour of the flowers round Zhivago's coffin:

> The kingdom of plants can easily be thought of as the nearest neighbour of the kingdom of death. Perhaps the mysteries of transformation and the enigmas of life which so torment us are concentrated in the green of the earth, among the trees in grave-yards and the flowering shoots springing from their beds. Mary Magdalene, not at once recognizing Jesus risen from the grave, took Him for the gardener.

'Gethsemane'

Coming as it does after the two poems on Magdalen, 'Gethsemane' can as little as those poems be considered a work of straightforward Christian piety. It is entirely possible, so far as I know, that Pasternak died a faithful son of his church; and among his last poems is one, 'In Hospital', which breathes a pure Christian devotion. But Zhivago is a different matter. Not only does he seem in the novel to embrace the noble but certainly heterodox faith of his uncle, the lapsed priest Nikolai Nikolaievich, but as a poet quite plainly Zhivago uses the Christian story as a myth, structural and archetypal, just as for instance Joyce uses the Odysseus story. The first poem in the sequence, 'Hamlet', a poem very explicitly echoed in the 6th stanza of 'Gethsemane', has established from the start that, whereas the Christian must believe the Christ-story unique and unrepeatable, Zhivago sees in it an archetypal pattern reproduced in the life of the tragic hero Hamlet and to some extent reproduced in his own life also. Lara sees herself at least once as standing in the same relation to Zhivago as the Magdalen does to Christ. And repeatedly Zhivago speaks of miracles, and wonder-working, with a careful ambiguity which has as much to do with the miracle of artistic creation as with the prodigies performed by Christ; indeed there is the same ambiguity about the very word, 'creation'. It is possible, though it would be perverse, to read all the overtly Christian poems in the sequence as celebrating the apotheosis of the heroic and martyred artist. All this surely invalidates Max Hayward's extraordinary observation (in *Encounter* for May 1958) that 'Zhivago is not a Jesus-like figure. He is more like an apostle, one of those disciples who could not keep awake during the vigil of Gethsemane...'

To be more specific, what Christ is made to say in the penultimate stanza of 'Gethsemane' seems to be quite blasphemously at odds with Christian dogma. Dogma holds, surely, that just as Christ when crucified escaped from time back into eternity, so the Crucifixion permits mortals who apprehend its significance similarly to escape the temporal dimension. Zhivago's Christ, on the contrary, goes to his crucifixion so as to be at one with the historical process, for the sake of something which works itself out wholly within time:

> See how the times turn allegorical,
> How they catch fire in very course of turning.
> In the name of the terror of their potency
> I seek the tomb in voluntary pains.

When he gives these words to Christ, Zhivago appears to be agreeing with Boris Pasternak not in the latter's Christianity but rather in what I call, not very happily perhaps, his apocalyptic Marxism. Christianity and historical determinism are perhaps reconcilable, though I think not without difficulty. In any case Pasternak, both when he writes as Zhivago and when he writes in his own character, seems to believe that at any given time there is a logic working itself out in historical events, and that no man lives so wisely and so well as he who has rightly divined whither history in his time is tending. And this is surely much nearer to a Marxist way of thinking than to the Christian way, since to the Christian one historical event in the past, the Incarnation, alone gives meaning and dignity to history; and history of itself tends nowhither, unless to the Second Coming.

I must not seem to be denying that the Jesus in the poem is indeed the historical Jesus of the gospels; or to be maintaining that on the contrary in this poem Jesus is an allegory of Zhivago. If I read *Doctor Zhivago* aright, it is not at all an allegorical work, but symbolical. And I conceive that in such a work just as Mary Magdalene can indeed be Mary Magdalene, and yet also Lara, and other women too, so Jesus can be very fully and seriously Jesus, yet also Zhivago, and also other men besides Zhivago. If so it will be quite proper, and indeed necessary, to ask such questions as: who was Zhivago's Judas? who was Zhivago's Peter? who were his disciples?

If we start by looking for Judas, what we find points, not to Zhivago as the Christ-figure, but to quite another character, and a minor one.

> With fire and sword and in the forefront Judas
> With all the treacherous kissing in his lips...

What these lines recall is a moment in the 1st section of Chapter Twelve, 'Iced Rowanberries'. The commander of the Red partisans in the tayga has used Sivobluy, one of his bodyguard, as an *agent provocateur* so as to trap the mutineers in his force. Betrayed and convicted, they are now to suffer summary execution, and as they are herded towards the precipice where they are to be shot they scream at Sivobluy:

> Judas! Christ-killer! If we are traitors, you are a traitor three times over, you dog, may you choke. You killed your lawful tsar to whom you took your oath, you swore loyalty to us and you betrayed us. Mind you kiss your devil, your Forester, before you betray him! You'll betray him all right!

Undoubtedly the force of this, and of the whole episode, is in the first place a triumph of realism, of verisimilitude: supposedly revolutionary heroes, the partisans employ against each other the most hated of all the strategies of the Tsarist secret police, the *agent*

provocateur; and when they håve nothing to lose they reveal themselves as still wholly Tsarist in sentiment. Compared with this, the
symbolical significance is only secondary. Yet it is insistent. For the
mutineers as a whole are a despicable rabble, yet they include two
better men, the old anarchists Vdovichenko and Rzhanitsky.
Rzhanitsky turns out to have secreted a revolver which, in a gesture
of furious defiance, he fires three times at the partisans ('aiming at
Sivobluy'); missing with all three shots he flings his revolver to the
ground, whereupon 'It went off a fourth time, wounding one of the
condemned men, the orderly Pachkolya, in the foot.' Here surely
is the Peter-figure, wounding the orderly in the foot as Peter cuts
off the ear of the high priest's servant.

This points to Rzhanitsky's associate, Vdovichenko, as the Christ-
figure. And sure enough:

> On the verge of the grave, Vdovichenko remained true to himself
> as he had been throughout his life. His head high, his grey hair
> streaming in the wind, he addressed Rzhanitsky as one *communard*
> to another, in a voice loud enough to be heard by all:
> 'Don't humble yourself! Your protest will not reach them.
> These new *oprichniki*, these master craftsmen of the new torture
> chambers will never understand you! But don't lose heart. History
> will tell the truth. Posterity will nail the Bourbons of the commis-
> sarocracy to a pillar of shame, it will pillory their dark deeds. We
> die as martyrs of the dawn of the world revolution. Hail, revolu-
> tion of the spirit! Hail, universal anarchy!'

Plainly, 'History will tell the truth' and 'Hail, universal anarchy!'
are Vdovichenko's ways of saying,

> See how the times turn allegorical...
> In the name of the terror of their potency
> I seek the tomb in voluntary pains.

And yet Vdovichenko counts for nothing in the story, is a marginal
character, one of the soonest forgotten.

Zhivago has no Judas. Nor has he any figure who plays Peter to
his Christ, as plainly as Rzhanitsky plays Peter to Vdovichenko.
But one might point to a Peter-figure in Vassya Brykin, the young
conscript who vanishes from the novel when he escapes from the
train which carries Zhivago to the Urals, only to reappear near the
end when Zhivago, coming back from the Urals, meets him again
in the charred ruins of his village and carries him along to Moscow.
This is told in the 3rd and 4th sections of the Conclusion; in the 5th
section we learn how Vassya learns printing and book-design, and
so produces the books which Zhivago writes, but how after a while
this disciple gradually deserts his master –

There came a time when the friendship between Yury and Vassya cooled. Vassya had developed remarkably. He no longer thought or spoke like the ragged, bare-footed, dishevelled boy from Veretenniki. The obviousness, the self-evidence of the truths proclaimed by the revolution attracted him increasingly, and Yury's talk, with its obscurities and its imagery, now struck him as the voice of error, doomed, conscious of its weakness and therefore evasive.

Yury was making calls on various government departments. He was trying to get two things: the political rehabilitation of his family and permission for them to return to Russia, as well as a foreign passport for himself and permission to fetch them from Paris.

Vassya was astonished at how lukewarm and half-hearted his efforts were. Yury seemed always to be in a hurry to believe that his efforts had failed; he spoke with too much conviction and almost with satisfaction of the futility of undertaking anything further.

Vassya's impatience with Zhivago's fatalism is surely like the state of mind in which Peter offered resistance to the mob when Jesus would not. And as Peter subsequently denied his master, so 'Vassya found fault with Yury more and more often and, although Yury did not take offence at being justly criticized, his relationship with Vassya gradually deteriorated. Finally their friendship broke up, and they parted company.' After this 'Yury gave up medicine, neglected himself, stopped seeing his friends and lived in great poverty'.

If Vassya Brykin is one of Zhivago's disciples, others are Misha Gordon and Nicky Dudorov, his boyhood friends who are entrusted with the epilogue in which we learn, twenty years after Zhivago's death, about the daughter he had by Lara. In a brilliantly realistic and penetrating passage (the 7th section of the Conclusion) we are shown how Gordon and Dudorov have had to do violence to themselves in order to come to terms with the regime. And Zhivago, at this point still alive in Moscow, perceives it also:

> To Yury the springs of their emotion and of their reasoning and the shakiness of their sympathy were as clear as daylight. But he could hardly say to them: 'Dear friends, how desperately commonplace you are – you, your circle, the names and the authorities you quote, their brilliance and the art you so much admire! The only bright and living things about you is that you are living at the same time as myself and are my friends!' – But how could anyone confess to such a thought?...

The answer is that Christ could confess to it when in 'Gethsemane' he says to his disciples who have failed him:

> You has the Lord appointed
> To live in my day...

There seems no room for doubt that when Zhivago gave these words to Christ he was voicing what he felt about Gordon and Dudorov.

What's more, in the next very brief section (the 8th), after Zhivago has disappeared, he writes to Gordon and Dudorov explaining that he has gone, as it were, into the garden to pray alone:

> He told them that in order to rebuild his life as completely and rapidly as possible, he wished to spend some time by himself, concentrating on his affairs, and that as soon as he was settled in a job and reasonably certain of not falling back into his old ways, he would leave his hiding-place and return to Marina and the children.

This explanation constitutes his 'Tarry ye here, and watch with me' – a request which they do not honour, since they immediately try to hunt him down.

That he none the less evades them is miraculous – 'Yet all the time he was living within a stone's throw, right under their eyes and noses, in the middle of the district they were combing for him' (Section 9). This is miraculous since, like all the other details of Zhivago's retreat, it is contrived by the superhuman agency of his half-brother Yevgraf. And my teasing out of sometimes tenuous parallels will be justified if it casts some light on this crucial and baffling figure, elusive and invulnerable.

Edmund Wilson is certainly right to refuse to take Yevgraf at his face value, as a realistic portrayal.[1] Pasternak has gone out of his way to make this impossible, deliberately destroying verisimilitude whenever Yevgraf makes his sparse but always momentous appearances, always as a *deus ex machina*. And plainly too it is of very great significance that Yevgraf's name in the Russian calendar means 'writer'. Mrs Lehovich, Mr Wilson's collaborator, decides that 'Yevgraf is Yury's creative genius'; and certainly this is very near to the whole truth about him. Yet if there is any substance at all to my reading of 'Gethsemane', it must appear that Yevgraf stands to Yuri Zhivago in the same relation as God the Father to God the Son. It is Yevgraf who could, who in the novel repeatedly did, dispatch 'a myriad of winged legions' to save Zhivago. This does not mean that he cannot be 'Yury's creative genius', but only that the nature of genius and of inspiration must be understood a little differently from Mr Wilson's understanding of it when he writes of Yevgraf as 'Yury's *alter*

---

[1]   Edmund Wilson, 'Legend and Symbol in *Doctor Zhivago*'. *Encounter*, June 1959.

ego, his creative, his poetic self'. What we want is a conception of poetic creativity, not as a potentiality within the person, but as a force applied to him or descending upon him from outside his personality. And this is just what we find in the 8th section of Chapter Fourteen, when Zhivago is writing his poems:

> After two or three stanzas and several images by which he was himself astonished, his work took possession of him and he experienced the approach of what is called inspiration. At such moments the correlation of the forces controlling the artist is, as it were, stood on its head. The ascendancy is no longer with the artist or the state of mind which he is trying to express, but with language, his instrument of expression. Language, the home and dwelling of beauty and meaning, itself begins to think and speak for man and turns wholly into music, not in the sense of outward, audible sounds but by virtue of the power and momentum of its inward flow. Then, like the current of a mighty river polishing stones and turning wheels by its very movement, the flow of speech creates in passing, by the force of its own laws, rhyme and rhythm and countless other forms and formations, still more important and until now undiscovered, unconsidered and unnamed.
>
> At such moments Yury felt that the main part of his work was not being done by him but by something which was above him, and controlling him: the thought and poetry of the world as it was at that moment and as it would be in the future. He was controlled by the next step it was to take in the order of its historical development; and he felt himself to be only the pretext and the pivot setting it in motion.

(Here again, in the last sentences, one notes the apocalyptic Marxism – if this is what Yevgraf is, and if he is also God the Father, it is a God who does not transcend history but on the contrary is a force within history, manifest only in the turnings round of time. It is not for nothing, perhaps, that Yevgraf's last manifestation is as a General of the Red Army in the second world war.) I conclude that Yevgraf is indeed Yury Zhivago's creative genius, but a genius seen as inhering not in the artist, but in his art and the medium of his art. That medium is language. But as the penultimate sentence makes clear, it is not narrowly the Russian language. Yevgraf is not the genius of the Russian language, nor of the Russian literary tradition; he is the genius of all language, and of the world's literature seen as a whole. After all, it could hardly be otherwise: if Yevgraf is to take the weight which the work as a whole requires him to take, he cannot be a personal, nor a national, nor even narrowly a human potency. What he must and does represent (he cannot be said to embody it, for he is not sufficiently 'present') is the creative potency of language considered as a natural force like wind or water.

The Poems of Doctor Zhivago. Manchester: MUP, 1965; New York: Barnes & Noble, 1965.

8   Parallels to Pasternak

It would be presumptuous and contradictory for us, having collected what we judge to be the best critical essays on Pasternak, to preface our selection by a critical essay of our own. That would suggest that having mastered what Tynyanov and Jakobson and Sinyavsky have to say, we can supplement, correct and synthesize them; as if we were schoolmasters and they our class of talented but still immature pupils.

What may be useful on the other hand is to take their insights, which they have expressed naturally and properly in the perspective of the Russian poetic tradition, and try to find whatever analogies there may be between that tradition as Pasternak inherited and augmented it, and the tradition of Anglo-American poetry as it was inherited and enriched by the British and American poets who were Pasternak's contemporaries. This is a sufficiently hazardous undertaking. But since there would be no point to this publication if we did not believe that Pasternak is important to readers who have no Russian, it must be true that there are bridges, if only we can find them, by which we may grope uncertainly from the poetry we know in our own language to the poetry in the unknown language of Pasternak.

I   PASTERNAK: THE EARLY COLLECTIONS[1]

At first sight, however, one is dismayed by the extent to which all the bridges are down. In respect of the early collections by which Pasternak made his name, there are in particular three areas in which misunderstanding is very likely, and yet may be avoided; three bridges which need to be repaired. They may be labelled as Sound, Symbolism and Syntax. And we may briefly consider these in turn.

It is Tynyanov in particular who shows how appreciative readers

---

[1]   *Twin in the Clouds* (1914); *Over the Barriers* (written 1914–16; published 1917); *My Sister Life* (written 1917; published 1922); and *Themes and Variations* (written 1916–22; published 1923).

of early Pasternak were enthralled by his compositions considered
as textures of sheer sound. This is at once a large stumbling-block
for Anglo-American readers. It is not that this feature is peculiarly
untranslatable, for in fact it is often possible for the translator to
create equivalent harmonies. The trouble is that in the present century many of us have been schooled either to disregard this dimension of poetry altogether, or else, more grievously, to suspect it.
We have been told to beware of poets who work upon us particularly
by means of euphony, onomatopoeia, alliteration, assonance. Ever
since I.A. Richards's *Principles of Literary Criticism* there have been
influential critics warning us that the semantic aspect of poetry must
be primary, and that the musicality of poetry can legitimately be
exploited only so as to point up and emphasize the play of meanings.
Only very lately have we begun to realize that the interplay of sound
and sense in poetry is too subtle to be schematized in this way. And
investigations of this interplay, such investigations as Tynyanov's,
still seem to us very risky:

> THE RISK: to suggest that the conquest of babble by the ear –
> to distinguish and organize, to make significant, to relate as
> experience, to name – is the origin of speech and emotion. Speech
> at this level articulates internal sensations. 'The inner voice' as a
> counterpart of the inner light. The recurrence of vowels and con-
> sonants, the tonal structure, is related to heart and alimentary
> tract in its rhythmic organization; it is expressive. It is 'moving'
> – melopoeia is the passionate system of the poem.[1]

In Pasternak's lifetime, Joyce's *Finnegans Wake* is the one ambitious
work of the English-speaking world which explores this region in
which sense grows out of sound, as much as sound grows out of
sense. The young Pasternak, on the other hand, explored this possibility constantly. In many of his early poems he dramatized 'the
conquest of babble by the ear' in search of meanings. And an American scholar, Dale L. Plank, has lately most valuably dotted the *i*s
and crossed the *t*s of Tynyanov's observation to this effect.[2]

Perhaps the poet in English who comes nearest to emulating Pasternak in this respect is Hart Crane. At any rate Hart Crane, for
instance in *White Buildings*, orchestrates his verses very voluptu-
ously. And not many English-speaking critics have been ready to
trust Crane's 'music' as the Russian critics in this volume have trusted
the music, the luxuriant clash and crackle of sheer sound, in Pasternak.

[1]   Robert Duncan, 'Notes on Poetics, Regarding Olson's Maximus', in *Agenda*, III
(Dec. 1964) vi, p.32.
[2]   Dale L. Plank, *Pasternak's Lyric: A Study of Sound and Imagery* (The Hague, 1966).

In Pasternak as in Crane the rich orchestration often goes along with synaesthesia, the mingling or deliberate muddling of appeals to the five senses. This is what Louis Zukofsky, when he writes of Crane, refers to as 'the Wagnerian ideal'.[1] And Zukofsky quotes Ezra Pound's description of this method of proceeding: 'You confuse the spectator by smacking as many of his senses as possible at every possible moment, this prevents his noting anything with unusual lucidity, but you may fluster or excite him to the point of making him receptive.' Some of Pasternak's poems seem to fluster or excite the reader into receptivity, rather than presenting him with one image at a time sharply edged and lucid. An example is 'Margarita', a poem from *Themes and Variations* (1918). British and American readers in our time are more suspicious of being flustered in this way than are for instance, French-speakers and Spanish-speakers, if only because the French and the Spanish poetic traditions have come to terms with surrealism, as the Anglo-American tradition has not.

But 'the Wagnerian ideal', as Zukofsky and Pound define it, does not account for more than a few of Pasternak's poems in which the texture of sound counts for a great deal. Apart from anything else many such poems, particularly in *My Sister Life*, are notable for sharply edged and immediately lucid images, particularly of land-scape and weather. Dale L. Plank, in painstaking analysis of several such poems, discovers that many of them 'are more densely, more consciously... organized in their sounds at first, less so as the poem progresses'.[2] In other words 'the conquest of babble by the ear' is something that happens in the course of the poem, as we move through it from first to last; the poem begins in 'babble' and ends in 'conquest'. And this brings us to the second of our broken bridges, that of 'Symbolism', specifically, of Pasternak's relation to the French *symboliste* poets. For Plank points out very justly that in the case of poems which progress in this way,

> We may assume that the poem's composition proceeded accord-ing to the plan described as follows by Valéry:
>> If I am questioned; if anyone wonders (as happens sometimes quite peremptorily) what I 'wanted to say' in a certain poem, I reply that I did not *want to say* but *wanted to make*, and that it was the intention of *making* which *wanted* what I said....
>> As for the *Cimetière marin*, this intention was at first no more than a rhythmic figure, empty, or filled with meaningless syl-lables, which obsessed me for some time....

[1] Louis Zukofsky, 'American Poetry 1920–1930' (1930), in *Prepositions* (1967) p.131.
[2] Plank, op. cit. p.26.

Russia had had its own Symbolist school of poets. For that matter Valeri Bryusov, himself an ex-Symbolist, recorded that as late as 1922 self-styled 'Symbolists' were advertising public readings of their poems, as were acmeists, futurists, expressionists, neo-classicists, realists, and neo-realists, neo-romantics, and comically many others.[1] And the Russian Symbolists were aware of having some intentions in common with the French *symbolistes*, though the Russian school and the French came to stand for such different things that the common title 'Symbolist' is misleading. Pasternak, however, if we except an early and not very decisive connection with Centrifuga, a group of moderate Futurists, never aligned himself with any consciously instituted school, and the things he has in common with French *symboliste* poets (Mr Plank convincingly finds parallels with Mallarmé and Verlaine as well as Valéry) are to be thought of as 'parallels', not in terms of derivations, allegiances or influences. Certainly Pasternak could never have subscribed to Valéry's categorical insistence that Art is superior to Nature. Quite the contrary, indeed, as we shall see. On the other hand in his autobiography *Safe Conduct* (1931) he declared something that Valéry would have subscribed to, when he wrote: 'The clearest, most memorable and most important thing in art is its coming into being, and the world's best works, while telling of the most diverse things, are in fact narrating their own birth.' And Plank shows how poem after poem by Pasternak is like Valéry's *Cimetière Marin* or Mallarmé's *Prose pour Des Esseintes* in having for subject nothing but its own way of coming to birth, sustaining itself, and drawing to a close.

Unless I misunderstand T.S. Eliot's 'Love Song of J. Alfred Prufrock', that poem is another of the same kind, as are the *Four Quartets* also. And indeed Eliot was so explicit about his kinship with the French *symbolistes* – Laforgue in his youth, Valéry in his maturity – that there is no excuse for Anglo-American readers when they find the *symboliste* poetic bizarre and sterile. Unfortunately, 'aestheticism' is a word of such ill omen in modern English usage, and a term which cloudily comprehends so much, that we commonly dismiss out of hand any poem which is related to 'life' so indirectly, so far below the surface, as are the poems written in the *symboliste* tradition. In order to save Eliot from the imputation of Art for Art's Sake, our philistinism has distorted him by insisting on looking for help with his poems anywhere but where he pointed, to France. And it is likely enough that we shall try to do the same with Pasternak. Accordingly it needs to be said that in Pasternak's poetry, no less in

[1]   Valeri Bryusov, 'Vchera, sevodnya i zavtra v russkoi poezii', in *Pechat' i Revolyutsiya*, VII (1922) pp.38–67.

his theory of poetry as we find it in Section VII of *Safe Conduct*, there is a marked strain of what the English-speaking reader will take to be haughty aestheticism.

The musicality of *symboliste* poetry is not always a matter of what I have called 'orchestration'. Valéry mocks any attempt to define *symbolisme* by pressing the notion of 'symbol', and declares instead that what defines it is 'the common intention of several groups of poets (otherwise mutually inimical) to "reclaim their own from Music"'.[1] And the context makes clear that Valéry has in mind far more than patternings of sound, important as that is to *symboliste* poetry and to all poetry. Even Verlaine, when he declared 'De la musique avant toute chose', may have intended to stress, along with orchestration of sounds, the *continuity* of music, its way of never stopping but to start again. In this way *symboliste* poetry, notably in Valéry as earlier in Baudelaire, is as much concerned with the unsounded rhythms of syntax, the swerving and coiling and unwinding of the poetic sentence, as with the sounded rhythms that are governed by prosody. And this is the third of the bridges that need to be built or rebuilt if we are to cross from the world of our poetry to the world of Pasternak. To Mayakovsky, according to Ehrenburg in his memoirs, it seemed in 1923 that Pasternak's poetry manifested 'application of a dynamic syntax to the revolutionary task'. And to Yevgeni Zamyatin writing in the same year on Pasternak's stories in prose (*Russkoye Iskusstvo*, II–III) it appeared that 'The shift he has made, the new thing he has given, that which is his own, is not in his plots (he has no plots) and not in his vocabulary, but on a plane where hardly any one else but he is working: in syntax.' However, the fullest and most valuable statement of this, again in 1923, came from Mandelstam:

> In poetry the truly creative age is not the age of invention but the age of imitation. When the prayer-books have been written then it is time for the service to be held. The last Poetic Breviary to have been issued for general use in Russia is Pasternak's *My Sister Life*. Not since the time of Batyushkov has such a mature new harmony been heard in Russian poetry. Pasternak is no mere thinker-up of novelties, no conjuror; he is the begetter of a new way of writing, a new structure for Russian verse, which corresponds to the virile maturity attained by the language. In this new harmony everything can be expressed, and every one, whether they want to or not, will use it, because from now on it is the common achievement of all Russian poets. Hitherto the logical

[1] Paul Valéry, 'A Foreword' (1920), in *The Art of Poetry*, trans. Denise Folliot (1958), p.42.

structure of the sentence has been growing weaker, along with the weakening of the poem itself, i.e. it was but the shortest way to express a poetic idea. Frequent poetic use wears down the customary path of logic until it becomes – as such – unnoticeable. Syntax, which is poetry's circulatory system, is attacked by sclerosis. Then there comes a poet who resurrects the virgin vigour of the logical sentence-structure. This was what Pushkin was amazed by in Batyushkov; and now Pasternak awaits his Pushkin.[1]

To be sure, the concern for syntax which produced in Pasternak's poetry the effects that Mayakovsky and Mandelstam respond to need not be the sort of concern for syntax that we find in Valéry. Indeed Mayakovsky's word 'dynamic' and Mandelstam's 'virgin vigour' suggest something rather different. And it may be in fact that there is a much nearer parallel to be found in English than in French. I have in mind a well-known letter of 1926 written by W.B. Yeats to H.J.C. Grierson. Here Yeats declares:

> The over childish or over pretty or feminine element in some good Wordsworth and in much poetry up to our date comes from the lack of natural momentum in the syntax. This momentum underlies almost every Elizabethan and Jacobean lyric and is far more important than simplicity of vocabulary. If Wordsworth had found it he could have carried any amount of elaborate English. Byron, unlike the Elizabethans though he always tries for it, constantly allows it to die out in some mind-created construction, but is I think the one great English poet – though one can hardly call him great except in purpose and manhood – who sought it constantly.[2]

This concern remained with Yeats until his last years, when it crops up in his letters to Dorothy Wellesley, and the effect of this preoccupation is to be seen in the poems which he wrote from 1916 onwards. His reference to 'Elizabethan and Jacobean lyric' is significant in a letter to Grierson, the editor of John Donne. For the syntax that has 'natural momentum' appears in Yeats's poems whenever we are aware of the presence of Donne. If his 'momentum' corresponds to Mayakovsky's 'dynamic' and Mandelstam's 'virgin vigour', it may be that in Pasternak as in Yeats we encounter a syntax that has to do, not with *symboliste* 'music', but with the dramatic or histrionic illusion of a man's presence and his impassioned speech.

Unfortunately, the grammatical structures of Russian and of English are so different that the translator despairs of producing any

[1]   *Russkoye Iskussivo* (1923), p.182.
[2]   *The Letters of W.B. Yeats*, ed. Allan Wade (New York, 1955) p.710.

equivalent to this feature of his style which Mandelstam and Mayakovsky thought so important. Five polysyllabic words can be ranged in two lines of Pasternak as massively as blocks of masonry – an effect available only in a highly inflected language, something that English, with its clutter of prepositions and particles, can hardly attain to.

II   PASTERNAK AND THE FORMALISTS

By 1922 Pasternak's reputation in Russia was already assured. What is striking, among Russian critics who respond to him in 1922 and 1923 (the first years after the Revolution when reliable publication of books and journals was resumed), is the stress on Pasternak's originality, his 'newness'. And there was no particular strangeness or difficulty, in those years, about acknowledging Pasternak's remoteness from political activity and at the same time seeing a profound affinity between the Revolution of 1917 and this poet's revolutionary attitude to his art, and his revolutionary handling of his medium.

For Bryusov in his 'Yesterday, Today and Tomorrow of Russian Poetry', yesterday was represented by Symbolism, today by Futurism, and tomorrow by 'proletarian poetry'; and when poetry emerged which expressed the 'new world-view' of the proletariat, then (Bryusov believes) Pasternak would be left behind as a 'poet of the intelligentsia':

> To the same extent that Mayakovsky, in the moods of his poetry, is close to the proletarian poets, Pasternak is without doubt a poet of the intelligentsia. In part, this leads to a breadth of creative range: history and the present age, the data of science and the talk of the day, books and life – all these things on equal terms get into Pasternak's poems and there, in accord with his special sense of what the world is, they are all set out as it were on one level. In part, though, this excessive intellectuality makes his poetry anaemic, pushing it towards anti-poetic reflections, turning some poems into philosophic discussions, sometimes substituting witty paradoxes for living images.

Bryusov, apparently concerned in this article to deny his Symbolist past and prove himself a supporter of the most modern, the Bolshevik cause, none the less acknowledges:

> Pasternak's poems have had an honour, accorded to almost no works of poetry (except those that were prohibited by the Tsarist

censorship) since about the time of Pushkin: they have circulated
in manuscript. Young poets have known by heart poems by Pasternak that have not yet anywhere appeared in print, and they
have imitated him more entirely than they have imitated Mayakovsky....

And accordingly Bryusov is eager to enlist Pasternak as a poet of
the Revolution *à son insu*:

> Pasternak has not written any poems specifically about the
> Revolution but, perhaps even without his knowing it, his poems
> are steeped in the spirit of the present; his psychology is not
> borrowed from books of the past, it is an expression of his own
> being and could have been formed only in the conditions of our
> life.[1]

Very strikingly Bryusov agrees with the resolutely a-political Mandelstam (with Tynyanov also) in seeing Pasternak as pathfinder and
trail-blazer, as pioneer and innovator, not as the 'classic' master,
Pushkin to his Batyushkov, who characteristically takes over and
consummates the innovations of others; an Ezra Pound, we may
say, rather than a Yeats.

However, the 1920s in Russia were the years of a school of gifted
critics who were not, like Bryusov, mainly concerned with the
significance of the Revolution nor yet, like Mandelstam, creative
writers concerned to understand their contemporaries so as to find
their own way forward. These were the Formalists. It is no accident,
for instance, though to the English-speaking reader it is very unexpected, that in the very years of the Revolution, immediately after
Pasternak's experiments with orchestration of sounds in poetry,
there should have appeared 'the pioneer study directed at the discernment of patterns in sounds in poetry and their classification',[2] Osip
Brik's 'Zvukovye povtory'.[3] Brik's studies are a contribution to a
revolution in poetic theory and critical method which parallels Pasternak's revolution in poetic method, as that in turn parallels the
Bolsheviks' revolution in political method and political structure.
And this is the revolution which called itself 'Formalism'.

The Formalist critics are represented in our selection by Tynyanov
and by Roman Jakobson. Formalist criticism as a whole gave no
specially prominent place to Pasternak's writing, yet there are
illuminating parallels between Pasternak's theory and practice and
Formalist doctrine. In the first place, according to Formalist doctrine

---

[1] Bryusov, op. cit.
[2] Plank, op. cit. p.19.
[3] In Osip Brik, *Sborniki po teoril poeticheskovo yazyka* (Petrograd, 1916-17).

what art does is *ostranenie*, making strange. Art by the distortions
it effects makes the world strange and novel, restoring to the reader,
who is blinkered and dulled by habit and linguistic cliché, a child-like
vision. In the words of Viktor Shklovsky: 'Thus in order to restore
to us the perception of life, to make a stone stony, there exists that
which we call art'.[1] There has to be some connection between this
and Pasternak, the poet who was acclaimed in the twenties by critics
and reviewers in Russia as above all a man who sees the world as if
'for the first time'. And in his poems Pasternak is constantly fasci-
nated by this capacity of poetry for renewing and refreshing perception – yet with this crucial difference, that for him it is poetry that
does this, not the poet; that it is the world which thus renews itself,
through the poet and his poem, but not at the poet's behest. Equally
the distortions, deformations or displacements by which reality
refreshes itself in poems are for Pasternak something that happens
in the world, something that the poet notices and records, whereas
to the Formalists the displacements are effected by the poet. To this
end, as they understand it, the poet may employ certain devices.
And indeed the notion of 'device' is central to Formalist criticism.
For them subject-matter is unimportant. And by taking the work
as device, or as a structure of devices, they proclaim their indifference
to the work in its aspect as a reflection of biographical circumstances,
psychological or social. There are closely related attitudes to be found
in Pasternak, and it is these indeed which can mislead the English-
speaking reader into thinking him an aesthete. Not that Pasternak
busies himself with detailed study of this or that poetic device. But
like the Formalists he declares himself to be centrally concerned, in
any work, with the presence of Art in it; not at all with the overt
subject-matter, still less with the personality of the author, or with
his representatives:

> When we suppose that in *Tristan, Romeo and Juliet*, and other
> great works a powerful passion is portrayed, we under-estimate
> their content. Their theme is wider than this powerful theme.
> Their theme is the theme of power.
> And it is from this theme that art is born. Art is more one-sided
> than people think. It cannot be directed at will, wherever you
> wish, like a telescope. Focused upon a reality that has been dis-
> placed by feeling, art is a record of this displacement. It copies it
> from nature. How then does nature become displaced? Details
> gain in sharpness, each losing its independent meaning. Each one
> of them could be replaced by another. Any one of them is precious.

---

[1]   Quoted in Victor Erlich, *Russian Formalism* (The Hague, 1965) p.76.

Any one, chosen at random, will serve as evidence of the state which envelops the whole of transposed reality. (*Safe Conduct*)

Tynyanov similarly notes how any one of Pasternak's images by itself is fortuitous (random and replaceable), yet the whole which they make up (the 'theme') is obligatory. This obligatoriness (*obyazarel'nost'*) is, however, in Pasternak's understanding total. For art 'is a record', it 'copies from nature'.

This humility at the heart of what looks like arrogance is what sharply distinguishes Pasternak not only from the Formalists but also from other gifted Russian poets of his time, from Blok, from Mayakovsky and Yesenin. This is what he means in *Safe Conduct* when he records that, as early as *Over the Barriers*, 'I abandoned the Romantic manner':

> But a whole conception of life lay concealed under the Romantic manner which I was to forbid myself from henceforth. This was the conception of life as the life of the poet. It had come to us from the Symbolists and had been adopted by them from the Romantics, principally the Germans.
>
> This idea had taken possession of Blok but only during a short period. In the form in which it came naturally to him it was incapable of satisfying him. He had either to heighten it or abandon it altogether. He abandoned the idea, Mayakovsky and Yesenin heightened it.
>
> In this poet who sets himself up as the measure of life and pays for this with his life, the Romantic conception is disarmingly vivid and indisputable in its symbols, that is in everything that figuratively touches upon Orphism and Christianity. In this sense something not transient was incarnate both in the life of Mayakovsky and in the fate of Yesenin, a fate which defies all epithets, self-destructively begging to become myth and receding into it.
>
> But outside the legend, the Romantic scheme is false. The poet, who is its foundation, is inconceivable without the non-poets to bring him into relief, because this poet is not a living personality absorbed in moral cognition, but a visual-biographical 'emblem', demanding a background to make his contours visible. In contradistinction to the Passion Plays which needed a Heaven if they were to be heard, this drama needs the evil of mediocrity in order to be seen, as Romanticism always needs philistinism and with the disappearance of the petty bourgeoisie loses half its content.
>
> The notion of biography as spectacle was inherent in my time. I shared this notion with everyone else. I abandoned it while it was still flexible and non-obligatory with the Symbolists, before it bore any implication of heroism and before it smelt of blood.

And in the first place, I freed myself from it unconsciously, aban-
doning the Romantic devices for which it served as basis. In the
second place, I shunned it consciously also, considering its brilliance unsuited to me, because, confining myself to my craft, I
feared any kind of poeticizing which would place me in a false
and incongruous position.

With this crucial passage (which incidentally brings out some of the
ways in which Russian Symbolism was radically different from
French *symbolisme*) we come at last to something which the Anglo-
American reader should be able to respond to eagerly. For what
Pasternak here set his face against is that which Louis Zukofsky in
1930 called, with obvious distaste, 'overweening autobiographies
of the heart'.[1] And our poetry ever since 1920 has been marked
generally by a revulsion against Romanticism conceived in this way,
on the grounds that it is 'overweening'.

It is important to get this clear. For Pasternak's writing, early and
late, is full of the lyrical 'I', and he has not shared the reluctance of
Zukofsky and of our poets in the Imagist tradition, to reflect upon
the experience which he renders, even as he renders it. Moreover
Pasternak dedicated *My Sister Life* to an arch-Romantic, Lermontov.
What does this mean, in view of the anti-Romantic stance declared
in *Safe Conduct*? George Reavey records how, in Cambridge in 1927,
he graduated to Pasternak from Yesenin:

> Pasternak, when I discovered him, seemed to have no public face
> ... he was all contained in the movement of his own verse, in the
> rhythm of the creative act, and this very act of apparently spon-
> taneous creation, and the resulting chain of his images, were what
> seemed to absorb him wholly.[2]

This may be taken in several ways. One way of mistaking it would be
to envisage Pasternak as self-absorbed in a tiresomely self-regarding
and egocentric way, with no interests outside the rarefied ecstasies
of his own sensibility and the drama of his personal, vocational
destiny. And an unsympathetic reader of Lermontov might recognize him in this description.

The apparent contradiction was removed in one way by Renato
Poggioli when he observed, 'The raw material of Pasternak's poetry
is introspection. Yet Pasternak treats the self as object rather than
as subject.' But this is still cryptic. Victor Erlich glosses it more
helpfully: 'His work does not so much project a coherent and
dramatically effective image of the poet as dramatize what Edgar

---

[1] Zukofsky, loc. cit. p.141.
[2] George Reavey, *The Poetry of Boris Pasternak, 1917-1959* (New York, 1959) p.45.

Allan Poe calls the poetic principle – the power which brings the poem into being.'[1] In other words, the 'autobiography' is not of the poet's heart, but of the heart of poetry. And it is against this background, with these weighty qualifications, that one must understand Pasternak's dedication of *My Sister Life* to the most confessional of Russian poets, Lermontov; his poem to the same effect, 'In Memory of the Demon'; and his explanation of this to Eugene Kayden.[2] But in any case Pasternak was quite explicit, not only in *Safe Conduct* but elsewhere:

> People nowadays imagine that art is like a fountain, whereas it is a sponge. They think art has to flow forth, whereas what it has to do is absorb and become saturated. They suppose that it can be divided up into means of depiction, whereas it is made up of the organs of perception. Its job is to be always a spectator and to look more purely, more receptively, more faithfully than anyone else; but in our age it has come to know pomade and the make-up room, and it displays itself from a stage...[3]

In this statement of the early 1920s, we see Pasternak once again implying that the poet is 'a living personality absorbed in moral cognition', and not 'a visual-biographical "emblem"'. This represents a deliberate turning away by Pasternak from the precedents of Blok, Mayakovsky and Yesenin, who all projected an image of the poet or of themselves as poets. Much more than any of these Pasternak eschews 'overweening autobiographies of the heart', and this marks him off from Hart Crane or W.B. Yeats by just so much as it aligns him rather with Pound, William Carlos Williams or Zukofsky.

III   PASTERNAK: THE MIDDLE PERIOD

In the 1920s Pasternak made several attempts to compose long poems. *The Lofty Malady* consists of two sustained passages which appeared in periodicals, the first in 1923, the second in 1928. The long poem *Nineteen Hundred and Five*, consisting of six sections with a prologue, was published as a book in 1927; and bound up with it was *Lieutenant Schmidt*, a poem in three parts about the revolt of the Black Sea Fleet in 1905. *Spektorsky*, consisting of nine parts with a prologue, was published as a book in 1931.

[1]   Victor Erlich, *The Double Image* (Baltimore, 1964) p.140.
[2]   Eugene Kayden, *Poems by Boris Pasternak* (Ann Arbor, 1959) p.ix.
[3]   'Neskol'ko polozhenii' ('Some Theses'), 1922; see *Sochineniya* (*Works*) (Michigan, 1961) III, p.152.

Nineteen Hundred and Five, with its public theme (the abortive revolution of that year), was welcomed by many who had found the earlier lyrics too difficult. Gorky probably spoke for many Russian readers when he wrote to Pasternak in 1927:

> To be frank, before this book I have always read your poems with a certain effort, for they are excessively saturated with imagery, and the images are not always clear to me; my *imagination* found it difficult to contain your images, wilfully complicated as they are and often incompletely drawn. You know yourself... that their abundance often makes you speak – or paint – too sketchily. In *Nineteen Hundred and Five* you are simpler and more chary of words, you're more classical in this book, which is filled with a pathos that infects me, as a reader, very quickly, easily, and powerfully. Yes, it is an excellent book. This is the voice of a genuine poet, and of a social poet, social in the best and profoundest sense of the word.

Even so, Gorky wrote again the next day to tell Pasternak that 'the "imagery" is often too small for the theme, and still more often it capriciously fails to agree with it; thus you make the theme unclear.'[1] The émigré D.S. Mirsky, on the other hand, had responded readily to *My Sister Life* and *Themes and Variations*.[2] And yet it is hard not to see the welcome which Mirsky gave to *Lieutenant Schmidt* as a stage in Mirsky's reconciliation with the régime, a reconciliation which in 1928 was almost complete. For, when he calls Pasternak 'a great revolutionary and transformer of Russian poetry', Mirsky goes further than anyone before in identifying Pasternak with the Revolution. Mirsky thought that in *Lieutenant Schmidt* Pasternak had 'given to the whole old tradition of Russian sacrificial revolutionariness its creative fulfilment'. That tradition, he thought, had culminated in Pasternak, or rather in this work of Pasternak's; and Pasternak was 'the starting-point of all future Russian traditions'.[3]

There is no way of knowing how far some of these poems represent a deliberate attempt by Pasternak to graduate from lyric to epic, nor how far, if this was the case, he was swayed by exhortations to this effect from Gorky or others. For as some of the early reviewers had recognized, Pasternak's talent was lyrical in an absolute sense. Of *My Sister Life* one reviewer exclaimed: 'Reality represented solely by lyrical means! Contemporaneity lives in this book as a scent, as

---

[1] Gorky's correspondence with Pasternak in *Literaturnoye Nasledstvo* (1963) LXX, pp.300, 301.

[2] D.S. Mirsky, *A History of Russian Literature* (1949) p.502.

[3] D.S. Mirsky, *Versty*, III (1928) pp.150–4.

a rhythm, as an unexpected epithet, as an apt definition, as a structure...'[1] And Dale L. Plank notes in Pasternak's lyrics 'the effort to
overcome the temporal successiveness of the poem itself by squeez-
ing in as much action as possible in the shortest possible space, the
fascination for things caught in flight, the constant preoccupation
with images of water, storm, the seasons, anything that represents
change and evanescence'. Plank comments:

> To the lyrical imagination chronology is chaos and is opposed to
> the order of the world's metaphorism. Pasternak's historical and
> biographical poems of the twenties..., as well as his prose, illus-
> trate throughout the displacement of the narrative and sequential
> by the momentary; the scraps of days and hours that refuse to
> cohere.[2]

Thus in these poems, Pasternak does not abandon his lyrical procedures but on the contrary attempts to build larger structures, and
to compass the rhythm and shape of whole lifetimes, by pressing
his lyricism further. It may be that the nearest parallel in Anglo-
American poetry is once again Hart Crane, who in *The Bridge* similarly tried to build a structure of epic scope by lyrical means.
Sinyavksy's comments on *Spektorsky* show something of what this
means in practice.

Nineteen Hundred and Five awaits a translator. For of recent years,
since the appearance of Robert Lowell's *Life Studies*, poetry in English provides an idiom equivalent in many ways to Pasternak's idiom
in his poem. This is true for instance of the curt and abrupt metre
which Pasternak finds. Up to this point in his career Pasternak had
been comparatively unadventurous in his metres. One of the exceptions, however, is a particularly splendid one, a sequence of lyrics
in *Themes and Variations* called 'Razryv' ('The Break'), of which
Mirsky wrote that 'For emotional and rhythmical force, these nine
lyrics have no rivals in modern Russian poetry.'[3] Aseev remarks of
this work:

> The lines are all fastened to one another by knots of intonation
> which carry the voice without pause for breath from one line to
> the next. The stops are conditioned solely by the taking of new
> breaths. Who will assert after this that a stanza thus constructed
> observes the principle of rhythm but not that of intonation?

This represents a recognition by a Russian critic as early as 1929 of

[1] Ya. Chernyak, in *Pechat' i Revolyutsiya*, VI (1922) pp.303-4.
[2] Plank, op. cit. pp.85-6.
[3] Mirsky, *History of Russian Literature*, p.502.

something that our criticism came to securely only in the 1950s, with Charles Olson's *Projective Verse*: the recognition that the distinction between metrical verse and free verse does not take us far enough to be useful. On the other hand intonational verse, in the sense that Aseev gives to that term, was certainly being written in English at the same time as Pasternak was writing 'Razryv'. Different as it is in every other aspect, Pound's *Homage to Sextus Propertius* (1917) is structured upon intonations.

Accordingly Plank is a little misleading when he says of the new collection of lyrics which appeared in 1932:

> Although the tone of the poems of *Second Birth* is strikingly different from that of Pasternak's earlier books – it is now reflective, even elegiacal – the sounds are, if anything, more intensely organized in their patterns and, especially, as metaphors. The illusion of spontaneity that distinguished the earlier books is now almost absent; but in its place we have, not a new poetics, but an application of the old poetics, perfected and even enriched, to the needs of a man speaking.[1]

For as we have seen 'the needs of a man speaking' determine the structure of 'Razryz' in *Themes and Variations*. And indeed if we take seriously Pasternak's tribute to Verlaine, we must suppose that Pasternak was concerned for the cadence of the speaking voice from the start, for Verlaine stands behind some poems that Pasternak wrote as early as 1912. Pasternak says of Verlaine:

> He gave to the language in which he wrote that boundless freedom which was his own lyrical discovery and which is found only in the masters of prose dialogue in the novel and the drama. The Parisian phrase in all its virginal and bewitching accuracy flew in from the street and lay down entire in his lines, not in the least cramped, as the melodic material for the whole of the subsequent composition. Verlaine's greatest charm lies in this directness and spontaneity. For him the idioms of the French language were indivisible. He wrote not in words but in whole phrases, neither breaking them into separate units, nor rearranging them.

Pasternak's reference here to 'prose dialogue in the novel and the drama' is interestingly near to that admonition which Ford Madox Ford gave to Pound, and transmitted through him to Eliot: the warning that in the twentieth century poets are in competition not only with poets of the past but also with the great realistic novelists of the previous century. Equally, one of the things that Wladimir

[1] Plank, op. cit. p.112.

Weidle objected to, in his intelligently hostile response to Pasternak, is the way in which Pasternak's verse is densely furnished with work-aday *things* in all their weightiness and angularity. And this may be just what Pound, true to his Flaubertian allegiance, aimed for in some of his *Cantos*, and what he admired in a pre-Flaubertian realist, George Crabbe. The novelist that Pasternak had chiefly in mind may have been Tolstoy. Or if it was a French novelist, it is less likely to have been Flaubert than Balzac. However, Pasternak's specifying *dialogue* in the novel doubtless means that he might not have thought, with Eliot, that 'Poetry must be at least as well-written as good prose'; but only that it must be as well-written as good *speech*.

With this exception, however, Plank's characterizing of *Second Birth* is very just. In particular 'the illusion of spontaneity' which at this point tends to disappear from Pasternak's lyrics is not anything that we need grieve for; for this illusion sometimes gave the earlier poems a flurried air and a raucous tone. It is the more important to realize with Plank that habits of luxuriance and daring wantonness, in imagery and orchestration alike, survive from the earlier poems into *Second Birth*, although there is seldom by this stage any question of synaesthesia, still less of surrealism. An example is a poem on the death of Mayakovsky, which is quoted almost in its entirety by Sinyavsky:

> They would not credit it, dismissed it as
> So much wild talk – then two advised them, three,
> Then all the world. There aligned themselves in the series
> Of a term run out and halted
> The houses of Mistress Clerk, of Mistress Huckster,
> Yards of those houses, trees, and on the trees
> The dulled rook, stupefied in the sun's eye, screamed
> His inflamed curses after Mistress Rook
> That, what the deuce, henceforward boobies should not
> Obtrude their offices, bad cess to them.
> Only upon the faces came a damp
> Subsidence, as a tattered fishnet crumples.
>
> A day there was, a blameless day, still more
> Blameless than a dozen you have lived through.
> They crowded in, they dressed their ranks in the forecourt
> Like a shot, as if a shot had dressed them,
>
> As if, though razed, there fountained out of channels
> Pike and bream, as when a mine explodes,
> So from the fire-squib charged and laid in the sedges
> Was this exhaled as from sediments still ungelded.

You slept, you pressed the pillow with your cheek.
You slept, and with clean heels, with raking strides,
Now with one turn of speed, now with another, you
Entered the constellations of young legends.
And among these you burst so much the more
Notably that you made it in one jump.
The detonation of your shot was Etna's
Upon its foothills, Craven and Mistress Craven.

Here the luxuriance is not a matter of logically incompatible simili-
tudes colliding and jarring against each other, but of extraordinarily
rapid as it were cinematographic 'cutting' from one similitude to
the next. The flow of association, from urban scenes to nursery-
rhyme to geological to sporting metaphors and back to the geological
volcanic metaphor of Etna in the last lines, is not, as in surrealist
writing, the uncontrolled association of the unconscious in dreams.
It may seem so, but this is an illusion brought about by the copious-
ness of the poet's invention, the rapidity and impetuosity of his
transitions. It is the quality we associate with Shakespeare above all,
and in a later poet such as Dryden only when we detect a Shakespearean note in him. An example of the wanton or arbitrary image
might be the unannounced swerve into a metaphor from fishing 'as
a tattered fishnet crumples'. Yet this too, in thoroughly Shakespearean fashion, is taken up into the poem as it were retrospectively
when we reach (in the original version which Sinyavsky quotes) the
later image of fishing by depth-charges:

As if, though razed, there fountained out of channels
Pike and bream, as when a mine explodes....

Pasternak and Mayakovsky had been close friends. And the tact
of their relationship is beautifully preserved in the way in which the
shot by which Mayakovsky killed himself, though it is central to
the metaphors of Pasternak's poem, is nowhere brutally stated.
Those who know how affectingly Pasternak wrote of Mayakovsky's
death in his prose memoirs may not notice how in the poem Pasternak writes not in the first place as a friend nor as a member of the
same circle, but publicly, seeing the poet's death as impinging upon
his society in the widest sense, affecting people not normally affected
by poetry at all. This, at least, is how I read the 'sediments still
ungelded', as levels of Russian society which Pasternak had thought
of as brutalized into spiritual inertia, which yet show themselves
still capable of fructification by virtue of the response they make
(however muddled – the rook's response of irrationally alarmed
irritation) to the death of the laureate poet. The rook's injunction to

his wife not to meddle is perhaps the finest stroke in the poem; it is true to life as we know it, yet true also the idea of *noli me tangere*, or of the poet as tabu because sacred.

It is the public quality of this poem which allows us momentarily to think of that most public of English poets, Dryden. Yet, of course, in Pasternak's case this is the exception that proves the rule. Pasternak as a whole is challenging to the Russian reader because, by writing for the most part so insistently as a private person, he flies in the face of the traditional Russian emphasis (much older than the Revolution) on how the writer has civic responsibilities. *Doctor Zhivago* was to explore the paradox that, in certain states of society, such an insistence on the rights of the private life may itself be a civic duty of a particularly exacting and dangerous kind. And the tumult which surrounded the awarding of the Nobel prize to Pasternak was to show, from the poet's own life, how fulfilling this duty can have momentous and explosive consequences in the public domain. There is no analogue to this in the Anglo-American tradition in the present century. For British and American poets are, as it were, condemned to the private life; and many of them have worried, so far to no purpose, about how to break into the public realm, to take on that civic responsibility which their societies indulgently deny them. The only partial exception among greatly gifted poets in English has been W.B. Yeats, whose society, because it was Irish, permitted him for a while civic responsibility, and the public oratorical style which befits a public rôle. The word 'huckster' in our translation is a Yeatsian word, and may be allowed to hint at the Yeatsian parallel.

IV   FROM 1934 TO THE END

The first All-Union Congress of Soviet Writers in August 1934 inaugurated a period when the tension between the private life and public responsibility was, for many Russian writers, stretched to breaking and beyond. A main theme of the Congress was that of the speech in which Maxim Gorky declared that the creative impotence of twentieth-century literature in Europe was to be explained by the fact that man had turned out to be 'a social unit, not a cosmic one', and that 'individualism, which turns into egocentrism, breeds "superfluous people"'. One speaker who spoke at some length about Pasternak was Nikolai Bukharin, whose words are interesting because they define the category – of exquisite but valetudinarian minor talent – which was the most indulgent that official spokesmen could find for Pasternak to the day of his death:

Boris Pasternak is a poet most remote from current affairs, even in the broadest sense of the term... a singer of the old intelligentsia, which has now become a Soviet intelligentsia. He unquestionably accepts the Revolution but he is far removed from the peculiar technicism of the period, from the din of battle, from the passions of the struggle. As early as at the time of the imperialist war, he had intellectually broken away from the old world... and had consciously risen 'above the barriers'. The bloody hash, the huckstering barter of the bourgeois world were profoundly loathsome to him, and he 'seceded', retired from the world, shut himself up in the mother-of-pearl shell of individual experiences, delicate and subtle, of the frail trepidations of a wounded and easily vulnerable soul. He is the embodiment of chaste but self-absorbed laboratory craftsmanship, persistent and painstaking labour over verbal form, the material for which is afforded by the precious things of the 'heritage of the past', by profoundly personal – and hence, of necessity, constricted – associations, interwoven with inward stirrings of the mind.[1]

The tone is plainly apologetic.

Pasternak's life during the 1930s can be reconstructed from partial and fragmentary evidence, as has been done for instance by Robert Conquest.[2] But neither Conquest nor any other has yet explained why Pasternak escaped the purges which carried off so many of his friends and colleagues, especially since from time to time he spoke out rashly. In his literary career the late 1930s are the years of his work as a translator. In 1935 appeared a volume of lyrics translated from the Georgian, which was praised in a review by Mirsky; and this was followed by another collection of Georgian lyrics in 1937. A volume of Selected Translations in 1940 included versions by Pasternak from Shakespeare, Ralegh, Keats and Byron. Translations of *Hamlet*, of *Romeo and Juliet*, *Antony and Cleopatra* and *Othello* appeared during the war. It is clear now that already in the 1930s Pasternak was at work on what was to become *Doctor Zhivago*, and that this was no secret within the circle of his friends. The playwright Afinogenov, for instance, wrote in his diary under 21 September 1937:

Conversations I have with Pasternak are unforgettable. He comes in and at once starts to talk of something that is important, interesting and real. For him the main thing is art, and nothing

---

[1] Nikolai Bukharin, 'Poetry, Poetics and the Problems of Poetry in the U.S.S.R.', in *Problems of Soviet Literature* (*Reports and Speeches at the First Soviet Writers' Congress*) (Moscow, 1935) p.233.

[2] Robert Conquest, *Courage of Genius* (1961) pp.36–40.

but art. That is why he doesn't care to go into town but chooses to live here the whole time, going for walks by himself or reading Macaulay's *History of England*, sitting by the window and looking out at the starry night, sorting out his thoughts, or else, finally, writing his novel. But all of this is inside art and for the sake of art. He is not even interested in the end-product. The main thing is the work at it, the enthusiasm for it; as for what will come of it – well, let's see many years from now. His wife has a hard time, they have to find money and live somehow, but he knows nothing about it, only sometimes when the money problem gets really acute, he gets down to work translating. 'But I'd do just as well being a commercial traveller....' Set him down anywhere you like, he'll still keep his open gaze on nature and people – like the great and rare verbal artist that he is.

It's just the same when you go to see him, he leaves behind everything that's petty and he hurls at you subjects, judgments, conclusions – with him everything gets delineated in a real and meaningful way. He doesn't read the newspapers – and this is queer for me, who can't get through a day without the news. But he would never spend all his time up to 2 o'clock in the afternoon, as I did today, doing nothing. He's always taken up with his work, with books, with himself.... And if he should ever find himself in a palace or on the plank-bed of a prison cell, he'll still be taken up like this, perhaps even more than he is here – at least then he wouldn't have to think about money and worries, but could give the whole of his time to thinking and creating....

A man of rare integrity, rare interest. And your heart goes out to him because he can find wonderful human words of comfort, not out of pity but out of his conviction that better things are on the way: 'And these better things will come very shortly – as soon as you put all of yourself into your work, and you start to work and forget about everything else....'[1]

The 'work' which so much mattered to Pasternak, at the time Afinogenov writes of, certainly was not his translations. It may have been some of the poems subsequently printed in *On Early Trains*, in 1943. But more probably it was work directed towards the novel that was not to appear until twenty years later. And *Literaturnaya Gazeta* published in December 1938 a piece of prose by Pasternak under the title, 'Two Excerpts from a Chapter of a Novel: A District behind the Front'.[2]

---

[1] A.N. Afinogenov, *Stat'i, Dnevniki, Pis'ma. Vospominaniya* (Moscow, 1957) pp.152-3.
[2] Other prose fictions by Pasternak are *Il Tratto di Apelle* (1915); *The Childhood of Luvers* and *Letters from Tula* (1918); *Aerial Ways* (1924) and *A Tale* (published in 1934).

In his *Essay in Autobiography*, Pasternak declared that all his verse before 1940 was written in a style no longer to his liking. And this is one among many pronouncements to similar effect. The most enlightening of them appears at a point in *An Essay in Autobiography*[1] where Pasternak says that it was his reading of the poems of Marina Tsvetayeva which crystallized his dissatisfaction with his own early verse; and he expresses that dissatisfaction by saying that, in the work he had come to dislike, 'I wasn't looking for the point of things, only for their incidental sharpness.' This is accurate self-criticism. *Ars est celare artem*; and in Pasternak's early poetry the art seldom conceals itself. Knowing itself to be brilliantly resourceful and brilliantly perceptive, it makes no attempt to seem otherwise. Why should it? However this unashamedness consorts rather uncomfortably at times with the illusion of spontaneity which these poems set out to create; for then the poem can seem to be self-congratulating at times quite raucously.

This set aside, however, the matter of Pasternak's revulsion from his earlier styles has been given too much prominence. It is common and indeed inevitable for an artist who keeps moving throughout his life, to regard his own youthful self as a stranger to the man he has become, and to resent it irritably if fame and esteem is given to that stranger too exclusively. Thus Thomas Gray in his later years was impatient with admirers of his *Elegy in a Country Churchyard*, and Yeats came to hate 'The Lake Isle of Innisfree'. Thus Pound, looking back in 1934, felt that his own poetry to that date counted for next to nothing when set beside Thomas Hardy's.[2] We are sure Pound was mistaken, though we like him for making the mistake; and this surely ought to be our attitude to Pasternak also. Certainly we must resist any suggestion, basing itself on these pronouncements by Pasternak, to the effect that the poems written since 1940 are superior to those before; that in *Doctor Zhivago* and the poems of his last years Pasternak at last found the ways of writing which he had been groping for unsuccessfully throughout his earlier years. *Doctor Zhivago*, and the poems which Pasternak gives to Yuri Zhivago, are no doubt the crown and consummation of Pasternak's artistic career, but not in any way that supersedes the earlier writing. To regard *My Sister Life* as in this way 'prentice work would be absurd. Equally, though those who can approach *Doctor Zhivago* down the perspective afforded by Pasternak's earlier writings will almost certainly think that this is the way to see *Doctor Zhivago* most accurately; yet, of course, this perspective is not open to the vast

[1] *An Essay in Autobiography* trans. Manya Harari (1959) p.105.
[2] Ezra Pound, *Guide to Kulchur*, ch.52.

majority of those who read Pasternak's novel, and our selection from critics of *Doctor Zhivago* shows that valuable insights can be achieved by looking at it down quite different vistas, for instance in the context of the nineteenth-century realistic novel.

As for the latest poems, it was Yuri Zhivago who claimed to have worked all his life for 'an unnoticeable style'. Boris Pasternak could not have claimed this, and did not claim it. Moreover, it is not in any writer's power to decide whether his style should be 'noticeable' or not. For this is all in the eye of the beholder, it depends upon the prepossessions as well as the attentiveness of the reader. In any case the talented translator of Pasternak's last collection, *When the Weather Clears*, was on the wrong tack when, after recalling Zhivago's wish for an unnoticeable style, he confessed, 'A major criticism of these translations is their failure to be as un-literary as the originals.'[1] For a perky or jaunty colloquialism, such as we encounter in many versions from Pasternak, makes a style even more 'noticeable' than literary stiltedness does. And it would be a bitter irony if the man of whom Afinogenov said 'For him the main thing is art, and nothing but art' were to be called to testify, on the score of certain late pronouncements taken out of context, in the cause of those who believe that art and literature are always guilty until proved innocent, and that they can prove their innocence best by going in disguise.

[1]   Pasternak, *Poems 1955-1959*, trans. Michael Harari (1960), prefatory note.

The Introduction to *Modern Judgements: Pasternak*, with Angela Livingstone. London: Macmillan, 1969; Nashville: Aurora, 1970.

9 Pushkin, and Other Poets

Pushkin: A Comparative Commentary, John Bayley. Cambridge: CUP, 1971.
Pushkin on Literature, edited and translated by Tatiana Wolff. London: Methuen, 1971.

Pushkin the untranslatable: the notion has been in the air ever since the first rumours of a great Russian poet reached early Victorian England. When, of late, Edmund Wilson and Vladimir Nabokov joined issue about it, the famous talking-point was engaging two livelier minds than ever before. And Nabokov's four volumes devoted to *Evgeny Onegin* – supposedly a translation with commentary, but really a sustained demonstration that the translation was impossible – are a comic masterpiece by one of the greatest comic imaginations of our time. If the translations are not getting any better (though in fact Walter Arndt's *Eugene Onegin* is more service-able than any of its predecessors),[1] at least critical discussion of this poet has been moving on to an altogether higher level of awareness and discrimination. And now John Bayley's 'comparative commen-tary' sets the seal on this development. With Bayley's help English readers capable of responding to a poet so sophisticated as Pushkin, whose procedures are so much at odds with our current assumptions, can – even if they lack Russian – construct for themselves an image of this poet more accurate, more faceted, more intriguing and chal-lenging, than they could construct from any extant translations – or from any translations we are likely to get. A critical commentary as good as this, focused so severely, so resolutely refusing to be distracted by side-issues, makes translation for most purposes unnecessary.

And yet I cannot think that John Bayley will succeed in creating an intelligent enthusiasm for Pushkin in England, any more than D.S. Mirsky did nearly fifty years ago. The times, as I read them, could hardly be less propitious for a recognition among us of the

---

[1] Walter Arndt (trans), *Eugene Onegin*. New York: E.P. Dutton, second revised edition, 1981.

radiant paradox that Pushkin embodies: the union of impregnable impersonality and reserve as an artist with eager and vulnerable frankness as a person. If Robert Conquest's charming talent were multiplied a hundredfold, we might have a British Pushkin: and we'd be mightily disconcerted by it. For all our thinking about poetry and its idioms seems to be dominated still by a simple-minded either/or, according to which 'impersonal' means 'aestheticist', and 'personal' means 'dishevelled'. Ted Hughes, for instance, says, with becoming hesitancy:

> I think it's true that formal patterning of the actual movement of verse somehow includes a mathematical and a musically deeper world than free verse can easily hope to enter. It's a mystery why it should do so. But it only works of course if the language is totally alive and pure and if the writer has a perfectly pure grasp of his real feeling...and the very sound of metre calls up the ghosts of the past and it is difficult to sing one's own tune against that choir. It is easier to speak a language that raises no ghosts.

Easier it may be. Pushkin seems to have thought it was too easy to be worth doing. As John Bayley shows on page after page, Pushkin's method was always to call up ghosts into his language, knowing very precisely just which ghost he was summoning at any given point; and indeed Pushkin's 'perfectly pure grasp of his real feeling' seems to have been indistinguishable for him from knowing what ghost to summon, how long to entertain him, and when to exorcize him so as to entertain another. But then, Pushkin had no worries about a duty 'to sing one's own tune': as Bayley says, 'in *Evgeny Onegin*, then, the style is not the man but a complex instrument manipulated by him.' And yet Pushkin is no olympian aesthete, imperturbably detached and paring his fingernails, as Nabokov would have us believe: his use of delicate parody has more to do with Chaucer than with Max Beerbohm. John Bayley, who points this out, reflects discouragingly that what Chaucer and Pushkin share is 'an artifice that can probably only be achieved in a poetic language at an early stage of its development, when freedom and formality are allies who can bring out the best in each other.' I hope this isn't true, and I don't believe it is. If we go for coarser effects, it's because we are lazy and lack conviction, and our public lacks taste.

Seeking for English analogues like Chaucer is what Bayley commits himself to when he calls his commentary 'comparative'. But it's inescapable in any case, because Pushkin advertises his own traffic with certain English authors – particularly Shakespeare (in his verse-dramas), Scott (in his prose fiction) and Byron. Byron is the case that is hardest to handle. As Tatiana Wolff says of Pushkin in her massive and well-ordered volume of selections, *Pushkin on Literature*:

> With the rise of interest in comparative literature a new niche was found for him: 'Russia's Byron'. Had this been said at the beginning of the nineteenth century, when Byron blazed like a sun in European eyes, it would have been understandable; but it was said when Byron himself had been allotted a modest position in the English poetic hierarchy, only just holding his own as a major poet.

I hope that other eyebrows than those of Professor Wilson Knight will be raised at the information that Byron's status as a major poet is in doubt; and in fact I believe that the formula 'Russia's Byron' goes back further than Mrs Wolff allows for. However that may be, it certainly seems impossible to write about Pushkin without being unfair to Byron, for Pushkin so obviously modelled himself on Byron that it becomes imperative to show that he surpassed him. John Bayley does better than most in giving Byron his due, but misses an opportunity when he applauds Pushkin's bold and sparse epithets in his lyrics to the sea, yet fails to acknowledge the same feature in Byron. 'Roll on, thou deep and dark blue Ocean – roll' is a verse that deserves to be rescued from a passing gibe by Henry James.

How good Bayley can be with his comparisons (and yet how demanding, how scornful of readers who will see in this procedure only name-dropping in an echo-chamber) comes out in a passage like this:

> Wordsworth's finest poetry puts on loftiness or a penetrating simplicity under the impulse of the poet's desire to communicate, so that incongruity seems almost like a needful aspect of the very urgency of communication. Wordsworth seems to blow his blasts as if absent-mindedly: his argument is too intensely scrutinized to justify a change of diction which in a more formal poet would signify the discarding of a sufficiently handled commonplace and the taking up of another. Keats's finest poems depend equally on a seemingly uncontrolled mixture of the sublime and the banal; and when, in *Hyperion*, he seeks to confine his utterance to an artificially sublime diction, it rises like that of *The Excursion* into an inflexible monotony.

> By reason of its very uncertainty, its absorption in the feel of its experience rather than in any attention to appropriateness of diction, romantic poetry can generalise and philosophise in a way that is not available to Pushkin. When Keats speaks of 'the feel of not to feel it', or Wordsworth of 'blank misgivings of a creature moving about in worlds not realised', they make a break-through

in the verbal exploration of human experience. Such things can be implied by Pushkin in the drama of narrative – Keats's phrase might describe the impression Tatyana gives in her Petersburg salon – but Pushkin's styles have no power to give the thing in itself. His generalisations are the weakest things in *Evgeny Onegin* and redeem their weakness only by not taking themselves too seriously: their elegance seems good-humouredly to patronise an emptiness for which it is itself largely responsible.

Bayley goes on to speculate that Pushkin lacks 'the ability of the English romantic poets to be clumsy with point and power' because 'in terms of a literary tradition Pushkin has only the eighteenth century behind him'. One sees what he means, of course. Yet to commiserate with a poet for lacking the ability to be clumsy (however powerfully) seems to be a reach of refinement which would have raised a laugh from either Pushkin or Keats, who each had, as Bayley points out, a 'briskly straightforward and unpretending personality'. And then again, of course, one wonders whether 'literary tradition', in isolation from other traditions that might be called 'socio-political' or 'ideological', can do quite so much as John Bayley suggests, whether in liberating a poet or constricting him. Bayley permits himself one comment of a socio-political kind which is venomous:

> Like all great artists he is the product of his age, and a more liberal social and political environment would not have made him a better one. The very negativism of tsarist tyranny was a liberating factor. The censorship that really deadens and kills is the positive one of a secularized state culture, with its apparatus of arts councils and writers' unions, a culture that decrees the proper style and function of literature.

Is it indeed this sort of set-up which gives us our undoubted ability to be clumsy, and our conviction that by being so – pointedly or not, with power or without it – we are at all events being sincere, being 'ourselves'? Thinking of the aristocratic robustness of Pushkin's attitude to his vocation (for a vocation it was, not a mere accomplishment), and of what John Bayley calls 'the heroic commonplace of Pushkin's own nature', it seems as if that might indeed be what is wrong with us.

Listener, 17 June 1971; reprinted in *The Poet in the Imaginary Museum*, ed. Barry Alpert. Manchester: Carcanet New Press, 1977.

10 'Mr Tolstoy, I presume?'
The Russian Novel through Victorian Spectacles

I apologize for the facetiousness of my title. And it is not just facetious, but also inaccurate. For the late-Victorian reader knew Leo Tolstoy not as Mr Tolstoy, but as *Count* Tolstoy; and in England that noble title meant that he was listened to with more patience and more respect than if he had been merely a classless intellectual like Dostoevsky. In the social democracy of the United States, of course, Tolstoy's aristocratic status had if anything the opposite effect. As witness a Mr Maurice Thompson, writing in the *Literary World* of Boston on 23 July 1887:

> ...Tolstoi is a rich man who prefers to live in brutal vulgarity, a man who pretends to hate riches, but clings to all his cash; a heartless theorist, who pretends to believe that no evil should be forcibly resisted; who makes a pretence of shoe-making in order to attract attention to himself; who dresses like a clown for the same purpose, and who writes novels as dirty and obscene as the worst parts of Walt Whitman's 'Leaves of Grass'...

However, the American reception of the Russian novel is not my subject. (It was significantly different from the British, and in many ways more intelligent and serious – for instance, Turgenev, who was partially available in English before either Tolstoy or Dostoevsky, got much more intelligent treatment in America than in Britain. This was because of the influence of Henry James, who knew Turgenev in Paris and greatly respected his work: one of James's essays on Turgenev is still, for my money, unequalled as criticism of a Russian author by a writer of the English-speaking world. And James's discriminating enthusiasm crossed the Atlantic, to be disseminated in the United States, chiefly through William Dean Howells.)

Nevertheless, Mr Maurice Thompson of Boston suits my purpose in several ways – and first because of the date, 1887. Before 1885, in England and America alike, translations from the Russian had been no more than a trickle; from 1885 onwards it quite suddenly becomes a torrent. Turgenev, so 'westernized', who lived for so long in Paris, a friend of Flaubert and of George Eliot (whom he visited in England), had been known to only a few unrepresentative readers, and to them as a cosmopolitan whose Russian-ness was almost accidental. But the first translation from Dostoevsky comes in 1881; and then in 1886 *Crime and Punishment* and *The Insulted and Injured*, in 1887 *The Idiot, The Friend of the Family* and *The Gambler*, two more stories in 1888, and in 1894 a translation of *Poor Folk* was given the accolade of a preface by George Moore. Similarly, one of Tolstoy's early books had been translated as early as 1862, and a translation of *The Cossacks* in 1878. But in 1882 came *War and Peace*, translated anonymously and very badly from the French; and between 1887 and 1890 there appear in London no less than eight works of fiction by Tolstoy, not to speak of many more of the non-fictional exhortations by Tolstoy the lay-preacher and moralistic sage. It was only with this sudden bursting of the dams in the 1880s that British readers became aware, not of a handful of talented writers who happened to be Russian, but of 'the Russian novel' as a genre unto itself, of a Russian tradition in novel-writing that was distinct from, and yet comparable with, the English tradition and the French tradition. And – more important still – an awareness of Tolstoy, to some extent of Dostoevsky also, now spread beyond the restricted circles of literary intellectuals so that Tolstoy became – as we see from journals of the time – a familiar, at least as a name and a controversial figure, to the man in the street.

Thus the arrival of the Russian novel in England was a *late*-Victorian phenomenon, the spectacles through which Tolstoy and Dostoevsky were read (and I shall suggest in a moment that those spectacles perch on many of our noses still, at the present day) were *late*-Victorian spectacles. If the translations had come in the high–Victorian period, of insular assurance and firm complacency, I should have had a very different story to tell. I can give an example of this, which I hope you will find entertaining. That freakish first translation of Tolstoy, way back in 1862, was reviewed in the *Saturday Review* by some one anonymous who bears a striking resemblance, I find, to the immortal Mr Podsnap hilariously created by Charles Dickens in *Our Mutual Friend*. The book was *Childhood and Youth*, Tolstoy's early essay in autobiography, and it was reviewed in a tone of grudging animosity. The reviewer seemed to be affronted by the moral tone of the writing. The translator had said that on this count the narrative was as wholesome as 'the fresh air of a fine day in spring'; and she had gone on to claim for her author that he was poet and philosopher no less than novelist. But she had also remarked:

he shares with most Russian authors a striking power of observation, and a tendency to that bold truthfulness which calls things by their right names, and avoids the confusion of moral ideas that arises from giving, to false sentimentality the appellation of sublime passion, and to corruption that of virtue, as we have been too much accustomed to see done, particularly in modern French literature.

Clearly, the translator realized that where she praised her author for powers of observation, she had to be careful to insist upon his elevated moral tone. It is interesting to see that, so early, this could be done most easily by distinguishing the Russian author from the French, also an 'observer'; for to elevate the Russians at the expense of the French was to be *de rigueur*, till the end of the century, for all but the hardiest spirits who would champion 'realism' in any form. The reviewer, at any rate, proved unwilling to agree that the 'realistic' method could be either philosophical or 'moral':

the translator, although possessing a very fair command of the English language knows very little of English tastes, or of the English standard of taste, when she announces to us that Count Tolstoi reveals himself to us as a poet and a philosopher. There is nothing to blame in the book. The incidents recorded are very trivial, and therefore probably true, and the whole production is insipid, unless we force an interest in it by reminding ourselves that it is improving to know how Russians write. But as a record of childhood it has its merits. It is not sickly or pretentious. Its merits are, however, mostly negative, and few compositions have less claim to philosophy. Perhaps, in the original, the language may be poetical, and there is an admirable tenderness of character shown in the childish history recorded, but that is the end of the poetry.

As for moral unpleasantness, the critic gives the impression of struggling hard to find something which he is sure must be there. The episodes of childish love, for example, have to be found 'simple and natural', though 'at the same time nothing can be more bald.' In the end, the taint is located in the account of the mother's funeral. One criticism of Tolstoy's treatment is just and acute – 'He relates, with his usual honesty, what passed in his mind at the time, and is easily able, with the experience of later life, to detect the insincerity which mingles so largely with the sincerest grief of the young.' But this reader seems not to care for duplicity in artistic method; rather he is concerned to safeguard the fabric of his own society:

In another passage he expresses himself more fully about his father, and tells us that, in spite of his being a model of deportment, he was addicted to many very serious weaknesses. We do not like this. It makes no difference whether a writer is a Russian, or a German, or an Englishman – whether he is or is not like a spring morning, or what may be his noble tendencies. He is not, we think, justified in telling his family history in this way, and in probing the feelings of parents in order that he may have the satisfaction of sketching his own childhood. It is no excuse to say that, unless he puts in the dark shades, the picture cannot be truthful. There is no reason why he should draw the picture at all. The world can get on very well without criticisms written by a son on the behaviour of his father at his mother's funeral. It would destroy all family confidence if we were all of us liable to be sacrificed in this way to the exigencies of literary art; and if this is the style in which sons who are like spring mornings write, most fathers would devoutly wish their own offspring should be like autumn evenings.

Thus Tolstoy is censured because he challenges the authority of the father in the Victorian home.

It was I suppose inevitable – it was at any rate fortunate – that Tolstoy and Dostoevsky were offered in bulk not to this mid-Victorian society still for the most part arrogantly riding high on the conviction of being 'top nation', but to the altogether more worried and insecure England of the 1880s, when for instance distinguished minds like Leslie Stephen's and Thomas Hardy's had lost their religious faith under the impact of Darwin and Herbert Spencer and the geologists. And in fact nothing is more noticeable, among the early enthusiasts for the Russians, than the readiness to embrace a new evangel from the steppes, from outside that western world which had gone sour on its denizens, had cracked apart or broken up around them.

Among the things that seemed to be cracking up or breaking down was the class-structure of Victorian England. The populace was demanding a say and a share of political power, and gradually over the next forty years (just the period when Russian writers were read most avidly and respectfully in England) the populace were to get what they wanted. Already in 1885 the Education Act of 1870 had begun to do its work of providing for nearly universal literacy. As a result there was a mass-audience for printed matter, literate but otherwise half-educated. The stage was set for the emergence of the modern journalist, catering for an undiscriminating mass-audience. Sure enough, they emerge; and have a lot to do with the way Tolstoy in particular speedily became known, as a name, to the man in the street. The crucial name is that of W. T. Stead, a name now largely forgotten, though he and other pioneers of modern journalism like

George Newnes and Alfred Harmsworth deserve the closest study from students of English literature in the late-Victorian and Edwardian periods. Stead was less successful than Newnes or Harmsworth; as a historian of modern journalism tells us scornfully, 'Even the greatest stroke of his career, "The Maiden Tribute of Modern Babylon", was not heralded with bold captions.' But Stead, if he lacked the dexterity of some one like the later Lord Northcliffe, was on to the same gold-mine of the mass audience. And he was interested in Tolstoy. From 1887 until the date of Tolstoy's death, innumerable 'Visits to Yasnaya Polyana' occupy the pages of British and American periodicals. And Stead's was one of the first; in his *Truth about Russia*, published in 1888, the last section is called 'Count Tolstoi and his Gospel', an account of a week's stay in Yasnaya Polyana. In the last chapter he reported a conversation with Tolstoy, in which the latter discoursed upon his scheme for a Universal Library, which should bring out the classics of European literature at a price to suit the leanest pocket. In the first number of his own magazine, *The Review of Reviews* (a sort of premature harbinger of *The Reader's Digest*), Stead claimed to be trying to take Tolstoy's advice in a modest way. Meanwhile Tolstoy had written *The Kreutzer Sonata*, a book now little read, which however created a furore all over Europe by its shockingly frank treatment of sex in marriage. The book now would raise few eyebrows – it is, with pathetic obviousness and very painfully, Tolstoy's unjustifiable generalization from experience all too peculiar, his own experience of marriage. E.J. Dillon had heard a reading of or from *The Kreutzer Sonata* in a Moscow salon, and obtained permission to telegraph the gist of the story to London. Dillon, being warned that Tolstoy was often unreliable in dealing with translators, wrote to him asking for permission to translate the full *Kreutzer Sonata*. Tolstoy replied that the American translator, Isabel Hapgood, had already been given permission to translate. Dillon, however, got permission to summarize, and sent his summary to the *Universal Review*. Quilter, the editor, was unhappy about the provocative nature of the story and pruned the summary before he allowed it to appear. Isabel Hapgood, having read the manuscript, refused in horror to have anything to do with it, and Tolstoy then entrusted the task to Dillon. The latter protested against a certain brutality of phrasing which had been censored even in the Russian version, but Tolstoy insisted that this must be retained. Meanwhile the summaries had caused a sensation and it was rumoured that garbled translations of *The Kreutzer Sonata* were abroad in Western Europe. At this juncture Stead wrote to Dillon asking him to translate *The Kreutzer Sonata* for the first number of *The Review of Reviews*. Stead was appalled when the translation arrived, and had to raise money to buy out his partner, Newnes, before he could publish even a garbled version of the latter part of Tolstoy's novel.

The work as it finally appeared in *The Review of Reviews* was certainly not worth the trouble and the money which Stead had spent on it. In a preface written by Stead before the manuscript arrived, he had maintained, on the basis of his conversation with Tolstoy two years before, that in the new work Tolstoy was severely moral, indeed puritanical, on the relationship of the sexes. This passage survives to the text as the first part of the published introduction, and Stead dramatically changes his opinion at the point when the manuscript reaches him. At a loss, he recalls the French pioneer enthusiast for the Russians, Melchior De Vogüe, and adopts from him the handy escape clause: that Tolstoy is puritan, certainly, but his puritanism is 'oriental'. And he goes, for support, to an anonymous lady with long experience of India. This correspondent, in a letter quoted by Stead, confirms that the attitude of Tolstoy is that of her 'Bengalee friends'. Like them, she asserts: 'He has no idea of that noble Anglo-Saxon type of love in which the physical attraction is hallowed and consecrated by all that is holiest and purest in imagination and in faith, and soul and body blend in one full chord to form the marriage tie.'. And in the end, what survives of the novel in the pages of *The Review of Reviews* is the merest muddle, in which it is impossible to tell where editorial summary ends and Tolstoy's writing begins. Thus was Stead trapped by ignoring what has since become one of the basic truths for successful mass-journalism – that the mass-audience, though it is just as prurient as the intelligentsia, is more hysterically prudish. And one cannot exclude a feeling of satisfaction; Stead had caught a tartar – the great writer, even in a bad book like *The Kreutzer Sonata*, is too uncomfortably honest to be processed into pap for the mass-audience.

This, alas, is as much as I have time for from the recorded history of how the Russian novel was presented to an English audience, and received by that audience. I want now to take a more Olympian stand and to suggest that in a properly long perspective of cultural history, the awakening of the Anglo-Saxon people to Russian literature – something which happened to all intents and purposes between 1885 and 1920 – should rank as a turning-point no less momentous than the discovery of Italian literature by the generations of the English Renaissance. The teacher of Russian literature to English-speaking youth today is a beachcomber along sands still wet from the incursion of that tidal wave. But we need to consider the configuration of the coastline which took such a drenching and emerged from it permanently altered; that is, we need to remember that the England which awoke to Russian literature was late-Victorian and Edwardian England. Tolstoy certainly, Dostoevsky more dubiously, and in the end Chekhov quite ludicrously, were forced into the niches which remained unfilled in the Victorian hall of fame – among the sages and prophets, the great moral teachers: Carlyle and Goethe, Emerson and Ruskin. There was a moment when Tolstoy was competing for his niche with Mrs Henry Wood, and Dostoevsky for his with Hall Caine. The Russian candidates were successful; and there they stand to this day, marmoreal and minatory, voluminously bearded, hectoring us about 'our duty to humanity', in all humility and in all arrogance. Tolstoy survived into the age of the electric telegraph and wretchedly therefore tried to marmorealize himself into the shape of the instructive effigy that the Anglo-Saxons had made of him. Like Carlyle, like Ruskin, and like Wordsworth (an English poet posthumously recruited into the same constricting pantheon), Tolstoy and Dostoevsky have had to endure the vengeful malice of later Anglo-Saxon generations determined to get their own back on the hateful figure of just that Victorian father; and so they have had their debunkers, their peering and prying biographers, their Freudian or Marxist explainers who explain them away. First the apotheosis, then the backlash – and all because they got translated at one time rather than another.

I suspect we get them clear for ourselves only by sinking them back more deliberately into the context from which they come. And for my own part I mean by that Russian context not in the first place social and political history, and yet not on the other hand literary history merely, but the history of the Russian imagination. Let us not imagine, for instance, that we have to counterbalance them merely by remembering their contemporary, 'Turgenev, the pure artist'. That is a worse libel on Turgenev than any that was perpetrated on Tolstoy or Dostoevsky. Beside their Hall of Fame, the Victorians had a side-chapel dedicated to those lesser deities, the pure artists, for whom one of several awful words was 'winsome'. Harmless because mindless, diffident (as well they might be), childlike because puerile, these were the hermaphrodites of aestheticism among whom astonishingly that burly huntsman Turgenev was accorded a place. Of the many litanies which survive designed for use at these emasculating shrines, the most appalling perhaps is that composed by Thackeray (in his *English Humorists of the Eighteenth Century*) for the shrine of Goldsmith – Goldsmith, whose incarceration in this boudoir enrages me only a little less than Turgenev's. (The odd thing is that Turgenev, translated in part fifteen years before Tolstoy or Dostoevsky, had been taken as a sufficiently robust character until the appearance of his more vociferously agonized compatriots compelled him to put on aestheticist petticoats.) No, the aestheticism of late-Victorian and Edwardian times is only the mirror-image of its philistinism; if the hall of fame had not been so gruff and overbearing, the palace of art would not have needed to be so mincing and so mawkish. There is no escape from the whole complex of museums by way of setting up 'pure artist' against 'prophet' – no, nor by trying to distinguish Tolstoy-the-Artist from Tolstoy-the-everything-else.

Unfortunately (and here we can stop jeering at our grandfathers) we have never properly reconstructed that temple precinct which we inherited from the last century: it still consists of a hall of fame for the great moral teachers, and a fragrantly hushed side-chapel for the 'pure artists'. Despite Blok and Mayakovsky and Babel and many another who must seem totally out of place in either of these chambers, the pantheon of Russian literature still somehow, it appears, must be accommodated in these two categories and no others. One book by Pasternak, *Doctor Zhivago*, has in the eyes of Anglo-Saxon enthusiasts revived the image of the Russian novelist as sage and prophet, delivering portentous apophthegms about Life and Humanity and Love and Nature. (I speak, you understand, not of that great and poignant though imperfect book of Pasternak's, but of the image of it peddled by reviewers and commentators.) And meanwhile the career of that other brilliant Russian novelist of our time, Vladimir Nabokov, has refurbished the little palace of the 'pure', the amoral, artist. (The author of *Lolita* is the harmlessly wicked sort of pure artist, an Aubrey Beardsley, whereas the wretched Turgenev was given the other role of the harmlessly good and noble – but the two types were always allowed for.)

We cannot absolve Nabokov, as we must absolve Pasternak, from some responsibility for this state of affairs. For he has deliberately darkened counsel, and that on the most crucial figure of all – the figure that has been conspicuous by his absence from all that I have said, as he is conspicuously absent from the image of Russian literature generally, outside Russia. I mean of course Pushkin. Nabokov's four-volume translation of *Eugene Onegin* with commentary is a monumental attempt to make 'a pure artist' of Pushkin. The wit and vigour and erudition of Nabokov make up a case that is formidable. And yet not at all convincing. The image of Pushkin which emerges from Nabokov's volumes – entertaining and intelligent and invaluable as they are – is of a cold voluptuary with a fine ear and a rhyming itch; which is to say, a figure that provokes no interest and commands no sympathy, whatever the technical wonders that he is alleged to have worked with Russian syntax, versification and vocabulary.

Nothing, it seems to me, was more depressing for the state of our understanding of Russian literature than the profound obeisance with which Nabokov's monument was greeted by our reviewers. For how could the resourceful amoralist whom Nabokov celebrated be that poet to whom Tolstoy and Turgenev and Dostoevsky had paid such profound respect? An ex-colleague of mine at the University of Essex, Stanley Mitchell, put the matter succinctly and, I think conclusively, in a BBC broadcast some years ago:

> ... what Tolstoy and all Russian writers with him, in particular Dostoevsky, envied in Pushkin was precisely his sense of harmony and hierarchy. Both his personality, mercurial and unobsessive, and his work, virile, serene, unpropagandist, were the objects of deepest longing.
>
> But while Russian writers longed for Pushkin and a lost literature of harmony, writers in the West seized precisely upon the *dis*harmonies, the perturbations, the nostalgias, the great spiritual ache of later Russian literature, to make these the objects of *their* longing.

In other words, Russian literature in even its broad outlines will not be known until Pushkin is seen and known for what he is, or at least for what all later Russian writers have taken him to be. And no amount of perceptive and adulatory Pushkiniana in the trade journals like *The Slavonic & East European Review* will meet the case; for these will not get this poet out of the hands of the professionals and into the hands of the amateur, i.e. *the reader.* Just as Shakespeare cannot be ignored by those who have no English, nor Dante by those who have no Italian, so Pushkin cannot remain the perquisite of those who read him in the original only. The respectful enthusiasm which greeted Nabokov's *Eugene Onegin* shows how far Pushkin is from being in this way part of the imaginative universe of every cultivated Englishman. Some of the earliest critics, notably George Saintsbury, had the temerity to declare openly that the prestige of Pushkin among Russians was a confidence-trick which we had a duty not to be overawed or taken in by. And sometimes one longs for such bluntness now. For as it is, we are hypocritical about him. An unusually frank and brave stranger wrote to me after I had reviewed the Penguin Pushkin.[1] He introduced himself as a professional teacher of Russian, who confessed that he taught Pushkin without conviction, suspecting all the time that his reputation was necessary to Soviet ideology and only for that reason was so impregnable.

The excuse offered for this state of affairs is (with a sigh overtly of

[1] *Eugene Onegin: a novel in verse*, trans. Babette Deutsch. Penguin Books, 1964. (The currently available Penguin translation is Charles Johnson's, 1979).

regret, but sometimes I suspect of relief) that Pushkin is 'untranslatable'. This excuse will wash no longer because, lost in the shadow of Nabokov's non-translation, is Walter Arndt's version of *Eugene Onegin*, certainly not a definitive version (for it gives us Pushkin more as Byron) but an immeasurable advance on anything before, and certainly capable at a pinch of being the text from which to teach something of Pushkin to those whose Russian is imperfect or non-existent.[1]

No, the real obstacle surely is not the famous 'untranslatability' but the situation I've been trying to outline, in which we have two stools only, those of 'moral sage' on the one hand and 'pure artist' on the other. Pushkin to his glory insists on falling between these two stools, or rather – more precisely – that in fact there is only *one* stool and he is occupying it.

The middle ground that we need to occupy if we are to grasp Pushkin is not a *terra incognita*; as is the rule with literary study, it is ground that has been occupied and mapped in the past, which by mere desuetude has been allowed to revert to uncharted wilderness. The words which Stanley Mitchell used already re-establish some of the landmarks – 'harmony and hierarchy', 'mercurial and unobsessive', 'virile, serene'. These are not terms that we apply to the allegedly 'pure artists'. And there are, when we choose to remember them, many such words – suavity and urbanity, frankness and boldness, ease and strength, vigour and activity and repose. They are terms as far as possible from the technical terminology that is wished upon us by those who want defensively to make literary study a professionalism among other professionalisms, under the banner for instance of 'stylistics'. They are words which we use of people, of personalities, more often than of books.

And it is interesting, and immediately to the point, to ask why these terms have fallen into disuse: it is because they describe a sort of personality and a sort of behaviour that was more highly esteemed in an age of aristocracy than in democracies. And Pushkin of course was an aristocrat. And so, I suppose, what I am saying is that Russian literature (and, more narrowly, the Russian novel – for Pushkin wrote novels in verse and prose, as well as lyric poems) needs to be seen to have had more than a Victorian and one or two post-Victorian phases; it was the voice of a gentry culture before it became the voice of the bourgeois conscience.

---

[1]   *Eugene Onegin*, trans. Walter Arndt. New York: E.P. Dutton, second revd. ed., 1981.

A talk given at Oregon State University, Cornwallis, 1972.

11   Tragedy and Gaiety

Mandelstam, Clarence Brown. Cambridge & New York: CUP, 1973.
Selected Poems, Osip Mandelstam, translated by David McDuff.
Cambridge: Rivers Press, 1973; New York: Farrar, Straus & Giroux,
1975.
Selected Poems, Osip Mandelstam, translated by Clarence Brown and
W.S. Merwin. Oxford: OUP, 1973; New York: Atheneum, 1974
(Penguin Books, 1977).
Chapter 42, Nadezhda Mandelstam; with *The Goldfinch*, Osip Man-
delstam, introduced and translated by Donald Rayfield. London:
Menard Press, 1973.

Clarence Brown's long-awaited study of Mandelstam deserves its
place in the same series or at least under the same imprint as John
Bayley's incomparable *Pushkin*. Among innumerable arresting and
instructive things one wants to quote, there is Brown's comment
on Mandelstam's poems of 1913: 'The humour is often explicit, but
more often it springs from an intangible sense of elation, a gaiety
of language, *that would never be absent from his poems again.*' The italics
are mine. But they seem called for, since what we mostly know is
the harrowing story of Mandelstam's last years told by his indomit-
able widow Nadezhda, in her memoir of 1970, *Hope Against Hope*.
A tragic destiny; but the poems at the heart of it are *gay*. It was
Mandelstam's glory that, this linguistic hilarity once discovered, he
refused, even in his blackest years when his overt themes were most
sombre, to do without it; as it was his calamity that even when he
wanted to exclude it (as presumably in his abortive and pathetic
'Ode to Stalin'), he couldn't. We may think by contrast how the
author of 'Sweeney Agonistes' gave up more and more of the game-
someness, positively the *gaminess*, of poetic language, so as to
become the author of *Four Quartets*. And yet in that development
wasn't Eliot merely acknowledging that the spirit of the age had
switched irreversibly away from the high-spirited audacity of the
international avant-garde in its heyday? Mandelstam, especially in
poems about Leningrad, acknowledged the change but couldn't or
wouldn't reconcile himself to it.

In this way Mandelstam is very remote from us. He is so 'modern' that he makes us feel 'post-modern'. All the same, he has lessons for us. For instance how 'literary' he is! How insistently he experiences life 'at one remove'! And how conclusively the spectacle of his career knocks all the frail props from underneath such common and vulgar objections to a poetry that concerns itself, explicitly and shamelessly, with 'culture'!

However, we can learn from him only when we have a secure grasp of him and his poetry. Nowadays he can be introduced into a literary conversation without seeming to up-stage anyone. But it's only in the perspective of martyrology that we know him, not at all in the perspective of poetry. And in fact we haven't got him right even as a martyr. We get him right only when we see him as one angle of a quadrilateral: Mandelstam, Akhmatova, Tsvetayeva, Pasternak. This constellation is hard for us to discern, if only because for so many years, first in Russian and then in Anglo-American opinion, Mayakovsky was promoted so as to overshadow and eclipse his peers. And indeed one urgent need we have is for one of our dependable Russianists to assess for us how far Mayakovsky stands up, now that these contemporaries of his begin to emerge from the shadows. But in any case they have as yet hardly emerged at all, the shadows still cling murkily about each of them. I haven't primarily in mind, what Clarence Brown rightly insists on, the extent to which official suppression and falsification still obscure the actual canon, and anything like a definitive text, of Mandelstam's work. I'm thinking more of our own sins of omission and commission, and particularly of our performance as translators. All of these poets have been mutilated (oh with the best will in the world!) by grossly insensitive translations that still circulate along with one or two that are respectable. Is Mandelstam going to have better luck than the other three?

Not, I'm afraid, if David McDuff is typical. To see how little he can be trusted, compare his number 59 ('I see a lake, standing sheer...') with Clarence Brown's discussion of what is admittedly a fiendishly difficult poem. Other spot-checks, and comparisons with W.S. Merwin's versions, are no more reassuring. One notes resignedly that it's McDuff's version that will get about in cheap paperback. Merwin reads much better. No wonder; he's a practised professional, and has Clarence Brown for collaborator. He alone, not always but often, makes *poems* (American ones, naturally); by which one means, quite simply, that his versions mostly make sense – perhaps not always the right sense and certainly not the complete sense, but at all events *sense*. Donald Rayfield's mostly don't; not surprisingly, since making sense is what his commentary does, very interestingly too. But with Rayfield the commentator taking this responsibility, what is there left for Rayfield the translator to do? Answer (in part): try to keep Mandelstam's rhymes – which is nearly always a mistake. Rayfield is indispensable however, for what he does is to give us a chapter omitted from *Hope Against Hope*, together with the poems that that chapter discusses. This is excellent; the Menard Press is to be congratulated, and so is Rayfield for doing a thankless and necessary job. (For Clarence Brown's discussions, it should be noted, don't extend to these late pieces.)

In the quadrilateral of names the classic polarity between St Petersburg and Moscow is represented with a symmetry that is positively disconcerting: Akhmatova and Mandelstam are Leningrad poets, Pasternak and Tsvetayeva are Muscovites. Let no one think this is accidental or trivial. If from the Olympian standpoint of Russian culture as a whole the Muscovite and the Petersburg emphases are doubtless complementary, to those actually caught up in the Russian literary scene the opposing alignment (Slavophil versus Westerner, rural versus urban, pious versus sceptical, vegetative versus lapidary – the polarity shows up in many forms in each generation) necessarily figures as competing, if not antagonistic. The undercurrent of hostility to Pasternak among some of Mandelstam's admirers is at least partly to be explained in this way, as are Mandelstam's seemingly gratuitous attacks on Tsvetayeva in the 1920s (ten years after he'd been in love with her).

But this polarity is crossed with another which has more to do with the martyrology than the poetry and yet has its bearing on the poetry too: on each side of the divide stood one who was intransigent, and another who strove so far as honour would permit to be accommodating. Here it is Tsvetayeva who lines up with Mandelstam, Akhmatova with Pasternak. All four were martyred before the end; but it was Mandelstam and Tsvetayeva who *looked* for trouble. On this issue we must be careful not to take sides; for if one of the four angles yawns apart, all the others are forced out of true. Mandelstam and Tsvetayeva, it seems clear, were outrageous. Impossible persons, both of them. It's one of the manifold virtues of Nadezhda's furiously honest memoir that it doesn't blink this fact. One sees it most clearly perhaps in their prose. I've had Mandelstam's 'Conversation on Dante' presented to me as a model of what criticism should be. Heaven forbid! It is a work of genius; it is even, I believe, irreplaceable as a series of insights into Dante. But I can think of nothing worse as a model of critical procedure, so joyously idiosyncratic as it is, and so discontinuous. Likewise in public life Mandelstam seems to have been so wayward that even a society much less bureaucratically rigid and cruel than Soviet society would have found him unemployable and in a profound sense unassimilable. Which is not to diminish by a hair's breadth one's loathing and contempt for what Soviet society did to him. (And the society did it, not just the State – that's another of the searing truths that Nadezhda's memoir drives home.)

This is a good place from which to force an entry into the poetry. For Mandelstam was all of a piece (whereas Pasternak, it seems, could be, in no dishonourable sense, prudent and shrewd outside poetry, as in poetry he wasn't). Roy Fuller in an Oxford lecture has decided: 'poetry seems to stand, even thrive on, outrageous imaginative collage, provided the poet remains in formal control'. It's not what we're used to hearing from Professor Fuller; at least that anxious provision for 'formal control' seems more characteristic than what precedes it. (And Mandelstam incidentally answers to the stipulation, though his satisfyingly clear and symmetrical forms are nearly always subverted, as it were, from inside.) Anyhow Fuller comes by his perception honestly. And there are precedents: Baudelaire for instance, deciding that the beautiful in poetry must partake of the bizarre. And certainly a quality of the bizarre, the outrageous, seems to be what elevates the young Acmeist Mandelstam above his pre-Acmeist self, as also above the appealing and talented doomed Acmeist leader Gumilyev, just as it is what raises the young Imagist Pound over his pre-Imagist self, and over a gifted and attractive fellow-Imagist like H.D.

The comparison isn't gratuitous. Ever since, twenty-five years ago, one first heard of Mandelstam from D.S. Mirsky, one has fidgeted and fumbled with the notion that between the Acmeist school in Russia and the exactly contemporaneous Imagist school in London there were analogies so many and so exact that one gasped to see the *Zeitgeist* so flagrantly in action. One is gratified but also a little deflated to find that the analogy is now a critic's commonplace. It should *not* be a commonplace, I think, given how striking a conjunction it is. And indeed for a Poundian of sorts like myself there is every temptation to let the extraordinary analogy run away with the rest of the review. Heroically resisting temptation, let's say only that for English-speakers the way into the Acmeist Mandelstam (and Clarence Brown believes that 'acmeist' he remained in some sense to the end) seems to be inescapably by way of the Imagist Pound. This ought to be a big help; but probably won't be, because England has certainly seen what Akhmatova protested at in Russia: the deprecating of Acmeism in the one case, Imagism in the other, as no more than a late by-blow or variant of Symbolism (to which in fact both movements were opposed).

Clarence Brown intelligently gets a lot of mileage out of the

Acmeist/Imagist analogy. Thus, when he endorses and adopts Gumilyev's pin-pointing of just where the Acmeist takes over in Mandelstam's first collection, *Stone* (1913; and only ponder the Poundian implications of *that* title!), he quotes T.E. Hulme's Imagist 'Autumn':

> A touch of cold in the Autumn night –
> I walked abroad,
> And saw the ruddy moon lean over a hedge
> Like a red-faced farmer.
> I did not stop to speak, but nodded,
> And round about were the wistful stars
> With white faces like town children.

And there is certainly a neat fit between this and Mandelstam's poem:

> No, not the moon, a luminous clock-face
> shines down on me, and how can I be blamed
> if the weak stars I register only as 'milky'?
>
> Batyushkov's hauteur also I don't care for;
> who, when they asked what time it was, returned
> compendiously, 'Eternity!' for answer.

But the fit is really too neat to be convincing, especially since the common element is thematic (moon and stars), and Mandelstam was at pains to relegate the thematic component of poetry to no more than parity with other elements. What's missing from Hulme is precisely the bizarreness of the conjunction, the audacity of the imaginative leap from Mandelstam's first tercet to his second; and for this we look in vain to any Imagist save Pound himself.

It's good that Batyushkov's name crops up here. For Batyushkov (1787-1855), Pushkin's contemporary, figures large in Mandelstam's thinking. And very properly too, since he is perhaps the most illustrious example before Mandelstam of a rare but recurrent and precious bent that the Russian imagination may take: quite directly towards the Mediterranean, by way of remembering the Greek city-states on the Black Sea, and Ovid's exile in what is now Romania. (Mandelstam's second collection was given with brilliant appropriateness – though it wasn't he that chose it – the Ovidian title, *Tristia*.) A Petersburg poet, yes; therefore a Westerner, just so. But the Westerner in Mandelstam can draw on vast imaginative and cultural resources because, instead of looking through Peter the Great's 'window on the west' out to the Baltic and across to Scandinavia, Holland or England, he looks instead south-westward, along a tunnel through the centuries which leads his eye directly past the Crimea to the Aegean and beyond, even (and indeed especially) to Italy.

Batyushkov and Pushkin had sighted along that telescope before him; Mandelstam looks through it long and steadily, with yearning yet without the disabling nostalgia of the internal émigré he was said to be, but was not. Something of this we knew already from his widow's memoir; now we can see it in such poems as 'Batyushkov' and 'Ariosto', both of them in Brown-Merwin versions lucid, grateful and affecting. And this might seem the point at which to recall that the poet's origins were Polish and Jewish; but Mandelstam, as I read him, would have violently repudiated any such gloss – this direct access to Mediterranean humanism is an avenue open to the *Russian* imagination, opened up through *Russian* language.

Postscript: Verse-translations of Mandelstam by James Greene, who I think is better than Merwin – and his sensibility as European as Merwin's is American – have altered my focus on Mandelstam. [See Chapter 12 below.] I should now put less stress on the bizarre in his poetry and more on the *roundedness* of the forms that he favours, both in nature and in art. This would be to emphasize not just his 'formal control', but the extremely traditional nature of his formality. And his yearning towards the Mediterranean would then come to seem, in a quite precise sense, *classical*.

New Statesman, 7 December 1973; reprinted in *The Poet in the Imaginary Museum*, ed. Barry Alpert. Manchester: Carcanet New Press, 1977.

12   Mandelstam's Classicism

Of Mandelstam's *Octets*, Robert Chandler has said that 'the inform-
ing energy of the poem stems from, is a part of, the universal impulse
to form, which leads equally to the creation of a petal or a cupola,
the pattern of a group of sailing-boats or a poem.' And Mr Chandler
may be right. Yet as I worked at the *Octets*[1] it seemed to me on the
contrary that Mandelstam was distinguishing one kind of form from
another, and was celebrating only those forms that are 'bent in',
arced, the form of a foetus or a cradle, specifically *not* the open-ended
and discontinuous mere 'pattern' (rather than 'form') that a group
of sailing-boats may fall into.

I stress this because I am inclined to see in it the clue to what is
distinctive about this poet, and what is distinctively daunting about
the challenge he presents to his translators. If I am right, Mandelstam's
poems themselves yearn towards, and achieve, forms that are 'bent-
in', rounded, sounding a full bell-note. Moreover, because what the
poems say is at one with the forms they find for the saying, we see
why it is that, as Clarence Brown tells us, for Mandelstam 'cognition'
is always 'recognition' – *re*-cognition, a return upon itself, a 'coming
round again'.

And nothing else, so far as I can see, will enable us to reconcile
Anna Akhmatova's firm declaration, 'he had no poetic forerunners',
with his widow's no less firm admonition: 'Mandelstam...unlike
innovators such as Mayakovsky and Pasternak...composed verses
in tradition, which is far more difficult to imitate'. What sort of a
poet can this be, who is 'traditional' and yet has 'no poetic forerunners'? We solve this riddle by saying that in his techniques Mandelstam was indeed unprecedented, yet the techniques were made
to serve a *form* – why not say simply, a *beauty*? – that rejoiced in
calling upon every precedent one might think of, from Homer to
Ovid, to the builders of Santa Sophia, to Dante and Ariosto and
Racine. For it is true, surely: the sort of form to which Mandelstam
vows himself alike in nature and in art, the form of the bent-in and

---

[1]   Donald Davie's version of Mandelstam's *Octets* has been published in *Agenda*, Vol.
14, No. 2, 1976; also in *Collected Poems 1970-1983* (Manchester and Notre Dame, 1983).

the rounded-upon-itself, is the most ancient and constant of all European understandings of the beautiful – it is what long ago recognized in the circle the image of perfection. This profoundly traditional strain and aspiration in Mandelstam explains why the Russia of his lifetime is seldom imaged directly in his poetry, and why, when it is so imaged, the image is overshadowed by others from ancient Greece or from Italy; it explains why domes and cupolas and shells (either whorled or scalloped) appear in his poetry so often; and it explains why the hackneyed figures of the sky as a dome and a vault, and of the sea as curved round the earth's curve, appear in that poetry so insistently and with such otherwise unexplained potency. If we were to call Mandelstam 'classical' this is what we might mean, or what we ought to mean. And nothing is further from what may reasonably be seen as the characteristic endeavour of the Western European and American of this century, in all the arts – that is to say, the finding of beauty in the discontinuous and the asymmetrical, the open-ended and indeed the adventitious.

Just here arises the peculiarly extreme difficulty of translating Mandelstam into English. Before James Greene's, the most readable and accomplished translation we had was by W.S. Merwin, done in collaboration with Clarence Brown. But this was, necessarily and properly, an *American* translation; a translation, that's to say, into that one of the twentieth-century idioms which is, and has been ever since Walt Whitman, and even in such an untypical American as Pound, pre-eminently vowed to the open-ended and the discontinuous. Yet Mandelstam is the most 'European' of all Russian poets since Pushkin. How could Merwin have succeeded? Yet he did – to the extent that he does indeed bring over, for a public that has not and cannot have any immediate access to the Mediterranean fountains of European consciousness, as much of Mandelstam as can survive that oceanic passage. Here however was a chance for that one of the English-speaking idioms which *is* part of the European consciousness: could the British idiom achieve what by its very nature the American could not? James Greene had his own difficulties; for current British idioms, insofar as they respect the integrity of the verse-line and the verse-stanza (and plainly that was what was involved), characteristically give *pattern* instead of *form*, or else – to put it another way – they preserve the arc of the poem's form only by 'filling in', by not having the content of the poem pressing up against the curve of its form with equal pressure at every point. (The opposite danger, which I have not escaped in my versions, is of packing the content against the verse-line so tightly that the verse is felt to be straining and as it were bursting at the seams.) James Greene was equal to the challenge. His measuring up to it is shown in the first place by his daring to do what every verse-translator must have guiltily felt he ought to do, but was afraid of doing – that's to say, by leaving untranslated those parts of poems for which he could find no equivalent in English verse that carried authority. His more positive virtues – particularly in finding English near-equivalents for the punning resemblances in sound which, for Mandelstam as for Pasternak, function as structural principles, given the richly orchestrated nature of Russian... these can be appreciated only by those who can check back against the Russian originals.

Here for the first time we have a faithful version, not of Mandelstam, but of as much of Mandelstam as this scrupulous translator is prepared to stand by – faithful as never before, because as never before there is no line of the Russian poems that is not made *poetry* in English. Previous British versions have been wooden; this one *rings* – it is bronze, properly Roman bronze.

Foreword to *Osip Mandelstam: Poems*, selected and translated by James Greene. London: Elek, 1977 (rev. 1980).

13   Ironies out of Poland: Zbigniew Herbert

More than twenty years ago, as soon as translations from Zbigniew Herbert began to appear, he enjoyed a very good press in Britain. Alfred Alvarez, W.L. Webb in the *Guardian*, and Ian Hamilton were three who applauded him, and demanded that he be attended to. In this the British were, as they still are, ahead of the Americans. So we did something right, and may as well smirk about it. For Alvarez and Webb and Hamilton did not delude themselves, nor delude us. The proof, if proof is still needed, is in Herbert's sixth collection, published in the original Polish in 1983 and now very valuably translated in its integrity and its entirety by John and Bogdana Carpenter, who ten years ago gave us Herbert's *Selected Poems* (the second such, for the first *Selected* came out from Penguin in 1968). This latest collection of thirty-five poems, called *Report from the Besieged City*,[1] affords the very rare spectacle of a poet in mid-career dismantling one poetic personality and replacing it by another, which surpasses the first. Or so it seems to me.

The transformation that I see has everything to do with irony. For the poetic personality of the relatively youthful Herbert (he was born in 1924) was what won us over, or some of us, in the 1960s. And that personality was nothing if not ironical. It is not hard to see how that would be more attractive to the British than to the Americans. For an ironical attitude is one way of keeping one's dignity in a situation of impotence. And whereas the chronically helpless or luckless Poles have found themselves in that situation through most of their history, the post-1945 British, living through a post-imperial twilight, suddenly found their situation not very different. (The USSR, the USA – there are great differences of course, but one or the other Big Brother limits the power of Poles and Britons alike.) Accordingly it has often been noted, sometimes

---

[1]   Herbert, *Selected Poems*, trans. Czesław Miłosz & Peter Dale Scott. Penguin Books, 1968; reprinted by Carcanet Press (Manchester) 1985. *Report from the Besieged City*, trans. John & Bogdana Carpenter. New York: Ecco Press, 1985; Oxford: OUP, 1987.

angrily and accusingly, what a high premium has been put on irony
in British poetry since 1945. Indeed there has been one poet, D.J.
Enright, who has so consistently relied on irony very like Herbert's
that he might well feel a sort of pique at how his home-grown
performances have earned at best a tepid respect, while the Polish
ironies have been applauded. In *Report from the Besieged City* Herbert
has learned to do without irony. And that is a transformation indeed.

Irony isn't a simple matter. Enright has lately devoted a whole
book to discussing it. It comes in different kinds. And until lately
only one kind was in favour with Zbigniew Herbert. Stanislaw
Baranczak, a Polish poet himself, has just now given us the first
book in English wholly concerned with Herbert's poetry,[1] and he
there makes a significant, perhaps a damaging, point: 'In Herbert's
case we are nearly always dealing with just one of the two fundamen-
tal kinds of irony: with "being ironical" rather than "seeing things
as ironic", in other words with so-called verbal irony rather than
situational irony.' Situational irony has also been called cosmic irony.
Neither expression is wholly satisfactory. It is what many of us
know best from the work of Thomas Hardy. Alike in his poems
and his stories Hardy claims to perceive, and asks us to recognize,
a kind of irony built into the very frame of things. For him irony
is not an attitude that we may adopt in the face of the cosmos, but
the attitude with which the cosmos confronts *us*. In Polish we can
find this in the Nobel prize-winner Czesław Miłosz (b. 1911), who
is surely one of Herbert's masters. In one poem, in *Bells in Winter*,
we find Miłosz (or if we want to be pernickety, his *persona*) travelling
to and reaching a famous shrine in France:

> I was a patient pilgrim. And so I notched
> Each month and year on my stick, since it neared me to my aim.
> Yet when at last I arrived after many years
> What happened there, many would know, I think,
> Who in the parking lot at Roc Amadour
> Found a space and then counted the steps
> To the upper chapel, to make sure that this was it:
> Because a wooden Madonna with a child in a crown
> Was surrounded by a throng of impassive art lovers.
> As I did. Not a step further. Mountains and valleys
> Crossed. Through flames. Wide waters. And unfaithful memory.
> The same passion but I hear no call.
> And the holy had its abode only in denial.

[1] *A Fugitive from Utopia. The Poetry of Zbigniew Herbert.* Harvard University Press,
1987.

Here we surely detect irony of a sort in the wooden phrasing of 'to make sure that this was it'; and more certainly it is ironical that on such solemn occasions we have to deal with such mundane questions as where to park the car. But this is an irony that the world faces us with, it's not anything we summon up out of our own resources. The same is true of the more momentous irony that Miłosz is leading up to: 'And the holy had its abode only in denial.' For this obviously means more than: 'The irony of it! Nothing happened when I got there.' If we were to tease this out, we might find ourselves saying: 'We know that the holy exists, because we can conceive of it and yearn for it. But we seldom or never find it. And just that – its absence, and the hole that that absence makes in our sense of ourselves and the world – is what makes it ever present to our consciousness. Thus God's absence paradoxically proves that He is necessary, and exists.' This logic has been followed through by many philosophers and theologians in this century, and if we want to find it in poetry in English we cannot do better than look at many poems by our own R.S. Thomas. Those poems, like this passage from Miłosz, are profoundly ironical while not in the least quizzical.

There is a strikingly exact parallel in a relatively early poem by Herbert, his 'Mona Lisa', which Baranczak properly and usefully considers at some length. Here too a Pole has not without difficulty escaped from Poland on a pilgrimage to a shrine in France, though whereas Miłosz's shrine was religious, Herbert's is secular, a work of art, Leonardo's painting hanging in the Louvre:

> Through seven mountain frontiers
> barbed wire of rivers
> and executed forests
> and hanged bridges
> I kept coming –
> through waterfalls of stairways
> whirlings of sea wings
> and baroque heaven
> all bubbly with angels
> – to you
> Jerusalem in a frame
>
> I stand
> in the dense nettle patch
> of a cook's tour
> on a shore of crimson rope
> and eyes

> so I'm here
> you see I'm here
>
> I hadn't a hope
> but I'm here
>
>> laboriously smiling on
>> resin-coloured mute convex...

That word 'laboriously' fixes the tone as quizzical; if earlier phrases ('all bubbly with angels') haven't alerted us already, now we know – what we have here is the other kind of irony, which Baranczak calls 'verbal'. Herbert is going to be ironical towards and about the painting; the painting will not look ironically at *him*. And so it proves: before the poem is over Herbert is addressing la Gioconda, the famous image, as 'fat and not too nice signora'. In the meantime we have been told why the masterpiece leaves the poet cold, just as the older poet was left cold by the Madonna of Roc Amadour: the reason is that Herbert is a privileged person, able to leave Poland (and return to it), whereas other Poles can't:

> so I'm here
> they were all going to come
> I'm alone
>
> when already
> he could no longer move his head
> he said
> as soon as all this is over
> I'm going to Paris...

This is affecting. The reason that Herbert gives is readily understandable, whereas the reason that Miłosz finds for *his* discomfiture launches us into metaphysics. Moreover we feel warmly towards Herbert, because he feels warmly towards his less fortunate compatriots; and we notice that Miłosz expresses no such concern for any of his fellow men. Accordingly, though in other poems Milosz does express his own kind of concern, he has been thought to be cold. It seems plain that he will never be as popular as Herbert with British readers, nor probably with Polish ones either. If we can see good reason for a poet to be quizzical, then his quizzical tone is something we are at ease with; whereas the much more blank or elusive tone of a Miłosz or R.S. Thomas leaves us disconcerted.

Herbert however was never satisfied with, or self-satisfied about, his mastery of the quizzical. In 'From Mythology', one of his

numerous prose-poems (for so they appear in English, though
originally he found a distinct category for them), Herbert showed
early on that he recognized how verbal irony could be used, defensively, by the oppressors as well as the oppressed. And 'Elegy of
Fortinbras', dedicated 'for C.M.', the poem that more than any other
won him English admirers – and rightly, for its even-handedness
reminds us of great political poems like Yeats's 'Easter 1916' – will
bear, as an admittedly subordinate meaning, the interpretation that
as Miłosz is Hamlet so Herbert is his more limited though more
effective successor Fortinbras:[1]

> I go to my affairs This night is born
> a star named Hamlet We shall never meet
> what I shall leave will not be worth a tragedy

Other poems, and prose-poems, do not escape the fate always lurking for the quizzical – that of becoming whimsical. But this happens
seldom. Mostly Herbert was very sure in his control of verbal ironies:

> nothing special
> boards paint
> nails paste
> paper string
>
> mr artist
> builds a world
> not from atoms
> but from remnants
>
> forest of arden
> from umbrella
> ionian sea
> from parkers quink
>
> just as long as
> his look is wise
> just as long as
> his hand is sure –
>
> and presto the world –
>
> hooks of flowers
> on needles of grass
> clouds of wire
> drawn out by wind

---

[1] It is only fair to say that Stanislaw Baranczak rejects this reading.

Here the poet ('mr artist') is being quizzical about himself. And so this is the irony that we call deprecating, in which the author foresees the objections that can be raised to himself and his habits, and forestalls them by voicing the objections before any one else can. This shows very plainly how verbal irony is a self-protecting device, and it is easy to resent it if we think that greater poets, and more generous people, lay themselves open. Herbert knows this. How little store he set by these self-protecting skills, even as he practised them, appears from another of his most ambitious earlier poems, 'Apollo and Marsyas'. For in re-telling the ancient myth of how a human musician challenged the god of music to a trial of skill, was defeated, and flayed for his pains, Herbert identifies himself with Apollo (as, cool and clinical, he could not fail to do – Apollo was god of science as well as of music and poetry); and yet in the poem our sympathies are evoked for the human victim who, flayed, 'relates / the inexhaustible wealth / of his body':

> bald mountains of liver
> white ravines of aliment
> rustling forests of lung
> sweet hillocks of muscle
> joints bile blood and shudders
> the wintry wind of bone...

Though it is Apollo who has 'absolute ear', Marsyas has 'immense range'. And when at the end of the poem Apollo looks back at the scene of the atrocity and sees all nature blanched in sympathy with Marsyas, we surely see Herbert not just sceptical of his own Apollonian skills, but appalled by them. He has become a poet imprisoned by his own accomplishment, and knowing it.

But to know it is one thing; to break out of the prison is something else. And it seems to have taken Herbert some years before he had access, like Marsyas, to 'the inexhaustible wealth / of his body.' This he has now attained to, for instance in 'Shameful Dreams', which is quite unironical:

> Metamorphoses downward to the sources of history
> the lost paradise of childhood in a drop of water
>
> escapes chases through corridors of mice
> an insect's travels to the bottom of a flower
> a sharp awakening in an oriole's nest
>
> or loping watchfully over snow in a wolf's hide
> and at the edge of an abyss a huge howling to the full moon
> sudden fear when the wind brings the scent of a murderer

the whole sun setting in a stag's antlers
spiral dream of a snake
vertical alertness of the flatfish

all of them are recorded in the atlas of our body
and incised in the rock of the skull like portraits of our ancestors
so we repeat letters of forgotten speech

we dance at night before statues of animals
dressed in skin scales feathers and plated armour
infinite is the litany of our crimes

don't push us away good spirits
we have blundered on the oceans and stars too long
we are exhausted beyond measure accept us to the herd

Can we trust the translators enough to think that this hard-won access to 'the atlas of our body' is mirrored in the long and looping rhythms, which seem to be without precedent in Herbert's earlier work? It is to be hoped we can, though the Carpenters, in their valuable but far too sparse notes, say nothing about the matter. In fact it is very remarkable that none of the four translators who have worked on Herbert, nor Baranczak in his book, have anything to tell us about how this poet exploits or fails to exploit the musicality (by which one does not mean the euphoniousness) of the Polish language. The first translators, Miłosz and the admirable Canadian Peter Dale Scott, insist that Herbert is readily translatable – and we may hesitantly suppose this to mean, among other things, that with Herbert the phonetic, the sheerly acoustic, dimension of his medium counts for little. The Carpenters, to the contrary, declare Herbert hard to translate, and perhaps the later Herbert poses more difficulties than the earlier, but nothing they say gives the impression that this greater difficulty has to do with matters of rhythm, cadence, orchestration of sound. So long as we are told nothing about this dimension of the poet's performance, the nagging doubt must remain that we are perhaps being conned; at least, that we have in him all the translatable virtues but none of the untranslatable. This if true would make Herbert a strikingly two-dimensional poet; and it is rather shocking that no one, to my knowledge, has pointed this out. What I want to believe is that the greater richness of the later Herbert is reflected in a richer, more various music. But until a Polish-speaker can assure of this (and demonstrate it, so far as it is demonstrable), our anxious doubts must remain.

In the 1970s Herbert began using a *persona* whom he called 'Mr

Cogito', and commentators were quick to compare this with Paul
Valéry's Monsieur Teste or Pound's Hugh Selwyn Mauberley. This
stratagem, when one first encountered it or heard about it, seemed
to confirm that Herbert would never break out of the quizzical or
deprecating irony that he had made his speciality. But in *Report from
the Besieged City* this is belied. In the 'Mr Cogito' poems in this
collection (there are others which, interestingly, were excluded),
'Mr Cogito' is not strictly a *persona* for the poet to hide behind, but
much more simply a device that enables the poet to speak frankly
in his own person without seeming pretentious or hectoring. In one
of these poems, 'Mr Cogito and the Imagination', Herbert relates
how he has overcome his excessive reliance on verbal irony:

> Mr Cogito never trusted
> tricks of the imagination
>
> the piano at the top of the Alps
> played false concerts for him
>
> he didn't appreciate labyrinths
> the Sphinx filled him with loathing
>
> he lived in a house with no basement
> without mirrors or dialectics
>
> jungles of tangled images
> were not his home
>
> he would rarely soar
> on the wings of a metaphor
> and then he fell like Icarus
> into the embrace of the Great Mother
>
> he adored tautologies
> explanations
> *idem per idem*
>
> that a bird is a bird
> slavery means slavery
> a knife is a knife
> death remains death...[1]

---

[1] Cf. in Miłosz's very beautiful book, put together between 1981 and 1984, the
saying of a Zen master, Saisho: 'before I began studying Zen I saw mountains as
mountains, rivers as rivers. When I learned some Zen, mountains ceased to be mountains, rivers to be rivers. But now, when I have understood Zen, I am in accord with
myself and again I see mountains as mountains, rivers as rivers.' Czesław Miłosz,
Unattainable Earth. New York: Ecco Press, 1986.

'The piano at the top of the Alps' is delightfully witty, but if Herbert is being quizzical here it is at the expense of an earlier self that he has left behind. This is not clear at first sight, because the later Herbert also 'adores tautologies', as in 'Prayer of Mr Cogito – Traveller':

> and in the ugly city of Manchester I discovered people who were sensible and good

> nature repeated its wise tautologies: a forest was a forest the sea was the sea rock was rock...

Enamoured of tautologies, was Mr Cogito in the past as wise as 'nature'? We can hardly think so, on the evidence of two poems that are found on adjacent pages of the first *Selected Poems*. In the first, called 'A Knocker', we read:

> for others the green bell of a tree
> the blue bell of water
> I have a knocker
> from unprotected gardens
>
> I thump on the board
> and it prompts me
> with the moralist's dry poem
> yes – yes
> no – no

More pointedly, in 'Three Studies on the Subject of Realism', the third 'study' goes like this:

> finally they
> the authors of canvases divided into the right side and the left side
> who knew only two colours
> colour yes and colour no
> the inventors of simple symbols
> open palms and clenched fists
> singing and weeping
> birds and projectiles
> smiles and grinning teeth
>
> who say
> later when we get installed in the fruits of our labour
> we will use the subtle colour 'perhaps'
> and 'on one condition' with pearly lustre
> but right now we are drilling two choruses

and on to the empty stage
under a blinding light
we throw you
with a shout: choose while there's time
choose what you're waiting for
choose
And to help you we imperceptibly give a nudge to the balance

The thought-police also deal in tautologies, and demand them: singing is singing, weeping is weeping – and death to the many poems that sing and weep at once. The ironist gets round this by saying 'Yes' but meaning 'No', saying 'No' in such a way as to mean 'Yes'. In a totalitarian state this is intolerable, and sure enough during Poland's most Stalinist years Herbert was either silent or silenced. Though we must not think that Herbert looks any more favourably now on propagandist poster art or on socialist realism in literature, Polish conditions have apparently eased enough for him no longer to think that mordant irony is demanded of him as a socio-political duty, a form of protest.

But there is more to it than that. For the ironist, like the propagandist, knows 'only two colours / colour yes and colour no.' This is the condition of his being able to say 'Yes' while meaning 'No'; and that is why his best tunes have the dull dry finality of a door-knocker striking a wooden door. The piano on top of the Alps has all the best tunes, variously beautiful but also variously true. It can weep and sing at once, it can say 'Perhaps'. And that is why, despite what his ardent admirers may have claimed for him from the first, if Herbert had remained a polished and pointed ironist, he could never have been or become a major poet. Now when he utters tautologies, as he does, they have a very different ring.

Because Herbert has unharnessed himself from irony, it becomes possible and necessary to see him as practising various genres. *Report from the Besieged City* includes epistles for instance, and several elegies. Two of these last, both as it were 'to the memory of an unfortunate lady', deal with, respectively, Maria Rasputin (daughter of 'the mad monk', famous evil genius of the last Tsarina) and Isadora Duncan (American dancer, married to among others the short-lived Russian poet Yesenin). These are ample and leisurely pieces, funny, witty, yet tender. And it would be easy to dismiss them as lightweight compared with other poems that say a thunderous Yea or Nay to perennial 'problems' like human suffering or human freedom. But this would be a mistake. Once the piano on top of the Alps begins to play, it uses the whole keyboard, minor keys and major, treble and bass; and just that indeed, the width of the gamut, is the point of the doctrine of genres – a point we have lamentably lost sight of when we think of all poems as indiscriminately 'lyrics', It is the range of tones in the book that conveys the satisfying illusion that it comprises many more poems than thirty-five. One of the epistles, specifically called 'a Letter' and addressed to Ryszard Krynicki, a fellow-poet (b. 1943), is unusually explicit, as the epistolary genre permits, about Herbert's discontent with his own earlier *persona* – in the light (so it seems to me, though I can't prove it) of what he sees as Miłosz's alternative and superior witness.

That witness too, I have suggested, is profoundly ironical, though in a very different sense from what is meant by calling Herbert an ironist. And it is worth asking if Herbert in his new phase has attained to that other sort of irony we have called 'cosmic'. I believe he has, notably in a grand and sombre poem in three sections, 'Mr Cogito – Notes from the House of the Dead'. Here Mr Cogito, who may as well be called 'the author', speaks as spokesman for a group of people who have been dehumanized, debased by systematic humiliations below the level of their own humanity. These people, whom it is easy to think of as prisoners in prison-cells, hear each night over a period of time a voice raised (as it were in another cell) which restores to them a sense of their human dignity. The person behind this voice is called by the group and by Mr Cogito 'Adam'. Certainly he is not Christ, for 'he didn't redeem / his followers'. At one point we are invited to liken him to David the Psalmist, though he neither petitions nor complains as of course the Psalmist does. Indeed this voice doesn't *say* anything; it merely utters, time and again, the same two or three syllables. It utters itself, its own identity, perhaps its name – as Yahweh bears the name 'I AM'. The voice after a while falls silent, and is thereafter heard only (uncertainly) by Mr Cogito:

> more and more slender
> quieter
> further and further away
>
> like music of the spheres
> the harmony of the universe
>
> so perfect
> it is inaudible

It would be foolish to try to paraphrase this. But it is surely related to the matter of the 'wise tautologies'. For after all (impatient common sense may complain) a voice that speaks only tautologies – 'a mountain is a mountain', 'rivers are rivers', 'a rose is a rose is a rose' – is in a real sense saying nothing. Speech, we perceive, is not the same as utterance. And this uncovers an irony 'in the frame of things', about the human being as the only creature with the gift of speech. Without speech we could not lie, and so the gift of speech is both our glory and our shame. Our human dignity resides not in this special gift, but in the gift of *utterance*, which we share with the rest of Creation. And we utter ourselves best either in tautologous statements, or else in inarticulate cries and ejaculations. We may not like this argument, nor altogether trust it, to see that it has force – and *ironical* force.

(At this stage a champion of Herbert might undertake to defend his habit, early and late, of suppressing punctuation in his verses. It might be said that this mirrors his distrust of the articulate. But I should not soon be persuaded. If he values inarticulate utterance, or articulacy that cancels itself out as in the tautology, he is very articulate about that preference. For Herbert writes in sentences, he *does* predicate, though by suppressing punctuation-stops he affects not to. Accordingly most of the time I find this indeed an affectation, and an annoying one, which I just have to put up with.)

The distance that Herbert has come (he's of mixed ancestry, and the 'Herbert' is indeed English or Anglo-Welsh, so this Polish poet is kin to George Herbert and Lord Herbert of Cherbury) can be seen by setting beside 'Mona Lisa', which we have looked at already, a much more concise poem, 'Babylon':

> Years later when I returned to Babylon everything was changed
> girls I had loved numbers of metro lines
> I waited at the telephone sirens were stubbornly silent
>
> so consolation by art – Petrus Christus the portrait of a young lady
> became more and more flat folded its wings to sleep
> lights of annihilation and of the city approached each other
>
> the festival of the Apocalypse torches the false Sybil
> absolved drunken crowds of worshippers of abundance
> the trampled body of God was dragged in triumph and dust
>
> this is the end of the world fully laden Etruscan tables
> they are celebrating unaware of fate shirts stained with wine
> in the end the barbarians came to slash the aorta
>
> city I didn't wish your death anyway not like this
> because the sweet fruit of freedom will go with you under-
>   ground
> and everything must begin with bitter knowledge with grass

The Carpenters in an invaluable note (we pay for the greater concise-
ness by being more dependent on annotators) identify Babylon as,
not exclusively indeed but in the first instance, West Berlin – where
hangs the picture by Petrus Christus. Here in fact Herbert is doing
what other refugees from the unfree world, like Solzhenitsyn, have
disconcerted us by doing – making it clear that their condemnation
of the unfree societies they have escaped from does not commit them
to unreserved approval of the consumer societies they have escaped
to. What ironies that situation could generate, whether at the expense
of the refugee/traveller, or aimed at either or both of the societies
being compared! But Herbert resists all such temptations; his tone
is not ironical in the least, but apprehensive and resigned, com-
prehensively *mournful*.

Poetry Durham, 1987.

The Translatability of Poetry

The Penguin Book of Modern Verse Translation appeared in 1966. The very idea of such an anthology is a novel one, and greatly to be welcomed; and the anthology, as edited by George Steiner, is extremely interesting and challenging. In his introduction, for instance, Dr Steiner asserts roundly: 'The period from Rossetti to Robert Lowell has been an age of poetic translation rivalling that of the Tudor and Elizabethan masters.' I don't know how one starts getting to grips with a claim so sweeping and so sanguine, and I am not going to try. What interests me for the moment is that this period, for which such claims can be made, has also been a period in which the mere possibility of translating poetry has been denied – many times explicitly but also by implication.

For the explicit denial we can go to Robert Frost, who defined poetry as 'what gets left out in translation', or to Robert Graves, who has endorsed Frost's definition. For a statement of the opposite case, I find myself having to go back to Doctor Johnson. In his *Life of Denham*, Johnson comments on the four lines from Denham's 'Cooper's Hill', which, he says, 'since Dryden has commended them, almost every writer for a century past has imitated'. After he has analysed and applauded the felicities of Denham's verses, Johnson observes: 'The lines are in themselves not perfect: for most of the words, thus artfully opposed, are to be understood simply on one side of the comparison, and metaphorically on the other; and if there be any language which does not express intellectual operations by material images, into that language they cannot be translated.' Clearly, Johnson is here taking a position directly contrary to that of Robert Frost and Robert Graves. He is applauding poetry the more, according as it more nearly approaches the presumably unrealizable ideal of infinite translatability. 'Poetry', says Frost, 'is what gets left out in translation' – and we may take it he means reasonably intelligent and scrupulous and skilful translation. 'Poetry', says Dr Johnson in effect, 'is what survives all translations short of the crassly stupid, unscrupulous and incompetent.'

The battle-lines are drawn and there is no reconciling them by negotiation. Still, there is room for parleys which may limit the conflict. First of all, then, it is clear that in this difference of opinion the word 'poetry' is as usual playing a double role: in the first place it is simply descriptive, defining what is not prose; in the second place it is evaluative, a hooray word, distinguishing poetry from more or less misleading imitations, from verse or from poetastry. In this second, 'loaded' sense of poetry, what Graves and Frost are saying is that *true* poetry or *genuine* poetry or *essential* poetry is untranslatable: in other words, that poetry is better, the less translatable it is. It's as well to get this clear so as not to lose touch with common sense altogether. For the fact is that what purport to be translations of poetry continue to appear, and they continue to be read – not least by those who would most stoutly maintain with Robert Frost that poetry is untranslatable. Indeed this is one of the things that is queerest about the whole business – our habit of talking differently on this question out of the two sides of our mouths.

It will be as well to let common sense have its say a little longer. Common sense and common experience will tell us that a poem is likely to be more translatable the longer it is: since a poem of some length normally calls upon structural devices less bedded in nuances of language than those devices which compose the structure of a twenty- or thirty-line lyric. For instance, the greatest poem of Poland, the *Pan Tadeusz* of Mickiewicz, is available in Everyman's Library in the thoroughly pedestrian but thoroughly readable prose translation of G.R. Noyes; and in that form it can be enjoyed as a very good, perhaps a great, novel. So much common sense should be ready to grant. And yet, having conceded so much, has it not conceded a great deal? For, after all, the distinction between verse and prose is not an ultimate one. An epic in verse, and a prose fiction of epic sweep and scope, are alike cases of *poesis*, or making with words. And what does it mean to say that we appreciate *Pan Tadeusz* in its English dress as a very good novel if it doesn't mean that we find in it generous feeling and a scrupulous regard for truth in portraying the human spectacle and the human condition, together with all the skills of arousing and sustaining interest by the narrative logic which guides one situation into another. Now, who is to say that all these features are not features of good poems as much as of good novels?

What are we to think of Paul Valéry, when he confesses: 'I would even go so far as to say that the more an apparently poetic work survives being put into prose and retains a certain value after this assault, the less is it the work of a poet'?

Surely we cannot help but detect, in Valéry as in Frost and Graves (however odd this grouping appears), an exponent of *la poésie pure*, one of the once so numerous and articulate tribe for whom only lyric poetry is true poetry, and poetry is magical, a bloom on the surface of words too precarious and fugitive to bear examination. We may be excused for suspecting, behind all proponents of the maxim that all poetry is untranslatable, the lineaments of this same familiar figure who, even as he offers to put transcendent value on poetry, in fact emasculates it by demanding of it a purity, from human and quotidian concerns, which it is poetry's glory never to attain.

So far I have dealt only with some people who are explicit about their belief that poetry is better the less translatable it is. But the same view can be implied by us when we are not formally considering translation at all. I will take as examples three well-known and justly applauded critical dicta from the recent past: first, Gerard Manley Hopkins esteeming Dryden for exhibiting 'the naked thew and sinew' of the English language; second, Ezra Pound condemning *Paradise Lost* because Milton in that poem treated English as if it were a fully inflected language, Latin; and third, Dr Leavis defining the distinction of Keats's 'Ode to Autumn'. My quarrel – or rather my hesitant discomfort – is not at all with the judgements in themselves, but with an assumption which seems to be implicit in the way they are expressed.

To take Dr Leavis first. He is talking about the line from Keats's Ode: 'To bend with apples the moss'd cottage-trees'. And he remarks, comparing Keats's use of English with Tennyson's: 'That "moss'd cottage-trees" represents a strength – a native English strength – lying beyond the scope of the poet who aimed to make English as like Italian as possible.' Bluntly, by 'native' in Dr Leavis's phrase about Keats ('native English strength') I understand 'untranslatable'; and I suggest that it's hard to take it any other way in view of the contrast which follows, with the allegedly Italianate Tennyson.

We can go on from this to challenge Pound and Dr Leavis alike to explain what is self-evidently reprehensible about treating English as if it were Latin (as Milton is said to have done) or (with Tennyson) as if it were Italian. I can imagine them replying that if a poet casts the language of his poetry in a different mould from the language of his conversation, he risks a perhaps damaging discontinuity between the person he is when he isn't writing poetry and the person he is when he writes it. One thing to say about this is that there is conversation and conversation: that the conversation of barristers, for instance, is quite different in the patterns it makes from the conversation of juvenile delinquents. But what is more to the point for our present purposes is to notice that this contention all but precludes the possibility that our native language should extend its grasp, so as to apprehend new sorts of experience, as those present themselves. We might remember T.S. Eliot saying that the models which at the start of his career enabled him to say what he wanted were just not available in English but only in French. If we object whenever a poet tries to use English as if it were French or Italian or Latin or Chinese, we are assuming that there are not extant in those languages any perceptions and apprehensions which have not already found embodiment in English. We are in the position of being invited to draw *ad lib* upon the treasure invested in the language we are heir to, but never of attempting to add to that precious stock. And we are declaring that it is dishonest to try to attain to apprehensions that we don't have already as our birthright.

I am suggesting that to credit a poet with 'a native strength' is something short – may be something rather far short – of the highest praise. If so, to write English as if it were Italian, or to translate Italian into English (not that these two operations are identical), is a risk some English poets need to take – for their own good, but also for the good of the native tradition.

So much for those who assert or imply that poetry is untranslatable. But this position has not gone unchallenged, even in our own day; and in fact we find at the opposite extreme some voices raised which seem to echo Dr Johnson's contention that poetry is infinitely translatable. This is an illusion, however. Really, these voices are saying something different: they are saying that poetry does not need to be translated, that it translates itself, automatically and somehow mystically, in the ear of a sympathetic listener. This is what the American poet Louis Zukofsky was saying in 1950 when he declared:

> And it is possible in imagination to divorce speech of all graphic elements, to let it become a movement of sounds. It is this musical horizon of poetry (which incidentally poems perhaps never reach) that permits anybody who does not know Greek to listen and get something out of the poetry of Homer: to 'tune in' to the human tradition, to its voice which has developed among the sounds of natural things, and thus escape the confines of a time and place, as one hardly ever escapes them in studying Homer's grammar. In this sense poetry is international.

And it was in this sense that poetry was taken to be international a few months ago, at the gathering called 'Poetry International '67', in the Festival Hall. Ted Hughes, who was one of the directors, declared in the broadsheet that he circulated at the time:

> However rootedly national in detail it may be, poetry is less and less the prisoner of its own language. It is beginning to represent,

as an ambassador, something far greater than itself. Or perhaps it is only now being heard for what, among other things, it is – a universal language of understanding, coherent behind the many languages, in which we can all hope to meet.

The generosity and urgency of these sentiments is something that we must all want to respond to. But if we try to get at the sense of what Ted Hughes was saying, I think we have to conclude that he was asserting what Louis Zukofsky asserted – that the poetry of Homer is accessible in the original Greek to listeners who do not know Greek.

As a matter of fact it is hard to rebut this contention. Nor is it necessary to do so. Let us admit that the poem as a structure of sounds 'comes over'. Let us leave aside the surely very real possibility that a poem in Greek thus 'comes over' where a poem in Chinese wouldn't. Let us leave aside also the familiar and fascinating specu-lations which have their claims upon us as soon as we isolate from poetry those features like sound-patterning which it appears to share with music – the speculations, I mean, about how music is expres-sive, and what it expresses. Let us leave this aside, noting only that to say Homer is accessible to a listener is not to say that he is com-prehensible to him or even that he is meaningful. And then let us concede for the sake of argument that *in some degree* the poetry of Homer is accessible in the original Greek to listeners who have no Greek. It then becomes precisely *a matter of degree*: and I contend that the degree to which Homer is thus accessible is inconsiderable and useless, that what 'comes over' in such a case is a tiny part of what Homer's poetry amounts to, and that Ted Hughes and Louis Zukofsky therefore are taking a tiny part for a vast whole, and inducing others to do the same.

Mr Colin MacInnes, for instance, was persuaded. When he attended 'Poetry International' he found out, so he declared, 'that language though vitally important, is not such a barrier as one might have thought.' And he explained further:

> If you heard one of these poets reciting his poem in a mother tongue of which you didn't understand a word, you *could* under-stand something of what he was saying: so much so that the subsequent translation seemed something of an anti-climax.

Here the word is 'understand': Mr MacInnes says 'you could *under-stand* something of what he was saying'. And so there once again looms in the offing the question, for my present purposes a sterile question, whether a listener who is affected by a piece of music, who 'enters into' that music, can be said to understand it. But where poetry is concerned, surely common sense will serve us. And common sense and common usage alike take understanding a poem to mean, among other things, understanding the sense of the words of which the poem is made. Now, clearly it cannot be true that if you have no Spanish, Pablo Neruda's presence and his voice will magically enlighten your darkness, so that you understand the sense of each Spanish word in the Spanish poems which he reads to you. If not, and if poems are structures not of sounds but of sounds-plus-meanings (that is to say, of words), then it is an abuse of language to claim that one understands, even partially, a poem composed of words whose sense you do not know.

We need not dispute that Colin MacInnes and others had an intense experience in the Festival Hall when Pablo Neruda or Giuseppe Ungaretti was before them, reading poems. Mr MacInnes construes this experience as (it is his own word) revelation; I believe that it was, that it has to be, delusion. What he apprehended was not meaning, but the illusion of meaning.

To return to my narrower concerns, on the other hand, what is particularly significant is Mr MacInnes's honest admission that 'the subsequent translation seemed something of an anti-climax'. Precisely! If poetry somehow translates itself, then translators are superfluous, officious and troublesome: an annoyance. I hold myself that translating is a noble office. For we may agree with Ted Hughes that poetry is not necessarily the prisoner of its own language; but it is the translator alone who can unlock the prison-door, and release poetry from one language into another. Translating is not quite impossible. But it is damnably difficult. And that is why, as has been said by others, the good translator of poetry is a rarer apparition even than the good poet. Poetry *is* translatable – just, sometimes, given luck, given above all a scrupulous and gifted and lucky (which is to say, inspired) translator.

Listener, 28 December 1967. Reprinted in *The Poet in the Imaginary Museum*, ed. Barry Alpert. Manchester: Carcanet New Press, 1977.

Index